DISCOVERING ANTIQUES

THE STORY OF WORLD ANTIQUES

 GREYSTONE PRESS/NEW YORK · TORONTO · LONDON

This superb full-color work is brought to you in its entirety from the original publisher, The British Publishing Corporation. Only the arrangement has been slightly altered. In fact, rather than disturb the text in any way, you will find the English monetary system used throughout the set. Here is a handy conversion table showing the value of a Pound ($£$) in terms of U.S. dollars.

DATES	U.S. Dollars equal to one Pound ($£$)
1939	$3.92 to 4.68
1940 to Sept. 1949	4.03
Sept. 1949 to Nov. 1967	2.80
Nov. 1967 to Aug. 1971	2.40
Aug. 1971 to June 1972	2.60
June 1972 to present	2.45 (floating rate)

20 shillings = one Pound ($£$)
21 shillings = one guinea

In February, 1971, the guinea was taken out of circulation.

TITLE PAGE PHOTO CREDIT: *Ivory netsuke* depicting Hotei with a fan, staff and boy, Japanese. (British Museum, London.) *Photo: Hamlyn Group Library*

Contents

CENTRAL EUROPE

The Vienna of Maria Theresa	Sir Charles Petrie	253
Eighteenth-Century Bohemian Glass	Gabriella Gros-Galliner	258
Kaendler at Meissen	William Hutton	264
Masterpieces in Ivory		269
COLLECTORS' ITEM: Playing Cards	Arthur Negus	272
Viennese Porcelain	Joan Jordan	274

CHINA AND JAPAN

The Meeting of East and West	Julian Reade	279
Ming Dynasty Porcelain	Anthony Derham	284
Lacquered Furniture	Jonathan Harris	289
COLLECTORS' ITEM: Seals	Arthur Negus	294
Ornamental Jade	G. Bernard Hughes	296
Arms for the Samurai	William Allan	301
China and Japan in the Eighteenth Century	Basil Gray	305
Ch'ing Dynasty Porcelain	John Cushion	310
Netsuke and Inro	Nicolas Wolfers	315
COLLECTORS' ITEM: Amber	Arthur Negus	320
The Porcelain of Japan	Michael Eveleigh	322
Japanese Wood-Block Prints	Jack Hillier	326
The Vogue for Oriental Art in Europe	William Gaunt	331
Japanese Ivory Carvings	Neil Davey	335
Metalwork in Nineteenth-Century Japan	Bon Dale	338
COLLECTORS' ITEM: Chess Pieces	Arthur Negus	342
Japanese Colour Prints	B. W. Robinson	344
The Porcelain of China & Japan	Michael Eveleigh	349
Shadow Play Puppets	Shelagh Weir	353

ENGLAND

The Age of Gloriana	John Buxton	357
A Taste for Riches and Ostentation	Edward T. Joy	362
The Ruff and the Pendant	James Laver	366
COLLECTOR'S CORNER	371	
MARKET TRENDS		373

1

Museum Photo

Charles VI
Born 1685
Holy Roman
Emperor 1711
Died 1740
Maria Theresa
Born 1717
Queen of Hungary
and Bohemia,
Archduchess of
Austria 1740
Died 1780

The Vienna of Maria Theresa

Sir Charles Petrie

Vienna emerged as a great artistic centre during the eighteenth century. Charles VI and the Archduchess Maria Theresa played a major part in the embellishment of this majestic capital and the promotion of culture generally among their subjects

Fig. 1 (frontispiece) *The Palace of Schönbrunn engraved by Karl Schütz, 1783.*
The magnificent Palace of Schönbrunn was redesigned by Johann Bernhard Fischer von Erlach (1656–1723), one of the foremost baroque architects in Austria in the last years of the seventeenth century.
(Österreichisches National-bibliothek, Vienna.)

Fig. 2 *Portrait of Maria Theresa by Martin van Meytens, mid-eighteenth century.*
(Germanisches Nationalmuseum, Nuremberg.)

The importance of Vienna as a centre of the Fine Arts dates from the end of the seventeenth century; previously it had suffered all the inconveniences of being a frontier city between West and East having withstood, in 1529 and 1683, two sieges by the Turks. In consequence, the only medieval buildings of note are the cathedral of St. Stephen and the church of Maria-Stiegen, while renaissance monuments are few.

Under the influence of Johann Bernhard Fischer von Erlach (1656–1723) and Lukas von Hildenbrandt (1668–1745), at the end of the seventeenth and the beginning of the eighteenth century, a brilliant style of baroque architecture came into being, stamping the city with the peculiar character which it still possesses. Von Erlach, it may be noted, received his inspiration direct from Rome, where he studied as a young man, and above all from the work of Bernini, the architect of the great colonnade of St. Peter's. From that period date the Palace of Schönbrunn, the Winter Riding School, the Imperial Library, the Belvedere and many other palaces. The monarchs who were responsible for the transformation of their capital were the Emperor Charles VI and his daughter, Maria Theresa, whose combined reigns stretched from 1711 to 1780.

Let it be said at once that neither in international nor in domestic affairs was Charles VI a success as a ruler. His reign passed in the endeavour to secure the unchallenged succession of his daughter (he had no sons) to the undivided Habsburg dominions; and with this end in view he drew up an instrument called the Pragmatic Sanction, to which he secured the adherence of the neighbouring Powers. Unfortunately for Maria Theresa, however, he omitted the precaution of reinforcing his diplomacy by arms or money.

Years before, Prince Eugene had warned Charles that the best guarantee of the Pragmatic Sanction was a strong army and a full treasury, but when he died, in 1740, he had neither. The treasury was all but empty and the taxes, oppressive and unproductive, were causing widespread discontent; as for the army, it was demoralised by defeat, its generals were discredited and its ranks were depleted to half their proper strength; it urgently needed the reorganisation and reforms which the financial situation rendered impossible. In effect, Charles VI, as a recent historian has aptly put it, 'moved through his last years with his head in the clouds, surrounded by a rabble of flatterers and deceivers'.

The Emperor was a considerable patron of the arts and sciences

Where the arts were concerned, the position was very different, for he was not only their patron but also their practitioner. In particular, like so many of the Habsburgs, he was devoted to music and he even composed an opera which was produced with great splendour in the theatre of the palace. The parts were performed by the principal members of the nobility, the Emperor himself played in the orchestra, and his two daughters danced in the ballet. His tastes and interests were varied: he was a considerable patron of the sciences, his orchestra was distinguished for the excellence of its musicians. He was also interested in printing, sculpture and architecture, and showed his keenness as a bibliophile by his purchase of the books of Prince Eugene, which he had housed in the Imperial Library, designed by Von Erlach and completed in 1726.

The erection of this building brought together as a team a brilliant galaxy of talent – painters, sculptors, wood-carvers and workers in marble and metal – to produce one of the richest and most stately halls in Europe. From the same period dates the great Karlskirche, with its soaring dome, set in the open fields beside the little river Wien, which is

Fig. 5 *Sphinx from the garden at Belvedere.*

Edwin Smith

Edwin Smith

Fig. 6 *Staircase of Prince Eugene's Winter Palace, Vienna, by Fischer von Erlach, 1695–96.* **Atlantes** *or male nude supporting figures which serve as columns were particularly popular with the central European baroque architects.*

Fig. 3 *Inner courtyard of the Hofburg, engraved by Karl Schütz, second half of the eighteenth century. The Hofburg was the Habsburg residence in Vienna from the thirteenth century. (Österreichisches Nationalbibliothek.)*

Fig. 4 *Prunksaal or State-room of the Imperial Library, Vienna (now the* Nationalbibliothek) *by Fischer von Erlach, completed in 1726 after his death.*

now no more than a conduit and largely built over. This church, still the greatest in Vienna after the romanesque and gothic cathedral of St. Stephen, was the special pride of Charles VI, and it was dedicated by him in 1713 to St. Charles Borromeo in thanksgiving for the end of the plague. In effect, the great building boom had struck Vienna long before Charles died, and when it came, both established and emerging talent enjoyed imperial patronage and encouragement.

Maria Theresa – the one Habsburg loved by Austrians and Hungarians alike

Such was the inheritance to which Maria Theresa succeeded at the age of twenty-three and, within three months of this event, Frederick of Prussia had seized Silesia; yet the very greatness of this disaster, and the terrific impact of modern organisations and ideas upon a system that was hopelessly medieval, produced changes that were highly beneficial to her dominions as a whole. By inclination, Maria Theresa was strongly conservative, but she pushed on the work of regeneration with resolute determination, especially where military matters were concerned. The result was that her efficient professional army which confronted Frederick in the Seven Years' War, though not yet equal to the Prussian, was immeasurably superior to that which had served her in the first Silesian conflict. Without, perhaps, the highest gifts of statesmanship, Maria Theresa possessed a remarkable talent for awakening enthusiasm in others, as well as a resolute will unshaken in a crisis and an unerring practical insight. Despite an unfaithful husband, an uninspiring court and a corrupt administration, she continued to win the respect even of her enemies, as well as to be the one Habsburg loved by Austrians and Hungarians alike, and to impart to her reign the aspect of a golden age of happiness and renown. Her court may be described as a highly idiosyncratic

mixture of glittering ceremony and informality.

As a mother, it must be admitted that she was not a success. Her eldest son, the future Emperor Joseph II, was on the one side a warm-hearted philanthropist, a 'do-gooder' who sacrificed everything to impulse and sentiment, and on the other, a ruthless bureaucrat who carried out his pedantic ideas with military precision and force. In effect, he failed on the throne because he was too much of an idealist and theorist; a great deal of the blame for this must be laid at his mother's door. For the shortcomings of her daughter, the ill-fated Marie Antoinette, she must also be held responsible in that the girl's education was scandalously neglected. She realised her mistake when it was too late. A letter has recently been published in which Maria Theresa warned the French Queen against her dangerous courses and her frivolity, even going so far as to say, 'One day you will recognise the truth of this, but then it will be too late'. The wretched woman did recognise it, but not before she was the Widow Capet waiting for trial and the guillotine.

Maria Theresa grew up in a Vienna that had already been transformed. By the time she was born, all the grand families had new palaces, some of them two; the summer palaces outside the walls and the winter palaces within them; with the exception of Eugene's summer palace, the Belvedere, they were not overwhelmingly pretentious. The splendour was indoors, where broad and imaginative staircases opened out into state-rooms: façades were cool and classical in a renaissance idiom, sometimes with an efflorescence of statuary along the skyline, but more often with an elaboratley conceived and executed portico with sunbursts or swags of trophies appearing to grow out of the stone. All this glory was inherited by Maria Theresa.

She is herself associated with three main buildings – the Hofburg, Laxenburg and Schönbrunn. The first of these, also referred to as *Die Burg*, had been founded before 1221 by Duke Leopold VI, the last but one of the Babenbergs, and was the residence of the Habsburgs from 1278 until the fall of the dynasty in 1918. It is an extensive pile of build-

7

8

Edwin Smith

Museum Photo

ings, embracing several courts and belonging to different periods; in consequence, there is no unity of plan. One of the chief inspirations behind it was the Hofburg where she had the state-rooms redecorated to her own taste.

Later, she spent as much time as she could at Laxenburg, which was originally an old castle in the beautiful country of the Danube, ten miles from Vienna and just off the main road to the Hungarian frontier. The Neues Schloss, which Maria Theresa started to have built in 1752, is a plain, two-storied building, utterly unpretentious, though it contains some charming rooms; since the fall of the monarchy, it has been allowed to become a ruin, but is now being slowly restored.

The Archduchess spent many hours watching the Palace of Schönbrunn grow

It is, however, with the Palace of Schönbrunn that the name of Maria Theresa will always be closely associated. It stands on the site of a six-teenth-century hunting-lodge, which was destroyed during the Turkish siege of 1683. A magnificent new building was commenced thirteen years later, but was left unfinished at the death of the Emperor Joseph I in 1705. The work was recommenced by Maria Theresa and, devoted as she was to the simplicities of Laxenburg, she soon came to prefer Schönbrunn. Like Philip II of Spain in the case of the Escorial, she spent long hours watching the building grow. She moved into her own apart-ments as soon as they were completed and after her husband's death she settled into the palace for good. One day, as she was sitting under the arcade leading to the gardens, she saw a youth climbing the scaffolding, which was expressly forbidden. It was the young Haydn, then a member of the choir-school of St. Stephen's Cathedral. Maria Theresa told the choir conductor to punish him soundly.

She interrupted a performance at the theatre with 'My Poldy's got a boy!'

The theatre was not patronised much in the latter years of Maria Theresa's life, though she encour-aged others to do so, and it is in this connection that a story is told illustrating her unconventionality. When Leopold, Grand Duke of Tuscany, her second son, had his first child (her first grandson, who was one day to be the Emperor Francis II), she hurried excitedly down the corridors of the Hofburg, and into the Imperial box at the theatre to interrupt a performance with the triumphant cry, 'My Poldy's got a boy!'

It is possible to hold several different views about the capability of the Habsburgs as statesmen, but there can be no difference of opinion about the part they played in the embellishment of their capital city and in the promotion of culture

Fig. 7 *Interior of the Winter Palace of Prince Eugene,* c.1713–16.

Fig. 8 *Display in the Winter Riding School* on 2 January, 1743, school of Martin van Meytens. (*Österreichisches Nationalbibliothek.*)

Fig. 9 **The Grotto,** *Schloss Weissenstein, Pommersfelden, designed by Johann Dietzenhofer (c.1665–1726), 1722–25. The shell-decorated grotto at Pommersfelden with its symbolic sculptures of the Elements and the Seasons by Zammels is a conscious attempt at creating a bizarre and exotic ambience.*

Fig. 10 **Design for a bed and a clock** *by Johann Jakob Schübler (1689–1741), Augsburg, 1720s. Schübler's pattern books had made a strong impact on German design. He could be described as the German Marot but his designs are much stranger and sometimes verge on sheer fantasy. (Victoria and Albert Museum.)*

Fig. 11 **Spiegelsaal,** *or* **Mirror Room,** *Schloss Weissenstein, Pommersfelden, designed by F. Plitzner, 1718. The rarity of the materials and the magnificent overall effect greatly enhanced the prestige of the patron.*

Fig. 12 **Porzellansaal,** *or* **Porcelain Room,** *Schloss Charlottenburg, Berlin, designed to house Frederick I's collection of K'ang Hsi porcelain. Frederick's magnificent collection of porcelain was destroyed by bombs in 1943. The present display has been acquired in recent years.*

generally among their subjects.

At the time of the building of the Palace of Schönbrunn and the Belvedere in Vienna, there emerged in Germany the final phase of the Baroque. One of the finest examples of decoration of this type can be seen at the Schloss Weissenstein, Pommersfelden (Figs. 9 and 11), designed by Johann Dietzenhofer and built mainly between 1711 and 1718. An architectural extravaganza, it was created for the building fanatic, Lothar Franz von Schönbrunn, Elector and Archbishop of Mainz. The designs of J. J. Schübler (1689–1741) illustrate this fantastic and almost grotesque style as extended to furniture (Fig. 10). The nobility avidly collected Chinese porcelain, which, emanating from the strange and exotic Orient, was in keeping with fashionable taste. Frederick I of Prussia was so proud of his fine collection that he had built a special Porcelain Room at Charlottenburg in which to house it (Fig. 12).

9

Scala

10

K. Hodله

12

Scala

Walter Steinkopf

K. Hoddle

Eighteenth-Century Bohemian Glass

Gabriella Gros-Galliner

Although Bohemia and Germany were torn by war throughout the early eighteenth century, they produced glass wares of great sophistication and beauty

Fig. 1 **Goblet and cover,** *Potsdam, early eighteenth century. Finely engraved with baroque designs and embellished with gilding.*
This elaborately decorated piece is saved from fussiness by its handsome, almost stark, outline.
(Victoria and Albert Museum, London.)

Fig. 2 **Beaker and cover,** *Bohemian, first half of the eighteenth century. Clear glass with ruby and aventurine enclosures, cut on the wheel. Complex and elegant techniques such as this were perfected in eighteenth-century Bohemia. (Victoria and Albert Museum.)*

Fig. 3 **Bottle, or decanter,** *German, second half of the eighteenth century. 'Milk' or opaque-white glass. Made in imitation of fine porcelain, this delicate piece is even decorated in the style of Meissen ware with a charming rustic scene. (Victoria and Albert Museum.)*

It is not easy to correlate the extrovert and superficial charm and glittering splendour of the early Rococo in central Europe with the somewhat repressive belief in the supremacy and absolute power of individual monarchy.

In Prussia, an early victim of the often ruthless régime was Johann Kunckel, the great chemist and manager of the Potsdam glass-house. The new Elector of Brandenburg (who became Frederick I of Prussia in 1701) had little sympathy with his father's protégé. He called Kunckel to account and demanded the return of all monies spent on experiments and costly research, which had produced the famous gold-ruby glass and revolutionary applications of gold-leaf decoration. Unable to meet such demands, Kunckel was forced to hand over all his savings and sell his own house. He died in 1703, a poverty-stricken, disillusioned man, but the influence of his work continued into the eighteenth century and, indeed, up to the present day.

Under Maria Theresa in Austria and Bohemia, a period of enlightened despotism existed. She instituted financial reforms and measures to foster commerce and agriculture, resulting in a renewed life in the glass industry, which had suffered greatly during the years of strife.

About the year 1700, certain areas in the Riesengebirge began to utilise water power as a means of industrial mechanisation. Bohemian and Silesian cutter-engravers benefited greatly from this innovation and their artistic skill made this the greatest period of Czech glass-engraving. The robust quality and bright sparkle of Bohemian crystal glass proved an ideal foil for the engraver's wheel, and by unanimous acclaim and universal demand the Bohemian product finally triumphed over the Venetian supremacy.

The prevalent ornamental motif was shell or *rocaille* decoration, already applied in high baroque art. In rococo design, the naturalism of this and other elementary forms was represented in a more flattering and elegant version. The straight line

was not permitted to stand unadorned: flowers, leaves, ribbons (*Laub und Bandelwerk*) and shell motifs filled every available space and corner. Pastoral scenes and vignettes of ruins, castles and grottos expressed the growing interest in architectural styles. Costly tableware for royalty and the nobility showed dutiful adulation in engraved portraits and inscriptions, often recalling victorious deeds.

The distinguished engraver Gottfried Spiller (died 1721), best known for his superb representations of the human body in intaglio engraving, produced some of his finest work at the Potsdam factory. His pupil, Franz Gondelach (born 1663), employed at the Hesse-Kassel glass-house of Landgrave Karl, was given the title of *Kurfürstlicher Glasschneider* (Glass Cutter to the Elector) by his grateful sovereign, an honour bestowed also on the great Caspar Lehman nearly a hundred years before. Gondelach's work is of astonishing variety in *Hoch und Tiefschnitt* (high relief and intaglio) augmented by diamond-engraving. Portrait busts in high relief have a sculptural quality that is obviously related to Gondelach's competence in the technique of rock-crystal engraving.

Portrait busts were a popular form of glass decoration, and an early technique practised in Brandenburg and elsewhere consisted of carved glass portraits in high relief pasted on to a suitably engraved vessel. The relation to the cameo techniques of antiquity and to nineteenth-century glass cameo development is clear.

The finest early eighteenth-century glass engraving was produced on Silesian soil. Friedrich Winter of Hermsdorf, brother of Martin who worked in the Potsdam area, combined *Hoch und Tiefschnitt* with intricate use of blank and matt-cut techniques. By the middle of the century, there was a profuse output from the great glass centre of Warmbrunn of high quality engraving produced mainly by the workshop of Christian Gottfried Schneider. Among outstanding Nuremberg glass of the early eighteenth century, is the work of Georg Friedrich Killinger, represented by impressive formal engraving of Venetian-inspired covered goblets. In contrast are Anton Wilhelm Maüerl's designs on bottles and decanters based on a series of *chinoiserie* copper-plate engravings by Paul Decker.

Among the major innovations in decorative cutting was the combined use of polished- and matt-cut, first introduced by Georg Schwanhardt (1601–67), which enhanced most effectively the

4

5

Museum Photo

6

Museum Photo

7

8

Museum Photo

reflective properties of the glass metal. The so-called *Kugelschliff* represents a very distinctive cutting technique coming into fashion during the first third of the eighteenth century. It takes the form of polished oval or circular depressions in intaglio cut, reminiscent of what are loosely known as 'printies' in eighteenth-century English glass, but more important in character and differently arranged.

In the 1694 guild register of Kamenicky Senov glass decorators, the art of *Kugelschliff* features quite distinctly and, though it is conceivable that the trained engraver was adaptable to a number of techniques, the guild apparently expected him to stick to his own particular accomplishment, at least for a certain time. It is an interesting fact that many professional painters turned to the art of glass

engraving, and this may in part account for the pictorial quality as well as the extraordinary skill and dexterity prevalent in eighteenth-century continental glass.

Kugelschliff in Bohemian and Silesian glass is most frequently applied to the underside of the base or foot. The German centres such as Branden-burg, Thuringia and Saxony favoured application to the body of the vessel, often in a neat row around the rim of the glass. A finely engraved lacy border became a fashionable feature by the middle of the century and is most frequently seen on Silesian specimens.

The massive goblet with generous bowl and knopped stem persisted until the late eighteenth century. During the last quarter of the century, there was a gradual emergence of the beaker or

Fig. 4 *Tea-bowl and saucer,* *probably German, perhaps from* *the workshop of Johann* *Friedrich Metzsch, Bayreuth,* *c.1740–50. Opaque-white glass* *with enamelled decoration,* *diameter of saucer 4¾ ins.,* *height of cup 2⅛ ins.* *The decoration, a scene of Cupid* *and Psyche, is in imitation of* *Meissen and Vienna porcelain.* *(British Museum, London.)*

Fig. 5 *Covered* **Zwischengoldglas** *goblet,* *Bohemian, mid-eighteenth* *century. Glass with engraved* *gold-leaf, height 10¼ ins.* *In this complicated technique,* *the gold-leaf decoration,* *depicting in this case the four* *seasons, is held safely between* *a plain inner glass and the* *faceted outer goblet.* *(British Museum.)*

Fig. 6 **Basin,** *Silesian or* *Bohemian, the decoration* *attributed to Ignaz Preissler,* *second quarter of the eighteenth* *century. Clear glass decorated* *with black picked out in gold,* *width 17½ ins.* *(British Museum.)*

Fig. 7 **Glass picture,** *German,* *early eighteenth century.* *Opaque-white glass painted with* *enamel colours.* *(Victoria and Albert Museum.)*

Fig. 8 **Beaker or ice-pail,** *probably Bohemian, c.1750–70.* *Opaque-white glass enamelled* *with four scenes depicting the* *Elements. Height 9 ins.* *(British Museum.)*

Fig. 9 **Mug,** *German, mid-* *eighteenth century. Opaque-* *white glass painted with* *enamels, height 5⅞ ins.* *(Victoria and Albert Museum.)*

Museum Photo

tumbler-shaped glass which, in its various modifications, was to become the basic form of nineteenth-century *Biedermeier* glass. The introduction of the 'Silesian' stem was probably due to the importation of glass under the Treaty of Utrecht in 1713. A moulded pedestal stem of four or more sides, it had no particular connection with Silesia but appeared in many areas of Germany.

The golden glitter of rococo elegance found a natural response in the decorative appearance of table glass. Additional gilding of cut and engraved glass became increasingly fashionable (Fig. 1). The popularity of new kinds of food and drink, and the growing variety of wines, necessitated a more considered elegance in fine tableware. The rich splendour of elaborately set out food amidst a glittering array of crystal glass was further enhanced, in the eye of the beholder, by the added presence of candelabra, chandeliers and mirrors. The tinkling of glass brought a fascinating musical sound to the rococo drawing-room, that of the 'musical glasses', or the glass harmonica. This instrument, which consisted of goblets tuned by partial filling with water and played by rubbing their edges evenly with a wet finger, was later mechanised by Benjamin Franklin by arranging musical glasses in a scale on a spindle, turned by a treadle.

Bohemia cornered the world market with superbly cut and coloured glass 'jewellery'

The first Bohemian chandeliers were produced about 1724 in the region of Kamenicky Senov and by the end of the eighteenth century the industry had created the ornate 'Maria Theresa' chandelier with layers of cut crystal drops and beads hanging from every part of its tiered branches. Although developed at a period when the brief era of Rococo had already receded, the 'Maria Theresa' chandelier typifies to this day the glittering rococo style. Cut-glass trimmings constituted a good part of Bohemia's export trade, and during this period the foundation was laid for its industry in artificial jewellery. From the famous centres of Turnov, and later Jablonec, Bohemia cornered the world market with superbly cut and coloured glass 'jewellery', imitating the work of the lapidaries who were among the first to turn to this particular field of decorative glassmaking.

Local mirror manufacture was so successful that Giuseppe Briati, one of Murano's leading mirror makers, became extremely worried about the effect of Bohemian glass on the Italian industry. In 1733 he came to Bohemia and, disguised as a porter, worked at a glass factory for three years to discover the secret of Bohemian techniques. On his return he obtained a patent and began to produce mirrors 'in the Bohemian fashion' at Venice, after he had been driven out by jealous Murano neighbours.

By the early eighteenth century, home manufacture began to outweigh local demands. One of the first German export ventures met with disaster, when a large glass consignment to be auctioned in London in 1709 was boycotted by the local Glass Sellers, who invaded the auction rooms and stopped the sale. Nevertheless, by about 1730 or 1740, a flourishing glass trade had been set up by Bohemian export companies representing several glass-works.

In addition to the attraction of quality and novelty, Bohemian glass prices were extremely competitive due to the relatively low wages of the workers.

These Bohemian glass export companies were unique establishments: patriarchal dynasties which, with their stringent laws and widespread and powerful interests were reminiscent of the tyrannical rule regulating the lives of the early Murano glass-makers. It was not long before warehouses became established in most major cities and ports of Europe and overseas.

Opaque-white, or milk glass was produced in imitation of porcelain

The earliest branches were set up in Cadiz, Seville and Madrid, and soon the Bohemian glass export empire embraced places as far apart as Amsterdam and Smyrna, Malaga and Mexico, Constantinople, Oporto and Petrograd. Such companies were family concerns, and younger members, often no older than twelve or fourteen, were sent abroad to study foreign fashions and eventually to manage foreign branches. They usually accompanied large consignments of glass, and only the older ones were permitted to travel by post-chaise. The younger members were made to walk all the way, in slow stages! Education was strict and tended to be religious. Bed and board were arranged with the local agency, and contact with local women was forbidden. Those who disobeyed were put on the first ship home. On completion of their foreign service, by which time they had reached the safe age of thirty-five or forty, these emissaries were allowed to return home to become associates or company owners. This feudal system proved enormously successful and the Bohemian glass trade established a world-wide monopoly.

Despite such good fortune, the trade could not remain unaffected by national and international changes and political disasters. The Silesians were not favourably inclined towards Bohemian glass pedlars and decorators, but Bohemian crystal glass proved superior to the Silesian product and almost indispensable to the Silesian cutter-engravers. When Silesia separated from Bohemia, Frederick II forbade the import of Bohemian glass and Silesians resorted to diverse methods for obtaining the desired raw material, which was often smuggled across. Nevertheless, a number of Silesian craftsmen were forced to work on Bohemian soil.

The thirst for riches had some unexpected consequences. When the alchemist Johann Friedrich Böttger (1682–1719) was ordered by Augustus the Strong of Saxony to transmute base metals into gold, he developed instead his precious 'white gold', and the first hard-paste porcelain factory was set up at Meissen in 1710. The desire for a cheaper imitation of this costly product resulted in the high popularity of opaque-white, or milk glass. This was no new invention; a variety of opaque-white glass was produced by Murano glass-makers during the fifteenth century, using the ash from burnt stag antlers. The Venetian *latticimo* (milk) glass was of a denser white and contained additions of tin oxide. Eighteenth-century milk glass was produced by the addition of bone ash, as was the new porcelain it was intended to replace and copy. Imitation it was, in both form and decoration; the glass character was entirely lost

10

Fig. 10 **Cup and cover**, German, c.1725. *Clear glass painted in unfired colours with coat of arms and supporters, height 9¾ ins. (Victoria and Albert Museum.)*

Museum Photo

(Figs. 3, 4, 8 and 9). The enamelling and gilding were usually done by decorators of porcelain, and the rococo motifs of flowers, birds and pastoral scenes were usually identical in style, although certain factories, such as Potsdam, showed a little more originality. Continental milk-glass never achieved the perfection of Bristol opaque-white, but it brought a little more elegance to the German glass styles of the period.

On an entirely different level was the gilding and enamelling in black and red of Ignaz Preissler (c.1675–1733) and his son, who were both employed on the North Bohemian estates of Count Kolovrat. Their decorative treatment of transparent glass vessels in a distinctive rococo style with overall scroll-work, *chinoiseries* and delightful vignettes depicting rural scenes, interprets most aptly the charm of this period (Fig. 6).

An exceptionally fascinating decorative technique matching the scintillating and graceful mood of the age is shown in *Zwischengold* glasses. These appear in the form of multi-faceted beakers or tall goblets (Fig. 5) and consist of two vessels fitting perfectly one within the other, the outer vessel having a cut-out base. The surface of the inner vessel is embellished by the application of gold-leaf, on which the desired motif is etched with a needle and the surplus removed, as in a silhouette. The base is similarly decorated, the beakers fitted into each other by means of a colourless resinous adhesive between the two walls, and the cut-out base is replaced. Care must be taken that no air bubbles become trapped during the fitting together of the beakers, which now afford perfect protection to the decorated surfaces. The rim of the inner vessel is of double thickness to a depth of about half an inch, forming a lip that fits and joins perfectly when placed in the outer beaker, which is half an inch shorter. The join may thus be seen on the outside of the vessel, and is usually disguised by the decoration (Fig. 12). Towards the middle of the century, *Zwischengold* glasses become more colourful with added enamelling and brilliant red or green lacquer backing to the gold or silver foil motif, in the manner of the *verre eglomisé* technique.

Rare earlier specimens of this glass are decorated to achieve a marble or agate effect which completely conceals the surface of the gold foil. The foil is usually left untouched on the reverse, so that the interior of the beaker will appear to be gilt (Fig. 15). Some of these rare vessels may have been made at the end of the seventeenth century; these have the join at the top of the rim, the two beakers being of equal height. The decorative themes are typically rococo, though crests and armorial emblems occur, especially on formal, tall goblets, and on very early specimens. A simplified technique consisted of inserting *Zwischengold* medallions decorated with red lacquer and gilding into the walls of glass vessels.

The highly artistic treatment of the famous *Mildner* glasses is akin to this technique. These very distinctive vessels were produced by Johann Joseph Mildner (1763–1808) of Gutenbrunn, Lower Austria, and were decorated by inserting relatively large *Zwischengold* medallions into the wall and base. The medallions were elaborately enamelled with portraits, emblems, initials or allegorical subjects. A red lacquer base and gilding were frequently applied to Mildner's *Zwischengold* medallions, which made a splendid contrast with his very rare beakers of opaque-white glass (Fig. 11). Finely painted parchment miniatures enclosed in glass

medallions and inserted into the walls of beakers were a further variant of Mildner's artistry. Most of these glasses are signed and bear inscriptions naming the subject, date and place of manufacture on the reverse side of the medallion.

During the second half of the eighteenth century a subtle change occurred in the glass industry. The neo-classical style, which was inspired by excavations in Central Europe, imposed its influence also on glass design of the period. The rich and lively ornamentation of high baroque and rococo gave way to forms of classic simplicity and refined elegance.

A distinct decline in both quantity and quality of artistically cut Bohemian glass was largely due to the meteoric rise of English lead crystal, which surpassed all foreign products in purity and brilliance. Moreover, English engravers had both the time and the opportunity to study and adapt themselves to all manner of cutting techniques, and their proficiency left little to be desired. Bohemia could no longer compete successfully, and by the late eighteenth century the effects of the French revolution and the Napoleonic wars caused a depression in the commerce and industry of the impoverished states. During this lull, there was a slow gravitation towards coloured glass and an experimental phase in the development of new techniques. Some of the greatest individual glass artists, such as Samuel Mohn and Friedrich Egerman, were born during this period. Only in the early part of the following century, however, did their work make its great impact.

MUSEUMS AND COLLECTIONS

Eighteenth-century German and Bohemian glass may be seen at the following:

AUSTRIA
Vienna: Kunsthistorisches Museum

CZECHOSLOVAKIA
Jablonec: Museum of Glass
Liberec: North Bohemian Museum
Prague: Museum of Applied Art
                 Museum of Decorative Art

GERMANY
Berlin: Kunstgewerbemuseum
Cologne: Kunstgewerbemuseum
Munich: Bayerisches Nationalmuseum
Nuremberg: Germanisches Nationalmuseum

GREAT BRITAIN
Cambridge: Fitzwilliam Museum
Edinburgh: Royal Scottish Museum
Lincoln: Usher Art Gallery
London: British Museum
                 Victoria and Albert Museum

U.S.A.
New York: Corning Museum of Glass
Ohio: Toledo Museum of Art

FURTHER READING

German Enamelled Glass by A. von Saldern, New York, 1965.
Der Nürnberger Glasschnitt des 17ten Jahrhunderts by E. Meyer-Heisig, Nuremberg, 1963.
Glass in Czechoslovakia by Karel Hettes, Prague, 1958.
Europaisches Glas by R. Schmidt, Berlin, 1927.
Das Glas by R. Schmidt, Vienna, 1922.

Fig. 11 **Tumbler** by *Johann Joseph Mildner (1763–1808), Gutenbrunn, Lower Austria, 1788. Opaque-white glass set with two medallions in gold and ruby colours, the rim mounted with a band of silver, height 4¼ ins.*
Made by one of the greatest of all glass-workers, this tumbler uses the Zwischengoldglas technique in a new way; the medallions are backed with gold-leaf and set into carefully cut roundels so that they are flush with the surface.
(British Museum.)

Fig. 12 Zwischengoldglas **beaker**, *German, early eighteenth century. Glass and engraved gold-leaf. Zwischengoldglas was a very popular technique in this age of ostentatious elegance. This beaker demonstrates the technique quite clearly; the join between the inner and outer glasses can be seen about a half-inch below the rim. The two parts were joined by a colourless, resinous adhesive which allowed the gold-leaf design to be seen on either side. (Victoria and Albert Museum.)*

Fig. 13 **Wineglass** *with thick enamelled decoration by Johann Friedrich Meyer, Dresden, eighteenth century.*
This charming baluster glass, a beautifully proportioned piece in its own right, has been decorated by one of the most illustrious of German glass enamellers. The exquisitely painted rustic scene is typical of the elegant fancies so popular at this time. (Pilkington Glass Museum, St. Helens, Lancashire.)

Fig. 14 **Tankard**, *with mark of Ehrenfriedersdorf, near Chemnitz in Saxony, early eighteenth century. Opaque blue glass with wheel engraving, the lid of pewter. (Victoria and Albert Museum.)*

Fig. 15 Zwischengoldglas **tumbler cup**, *German, c.1720. Glass and gold-leaf. This rare early specimen uses a complex technique by which the gold-leaf is almost completely concealed on the surface, but is left untouched inside to give the appearance of a gilt interior. (Victoria and Albert Museum.)*

Kaendler at Meissen

William Hutton

Fig. 1 **Tea-urn,** c.1740–45.
The scene, probably by the painter J. G. Heintze, shows the town of Meissen. On the hill above the Elbe stands the Albrechtsburg Fortress where the newly established factory was first housed in 1710.
(Private Collection, London.)

⚔
Crossed swords mark adopted 1724, in blue or black enamel.

Johann Joachim Kaendler was the man responsible for the triumph of Meissen. For more than fifty years the porcelain produced there was unsurpassed by the work of any other European factory

The European porcelain figure was conceived at Meissen soon after the material itself, for an inventory of 1711, the year after the factory began work, already lists several models, including a tiny but impressively baroque figure of Augustus the Strong, Elector of Saxony, King of Poland and the patron for whose satisfaction Meissen was established. Until about 1715, when it became possible to make white porcelain in some quantity, this and other models were made in the agate-hard red stoneware developed during the search for a material similar to Oriental porcelain.

The earliest figures at Meissen lacked any consistency of style, and this situation prevailed until 1727. Some are adaptations of Chinese types, while other models are related to small works in ivory, wood and metal of varied character. Generally these early figures were experiments by the factory, standing apart from the tablewares.

The Elector Augustus indulged a passion for luxury and display that achieved international repute even in an age accustomed to overweening splendour among princes. To house his immense accumulation of Oriental porcelain, he bought

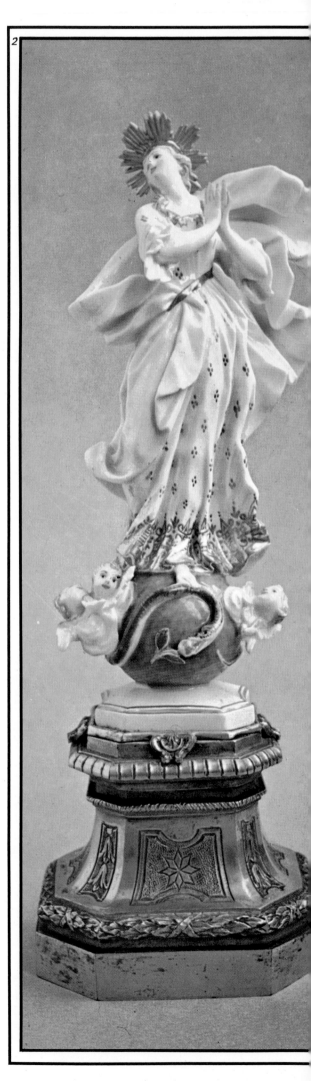

Fig. 2 *Virgin of the Immaculate Conception* by J. J. Kaendler (1706–75), 1737. Painted with enamelled colours and gold, height 7⅝ ins. without base. This was a popular theme for religious sculpture in the eighteenth century, here rendered on a scale suited to private devotions. (*Victoria and Albert Museum, London.*)

3

K. Hoddle

Fig. 3 *Allegory of Summer* by F. E. Meyer, c.1752. Painted with enamelled colours and gold, height 5½ ins.
From a set representing The Seasons, Meyer's slender figure illustrates the light spirit of the Rococo and contrasts with the more monumental late baroque style of Eberlein's allegory in Fig. 11.
(*Victoria and Albert Museum.*)

4

K. Hoddle

Fig. 4 *Shepherd with Bagpipes,* possibly by J. J. Kaendler, mid-eighteenth century. Painted with enamelled colours and gold, height 10⅛ ins.
The vitality of this figure suggests that Kaendler was the modeller. It well indicates his superiority over later and lesser artists who produced so many insipid pastoral figures.
(*Victoria and Albert Museum.*)

from a nobleman in 1717 a recently-built small palace across the Elbe River from his Dresden residence. It is best known as the Japanese Palace, and this was the first time that an entire building had been given over to porcelain, although richly decorated rooms designed to show off Oriental pieces had for some years been a standard feature of royal and noble houses. Augustus' programme, entirely fantastic in its scope and insensate ambition, eventually awarded the ground floor to Far Eastern wares, and the upper storey to those of Meissen. Each room was to be devoted to a separate colour of painted porcelain carefully arranged in a rich setting of stucco and carved and gilt wood.

The Elector's plans for his factory went further, encompassing a chapel with an altar, pulpit, large figures of the Apostles and even organ pipes in porcelain, and a gallery with life-sized animals and birds interspersed with huge, grotesque vases. Only parts of all this were realised, but these parts are among the prodigies of porcelain.

Shapes and designs changed with the modellers

In the 1720s, the basis for both the factory's artistic prestige and commercial success was established by J. G. Höroldt (1696–1775), who combined artistic with administrative gifts. His brilliant development of painted decoration, using *chinoiseries* of his own invention and versions of Oriental designs, was carried out on shapes offering a maximum smooth surface.

The factory's commission increasingly felt the need for tableware designs reflecting current taste, and in 1727 a young Dresden sculptor, Johann Gottlieb Kirchner (born 1706) was appointed as the factory's first trained modeller specifically to refresh the dated repertoire of forms. While he produced a few interesting pieces such as clock-cases, his work habits were too independent and after a year he was released and succeeded by the ivory carver J. C. L. Lücke, who proved even less satisfactory. For a year Meissen was without a modeller. Meanwhile the Japanese Palace was being enlarged to accommodate Augustus's plans, and in 1730 Kirchner was persuaded again to leave sculpture and return to the creation of great animals and vases in porcelain. To speed this project, another young Dresden sculptor, Johann Joachim Kaendler (1706–1775) was appointed to Meissen by Augustus whose notice he had gained while working in the Dresden Castle.

Kaendler was trained under Benjamin Thomae, one of the sculptors assisting Balthasar Permoser with the embellishment of the Zwinger (a series of linked pavilions and galleries for Saxon court festivities) where sculpture played nearly as important a role as architecture. Kaendler's adaptability to new tasks, indeed his quickness to see and exploit new possibilities for porcelain with an almost inexhaustible imagination, soon marked him as the up and coming man. Both he and Kirchner worked on the animals, but though Kirchner was made chief modeller, he was constantly at odds with the factory system and finally left Meissen in 1733. The full extent of his work is not known, for unlike Kaendler he was loath to keep records. Even so, it is clear that Kirchner, in his work at Meissen, laid the basis of a European porcelain figure-style and led the factory away from undue Oriental

Meissen Porcelain

7

5

6

8

9

10

Fig. 5 **Apollo vase** by Kaendler, 1744. Unpainted, height 20⅝ ins. From the set of the seven Planets, this vase was made for the Empress Elizabeth of Russia who sent Meissen many orders. (Victoria and Albert Museum.)

Fig. 6 **Goat** by Kaendler, 1732. Unpainted, height 21⅛ ins., length 28 ins. This piece was made for Augustus's Japanese Palace, in which the King housed his vast collection of porcelain. (Victoria and Albert Museum.)

Fig. 7 **Plate from the Swan Service** by Kaendler, 1738. Painted with enamelled colours and gold, diameter 11¾ ins. This plate is completely covered with beautiful relief work from which the service takes its name. (Victoria and Albert Museum.)

Fig. 8 **Angry Harlequin** by Kaendler, c.1738. Painted with enamelled colours, height 7⅝ ins. This Harlequin was transformed from an engraved illustration in a French book on the Commedia dell' Arte, the Italian comedy which became popular throughout Europe, and particularly in France, at the end of the seventeenth century. (Fitzwilliam Museum, Cambridge.)

Fig. 9 **Potter**, probably modelled by Kaendler and P. Reinicke, c.1750. Painted with enamelled colours, height 7½ ins. This comes from a series of eighteen figures symbolising various trades. (Fitzwilliam Museum.)

Fig. 10 **Woman carrying a child** by Kaendler, 1744. Painted with enamelled colours, height 8½ ins. Here Kaendler adapted a French engraving of 1739 of a peasant woman from Savoy. (Fitzwilliam Museum.)

influence and the realm of eccentric curiosities. Kirchner's elongated proportions and simplified modelling speak of a man who remained a sculptor at heart and they are in contrast to Kaendler's more compact modelling and agitated surfaces. Indeed, with his protean ability to adapt external ideas to his own purposes, Kaendler may well have recast some of Kirchner's models. His lovely *Virgin of the Immaculate Conception*, exceptional in that it was designed for a separate base, seems to reflect Kirchner's style (Fig. 2).

Kaendler brought to his first great task a mastery of baroque modelling and the gift of acute observation from nature. His *Goat* (Fig. 6) is one of the most impressive of the Japanese Palace animals, in which specific character was repeatedly translated into masterful sculpture. For porcelain, these figures were of enormous proportions and it proved impossible to eliminate the deep cracks caused by shrinkage in firing. In any event, Augustus's death in 1733, and subsequent shifts in direction, drew Kaendler to other tasks, though this work went on for a few more years, and from it sprang the race of smaller Meissen animals and birds which presently spread throughout Europe. The great animals are monumental achievements in every sense, and they include some of the masterpieces of animal sculpture.

Production of spectacular and ambitious dinner services was begun

Augustus the Strong was succeeded by his son, Augustus III, who fully maintained the glitter of the Dresden court, but his chief enthusiasm was for his great collection of pictures, which still testifies to his discernment. The factory's true guiding spirit now became Count Heinrich von Brühl, the new King's chief minister, and nominal director of the Meissen factory. As enlightened a patron as he was poor a statesman, Brühl recognised Kaendler's genius and promptly supported his contention that much could be done to improve tablewares with relief- and figure-modelling.

Kaendler now embarked on the great series of relief patterns that took Europe by storm with a magnificent service for Brühl's political rival Count Sulkowski, using for the dishes a wickerwork border which, with modifications, became one of the factory's most lasting patterns. While some of the Sulkowski pieces show an awareness of designs in contemporary silver, no such influence is evident in the profoundly original service made for Brühl himself from 1737 to 1741, as an extended allegory on the theme of water. This was the celebrated *Swan Service*, which comprised some two thousand two hundred pieces in thirty different forms. It is the most spectacular of all porcelain services, and takes its name from the subtle swan reliefs that appear most conspicuously on the plates (Fig. 7). There were five tureen models lavishly embellished with marine deities and shell festoons, sweetmeat dishes supported by mermaids, candlesticks, platters and bowls of many types, as well as vessels for tea, coffee and chocolate. Nowhere is the beautiful porcelain material itself better displayed than in this service, where the only painting is the Brühl arms, scattered Oriental flowers and slight gilding.

Kaendler also applied his fertile imagination to

the fusion of vase forms with sculptural decoration in a series of monumental vases. An ambitious *Elements* series was made for Louis XV of France in 1741–42. More restrained is the *Apollo* vase (Fig. 5), a version of one in a set of seven *Planets* vases modelled for the Empress Elizabeth of Russia in 1744. Works of this sort often had little or no painted decoration. Cultivated tastes appreciated the material for its own sake, and its glittering whiteness was an admirable foil to marble, lacquer, gilt furniture and panelling.

It is characteristic of Kaendler's capacity that while he was developing the great table services he also broke fresh ground, with profound consequences for the future with the first independent small figures, among the earliest of which are peasants playing musical instruments (Fig. 4). This was in 1736, and before the year was out he had also produced the first of his groups satirizing court manners and modes, in which the bulky crinoline skirt is often a conspicuous element; but Kaendler kept to general allusions and these are not in any way portraits. At the same time, Kaendler found perhaps his most famous theme of figure modelling in the traditional theatre of the Italian Comedy (*Commedia dell' Arte*), with its host of vivid stock characters, and his understanding of the earthy quality of their stage play inspired figures that seem to exceed the normal bounds of porcelain to convey an almost raucous vitality (Fig. 8).

Begun as an experiment, by 1740 the figures had found considerable success and, from this time on, they were central to the factory's work. A reason for their warm reception in Germany was the suitability of porcelain as table decoration, where they replaced the wax and sugar figures long customary there. Toward 1745, Kaendler used some French engravings for a series of figures which are not only picturesque, as intended, but also seem to have engaged his sympathy to an unusual degree.

In the middle of the century Meissen reached its peak, constituting Saxony's greatest source of income

The output of Kaendler and his colleagues in the 1740s was phenomenal. Besides special work for Brühl, the Court and foreign notables, they were often engaged with new relief patterns for tablewares, and there was a constant flow of figures drawn from mythology, the world of allegory, gallant pastorals, exotic peoples, peasants and gardeners. From 1735, Kaendler had a valued assistant in Johann Friedrich Eberlein (1696–1749), who helped with the *Swan Service* and also provided a series of other models of which the *Five Senses* (Fig. 11) is of particular distinction. Eberlein's work is separately recorded, but that of Peter Reinicke (at Meissen from 1743) is largely submerged by Kaendler's, who in any case 'corrected' all models before final approval.

As work records for 1749 to 1763 were lost in the Seven Years' War, we lack evidence for chronology and authorship in this period. In the early 1750s, Meissen reached its apogee of prestige and commercial success, employing nearly seven hundred people and constituting Saxony's greatest source of income. It was at this time that 'the Dresden' became generally available in England, where the figures, in particular, were copied at Chelsea, Bow and Derby, and already for some years Parisian luxury merchants had mounted Meissen figures with gilt-bronze as clocks and candelabra for sale to an international clientele. One suspects that the operating pace had become so fast that the quality at Meissen suffered, and after having sustained a remarkably high creative pitch for nearly thirty years the factory's inspiration may have begun to run thin. These are the years when the proverbial 'Dresden' shepherdesses and cupids first appeared as charming novelties. Colours tend towards pale tones of yellow, mauve and turquoise patterned with Oriental flowers in place of the earlier strong colours, applied with judicious restraint.

The best work of the period is, nevertheless, of a high order. A fresh style of figure modelling, with small heads and long, slender proportions, is due to Friedrich Elias Meyer (born 1724), who joined the factory in 1748. Meyer's graceful, elegant style (Fig. 3) is more truly rococo in spirit than Kaendler's more passionate interpretations of pastoral themes (Fig. 4). A sign manual of this new direction was the introduction in about 1750 of rococo-scrolled figure bases, which were then used for new models until the rise of neo-Classicism in the 1770s.

The supremacy of Meissen was threatened and prestige was gradually lost

The years around 1750 also saw the rise of several rival factories in Germany, Italy and France which threatened Meissen's near-monopoly, and when Saxony easily fell to Frederick the Great of Prussia in 1756 the stage was set for their ascendancy, notably that of Sèvres, to whom the palm of artistic leadership now passed. Meissen destroyed its kilns in the face of the enemy, but in a few months the factory was again operating, and until 1763 Frederick acted as its last great patron.

Frederick was a lover of porcelain, with dreams of his own factory, and while he was unsuccessful in luring Kaendler to Berlin, several men, including Meyer, went to the new factory there which Frederick took over in 1763. At Meissen he not only ordered many figures and vases from existing models, but, of greater importance, commissioned six large table services. Kaendler also modelled for him a series of large mythological groups, and these ambitious tasks must have provided a welcome challenge, for he brought to the realisation of some of them, at least, his full powers of imagination and composition.

The work for Frederick was the swan-song of Meissen, for with the return of peace in 1763, the factory entered a long and uneasy period of trying to find its place in a commercial situation where its ideas now seemed dated. Meissen no longer set the pace, and it was forced to assimilate outside ideas, chiefly from France.

Kaendler lived on until 1775, but although he was respected and occasionally still received important commissions, his baroque sense was never really at home in the age of neo-Classicism. The long triumph of Meissen owed more to him than to any one other man, and for this accomplishment he ranks as an important artist in his century.

11

Hawkley Studio

Fig. 11 *Allegory of sight by J. F. Eberlein, 1745. Painted with enamelled colours, height 8½ ins. The Five Senses are shown as standing women with appropriate attributes. Here, Sight is depicted with a telescope, a mirror and an eagle. (Cecil Higgins Art Gallery, Bedford. By permission of the Trustees.)*

HINTS FOR DATING MEISSEN

From 1723 the Meissen factory mark was the crossed swords of Saxony in under-glaze blue. Valuable evidence for dating tablewares are the impressed symbols used by throwers and moulders in the 1730s, replaced in 1739–40 at Kaendler's insistence by impressed numerals. Under the flat bases of figures the swords mark is often faint, or burned off in firing as it was unprotected by glaze, and, for this reason, the mark was placed on the base edge from about 1745. From about 1765 to 1775, a dot was usually placed between the hilts, and then until about 1814 a star was commonly placed beneath the swords.

A large proportion of the original moulds have survived at Meissen, and from the 1850s to 1914, in particular, figures and wares taken from them formed much of the production and are often found today. The figures may be distinguished from their ancestors by the tendency to have small white surfaces exposed, by the muddy pinks, greens and browns and by the presence of such colours as chrome green and maroon which were unknown in the eighteenth century. A further aid to their recognition is the large script mould numbers incised within open glazed bases, often accompanied by impressed numbers.

MUSEUMS AND COLLECTIONS

FRANCE

Paris:	Musée du Louvre
Sèvres:	Musée National de Céramique

GERMANY

Ansbach:	Residenz
Dresden:	Porzellan-Galerie
Hamburg:	Museum für Kunst und Gewerbe
Munich:	Bayerisches Nationalmuseum

GREAT BRITAIN

Bedford:	Cecil Higgins Art Gallery
Cambridge:	Fitzwilliam Museum
London:	British Museum
	Fenton House, Hampstead
	Victoria and Albert Museum
Wiltshire:	Longleat

HOLLAND

Amsterdam:	Rijksmuseum

U.S.A.

Connecticut:	Wadsworth Atheneum, Hartford
New York:	Metropolitan Museum of Art

FURTHER READING

German Porcelain and Faience by Siegfried Ducret, London, 1962.

Die Meissner Porzellantiere im 18. Jahrhundert by Carl Albiker, Berlin, revised 1959.

Meissen and other Continental Porcelain in the Collection of Irwin Untermyer by Yvonne Hackenbroch, London, 1956.

Dresden China by W. B. Honey, London, revised 1954.

European Ceramic Art by W. B. Honey, London, 1952.

German Porcelain by W. B. Honey, London, 1947.

Masterpieces in Ivory

The art of ivory-carving has always been held in high esteem. Ancient civilisations realised the potential of the smooth, unctuous substance with its subtle colour variations and were quick to exploit these qualities to aesthetic ends. The material was derived from various sources – elephant tusks, hippopotamus and walrus teeth and the tusks of fossils.

Early Christian ivories exist from the fourth century A.D. and the popularity of ivory as a material in which to carve religious images persisted throughout the Middle Ages and the Renaissance. Secular objects were also made of ivory – statuettes, chessmen, mirror-cases, combs and knife-handles.

It was during the seventeenth and eighteenth centuries that Germany and Austria became the main centres of the art of ivory-carving. The illustrations on the following pages show the many uses to which carved ivory was put by central European artists. The sources of the style lie within the tradition of European sculpture and the quality of the work cannot be denied. The carvings, whether secular or ecclesiastical, whether in relief or free-standing, are some of the finest examples of craftsmanship of this period.

Fig. 1 *The dead Christ supported by an angel and two* putti, *South German, early eighteenth century. Ivory and lapis lazuli. (Victoria and Albert Museum, London.)*

Fig. 2 **Orpheus and Eurydice** by Johann Leonhard Baur (1681–1760), 1760. Height 9½ ins. Signed and dated on the base. This important carving is the only authenticated piece in ivory by Baur. It is said to represent Eurydice indicating to her husband the serpent's sting which was to cause her death. There is some doubt, however, for the male figure does not carry the lyre which would positively identify him as Orpheus. In style, the group is reminiscent of the work of Giovanni Bologna, the famous mannerist sculptor. (Victoria and Albert Museum.)

Fig. 3 **Handle of a hunting-knife**, German, late seventeenth or early eighteenth century. Height 5¾ ins. The handle is carved in the form of a grotesque head with horns. Below, on the neck, is a medallion with an ox-skull in relief. Ivory was often used for the handles of knives and forks. The animalier form and the skull both suggest that this piece was attached to a hunting-knife. (Victoria and Albert Museum.)

Fig. 4 **Tankard**, German, late seventeenth century. Ivory drum mounted in silver-gilt, height 10¾ ins. The ivory drum is carved in relief with the Triumph of Silenius and a figure of a seated boy forms the knop. German tankards of elaborately carved ivory form an interesting group. The carving here is detailed and of fine quality. (Victoria and Albert Museum.)

Fig. 5 **Chinaman**, possibly from Dresden, first half of the eighteenth century. Ivory inlaid with paste. Nowhere was the passion for the East greater than in Germany. This figure, with its deeply cut draperies and inlaid paste in imitation of precious stones, illustrates a German's impression of the appearance of a Chinaman. (Victoria and Albert Museum.)

2

Museum Photo

3

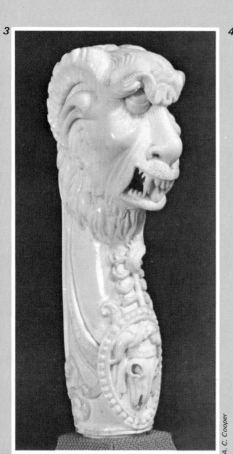

A. C. Cooper

4

5

Museum Photo

Fig. 6 **The Nursing of the Infant Jupiter by Amalthea** by Ignaz Elhafen (c.1650–c.1725), late seventeenth or early eighteenth century. Signed by Elhafen, probably a Bavarian who worked in both Rome and Düsseldorf before he was summoned to Vienna by the Elector. His work is characterised by his love of nymphs and satyrs and by his excellent modelling. In this relief of the Nursing of Jupiter, the background figures are very delicately handled in extremely low relief, whereas the foreground figures are in high relief, some parts of which are virtually free-standing.
(Victoria and Albert Museum.)

Fig. 7 **Triton** attributed to Mathias Steinl (1644–1727), c.1675. Height 4¾ ins.
This finely carved, small figure recently attributed to Steinl is indicative of the influence of the Italian Baroque penetrating into Germany. This is the type of figure, albeit much reduced in scale, that can be found in the great fountain statuary of artists like Bernini. It has been suggested that this triton might have originally been incorporated into a group. Alternatively, it might have been surmounted by a salt.
(Victoria and Albert Museum.)

Fig. 8 **Pastoral staff** by Joseph Teutschmann (1717–87), eighteenth century. Height 10¼ ins.
Finely carved with cherubs, the crook has typically rococo scroll-work. One of the cherubs wears a mitre and bears the coat of arms of Theobold Ritlinger, Abbot of the Cistercian Monastery of Aldersbach in Lower Bavaria.
(Victoria and Albert Museum.)

6

7

A. C. Cooper

Museum Photo

8

9

Museum Photo

Museum Photo

Fig. 9 **Bust of a woman** by J. C. L. Lücke (c.1703–80), mid-eighteenth century. Johann Christoph Ludwig Lücke was a member of a family of ivory-carvers from the Dresden area. He worked as a modeller at the porcelain factories of Meissen and Vienna where he described himself as 'principal director of the whole factory'. His chief work was, however, in the field of ivory-carving and included many portrait busts.
(Victoria and Albert Museum.)

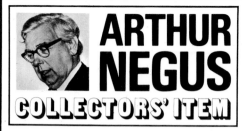

ARTHUR NEGUS
COLLECTORS' ITEM

PLAYING-CARDS

Playing-cards were used for amusement at the Italian and German princely courts at least by the beginning of the fifteenth century. Thereafter, the development of woodblock printing enabled many more cards to be made, giving them a more popular appeal and preparing the way for the mass-produced cards of the seventeenth century and after.

Because of the rapidity with which card-playing became an accepted – even a necessary – social talent, many different suit marks were developed. Italy, Germany, Austria, Poland and Bohemia all produced varying patterns and arrangements of suit marks.

Packs of cards were designed to reflect the political or social preoccupations of the moment. In Germany, divided as it was into many small states, heraldic cards were very popular. In Spain, with her rapidly expanding Empire, geographical cards were in great demand. Some were educational cards with historical and classical figures, some political like those directed against the Popish plotters of Charles II's reign or Deakin's 'political struggle' of the 1880s marking the Home Rule crisis.

The most decorative packs were made in the eighteenth century: in Paris alone over 200,000 different designs were produced in 1754, and the French armies in Canada, cut off from home by the British fleet, used cards as money during the last months before the fall of Quebec. During the French Revolution, a precedent was set when the traditional King, Queen and Knave were replaced by *Sages, Vertues et Braves.*

Collecting Hints

Beware of the 'made-up pack', put together from miscellaneous old cards. It is not an easy thing to do well, but it has been done. Look out for the names of the historic card-makers – Wokaun of Prague and Gobl of Munich are two that have fallen by the wayside; Piatnik of Vienna, Grimaud of Paris and the British De la Rue are three of the oldest to survive. Remember that all cards before 1890 had square corners, and that double-headed court cards did not come in until 1840.

Where To Buy

Sales of antiquarian books often include sets of playing-cards, and in general bookshops are a better bet than regular antique shops.

Prices

Eighteenth-century packs sell for between £50 and £300, and more recent ones for rather less, depending on condition and place of manufacture.

Above: *Dr. T. Schroeter's emblematical cards, mid-nineteenth century, with the emblems of four Germanic monarchs on the court cards: Maximilian I and Rudolph V, Habsburg, Friedrich Barbarossa and Karl der Grosse.*

Below: *Left to right:* **Popish plot card,** *English, 1679–80.* **French tarot card.** *'Timothy Ticklewits' Merry Budget of New Puzzles by G. Martin, early nineteenth century.* **Bubble card** *by Carington Bowles, satirising projected salt mining, 1720s.*

Opposite: *Above:* **Court cards,** *French, nineteenth century, with figures from Dumas.* Below: **Card case,** *English, nineteenth century.*

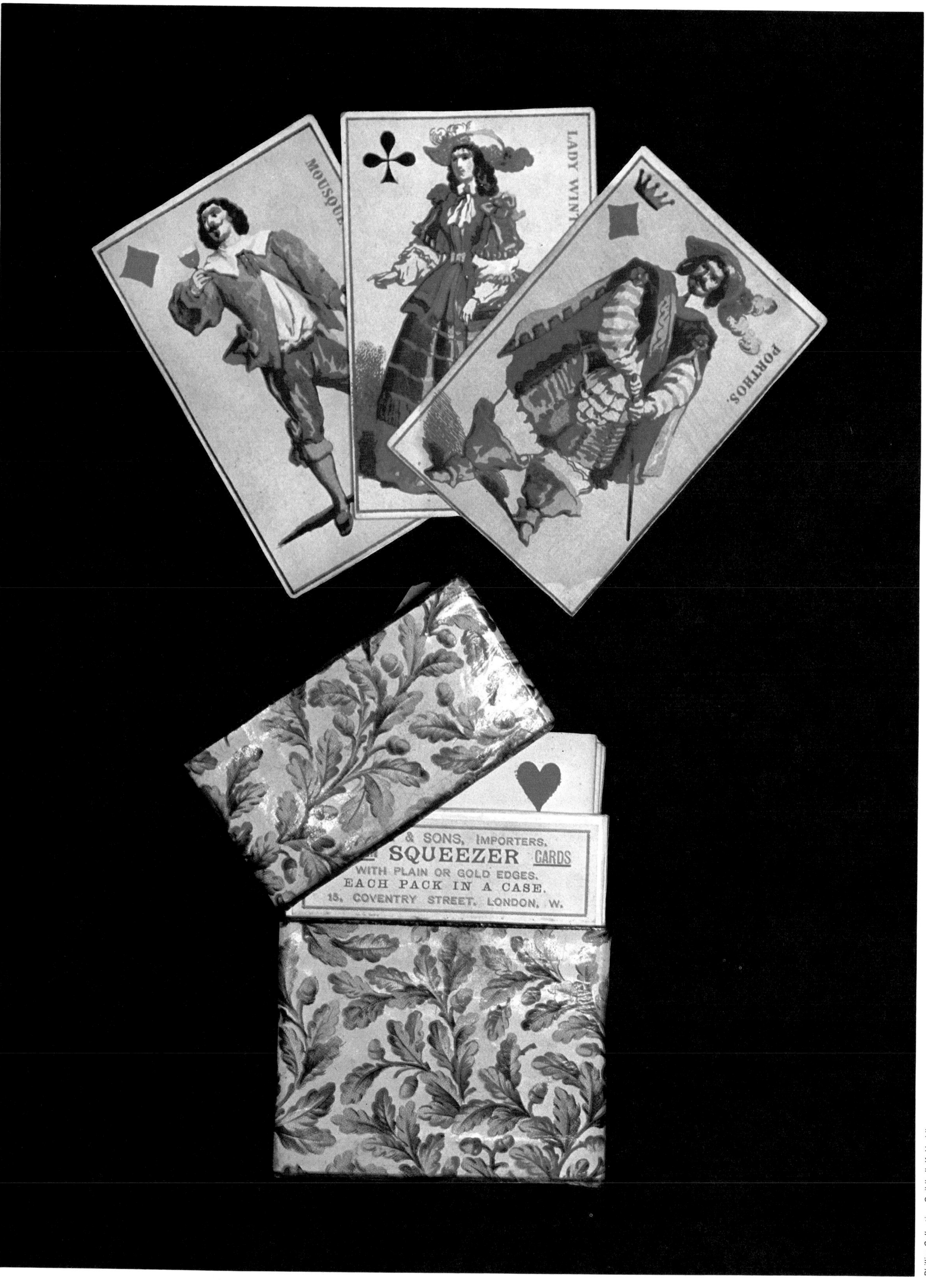

Phillips Collection, Guildhall: K. Hoddle

Viennese Porcelain

Joan Jordan

Using many of the Meissen techniques, and even some of their craftsmen, the Vienna porcelain factory began to produce individual and intricate wares in hard-paste

In 1704 Vienna gradually awoke from a politically enforced quiescence of the arts; the Turkish infidel at the gates had been vanquished and the scourge of plague had subsided.

Desirable socially and part of a self-supporting economy, the small factory of Claude Innocent du Paquier took its place in this setting. It was situated in the suburb of Rossau, not far from the Liechtenstein Palace. Du Paquier, until 1744 the sole proprietor of this factory which boasted only ten workers and one kiln, was of Flemish extraction and was born at Trier in Germany.

The factory received no assistance from the State, but the Emperor bought much Vienna porcelain and guaranteed wide privileges to the factory for twenty-five years, provided that Austrian artists were employed, and that the materials were obtained from the Austrian hereditary territories.

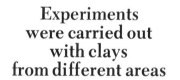

Experiments were carried out with clays from different areas

Du Paquier had made researches into the secrets of porcelain manufacture, albeit unsuccessfully. In 1717, through the Austrian representative in Dresden, the Count von Virmont, the services of the Dresden gilder and impostor 'arcanist' (one who knows the secret of making porcelain), Christoph Konrad Hunger, were obtained. Hunger was not, in fact, employed at the Meissen factory until 1727, and such knowledge as he possessed concerning the constitution of the paste and the management of the kilns was obtained through his friendship with Böttger, who, in 1708, had discovered the secret of true hard-paste porcelain at Meissen. He worked as Böttger's gilder and as an independent decorator. He was in Venice in 1720 and doubtless helped to establish the Vezzi factory, the third hard-paste factory in Europe.

Eight years after the Meissen patent of 1710, a patent was taken out by Du Paquier and his three partners, one of whom was Hunger. Clay from Passau was used, but at first this seems to have proved unsuitable. Meissen received a bitter blow in the loss of her kiln master and arcanist, Samuel Stölzel, who was brought to Vienna by Du Paquier and given his own carriage and the princely sum of one thousand talers a year. On the advice of Stölzel, kaolin from Aue, near Schneeberg in the Erzgebirge, was employed. This clay which had, it is said, been used to make hair powder, was the clay used at Meissen. Subsequently clay from Hungary was used, and the different sources account for the variable colour of the body. The kiln designs were brought to Vienna by Tiemann, Böttger's half-brother. Thus the second factory in Europe to make true hard-paste porcelain came into being.

Early Vienna porcelain resembles that of Meissen, but can be distinguished by the tone of the body. This is usually greyish or bluish, although some of the early wares have a creamy tone. Meissen was at first a yellowish ware, but subsequently it became pure white due to the inclusion of a feldspathic stone. W. B. Honey has pointed out that 'Meissen glaze, on close examination, is often found to be hazy with minute bubbles', and that this feature, with its colour, helps to distinguish it from early Vienna or Venice. The glaze of Du Paquier porcelain is flat and greenish when applied thickly, and the foot rims are rough and unglazed.

Silver shapes were relied upon in the absence of a tradition of porcelain forms. Handles of scroll and counter-scroll design were not finished with the same neatness and care as Meissen handles and were apt to behave irrationally and to bulge out unexpectedly. They were also of fish (Fig. 6), panther (Fig. 2) or dragon form; masks were applied to the vessels (Fig. 1) and small figures and animals (Fig. 3) or, in the truly baroque idiom, Roman emperors (Fig. 16) topped the objects or crouched in odd corners. They were of squat proportions resembling the limitations of the figures of Georg Fritzsche at Meissen. The applied figures were frequently gilt (Fig. 1) or silvered to simulate metal; indeed the use of silvering is a characteristic feature of Vienna, predominating over the use of gilding, but, in the course of time, it has oxidised to black. Chocolate beakers, teacups and coffee-cups were made, but rarely dinner-services, since it was the preference of the aristocracy to eat off silver dishes.

The earliest dated piece which has survived is a two-handled chocolate-cup of tall proportions with a slightly everted lip. Like the cup, the saucer is decorated with flutes. These form a petal-like relief design around the inner ring, raised to form a gallery to hold the cup firmly, a type of saucer known as a 'trembleuse' which was very popular at the royal French factory of Sèvres.

Apart from architectural devices, such as gad-rooning, fluting and cornices sometimes coloured to simulate marble, inspiration was sought from Dutch delftware. The form of a tulip vase was taken by Vienna and translated into a hard-paste version (Fig. 10). The decorations are naïve but of great interest since the colours used are under-glaze blue and over-glaze puce. Under-glaze blue was a constant challenge to the technical abilities of the European manufacturers, since kiln temperatures were critical and it was difficult to control the cobalt blue and to prevent it from running into the surrounding areas. Its use had, by this time, reached a point of great technical excellence in China in the K'ang Hsi wares.

The vase in Fig. 10 shows three features which became of paramount importance at the Vienna factory; plastic decoration depicted in the dragon's head handles, so unhappily joined to the outer bulb holders; baroque scroll-work decoration and Japanese 'sprigs'. Hunger claimed the exclusive secret of under-glaze blue as his, but in fact the Meissen factory was not noted for this colour and it was David Kohler who produced a good clear blue there just before 1725. The secret was then partly lost when Kohler died, and not rediscovered until

Fig. 1 *Tureen and cover, Vienna, c.1735, from the Russian Imperial Collection. (Victoria and Albert Museum, London.)*

Fig. 2 *Coffee-pot, Vienna, 1725–35. Polychrome. (Österreichisches Museum, Vienna.)*

Fig. 3 *Clock-case, Vienna, 1725. Polychrome, height 16½ ins. (Museo Civico, Turin.)*

Museum Photo

G. Rampazzi

Viennese Porcelain

Fig. 4 **Wine-cooler**, Vienna, c.1720–25. White decorated with applied flowers in high relief. Height 4¼ ins. (Österreichisches Museum.)

Fig. 5 **Tureen**, Vienna, early eighteenth century. Height 5½ ins. Formed as a tortoise ridden by a Chinaman, this delightful tureen is an example of the Viennese love of fanciful wares. (Österreichisches Museum.)

Fig. 6 **Tray**, Vienna, c.1740. Schwarzlot decoration enriched with gilding. Handles in animal form, such as the fish on this piece, were much appreciated. (Antique Porcelain Company, London.)

Fig. 7 **Ewer**, Vienna, c.1730. Decorated with under-glaze blue. Height 7 ins. Inspired by Chinese models made between about 1575 and 1600, vessels of this sort were very popular in eighteenth-century Vienna. (Victoria and Albert Museum.)

Fig. 8 **Bowl and cover**, Vienna, c.1730. Polychrome decoration, height 6 ins. The delightful figures are in the popular chinoiserie style. (Victoria and Albert Museum.)

Fig. 9 **Cup**, Vienna, c.1735. Polychrome fruit and flower decorations, height 3¼ ins. This attractive cup has the fluting so often found on pieces of this period. (Victoria and Albert Museum.)

Fig. 10 **Tulip vase**, Vienna, c.1721. Decorated with under-glaze blue and over-glaze puce, the gilding now mostly rubbed away. Height 9½ ins. Derived from similar Dutch pieces made in Delft, this extraordinary vase has three very important Viennese features: plastic decoration in the form of dragon handles, baroque scroll-work decoration and Japanese 'sprigs'. (British Museum, London.)

after 1732 at Meissen.

Vessels formerly known as sauce-boats were made, but they are, in fact, *Bourdaloues*, or oval chamber pots. A Jesuit preacher of the seventeenth century, named Bourdaloue, found the necessity for such a pot due to the great length of his sermons. His maid attended him with the requisite vessel.

Figures were copied, and some even cast, from Meissen originals and are of exceeding rarity. Some figures from the *Commedia dell'Arte*, Chinese characters, little puppet-like musicians, each placed between a two-tree-trunk candelabra, a tureen in the form of a tortoise ridden by a Chinese figure and another of a chicken, are apparently unique specimens.

It was not considered inappropriate to use extravagant gold or silver mounts for porcelain and thus some of the exquisite painting was often obscured. Few pieces are now in existence to bear witness to the value set on the porcelain by this practice, but many contemporary references remain.

Such pieces were offered as prizes at the cross-bow shooting matches (*Kranzlschiessen*) which were a feature of Viennese life during the summer and autumn months. The Austrian official gazette, *Wiener Diarium*, published the prize list before-hand and we learn that 'porcelain objects mounted with silver or gold, or tea, coffee or chocolate services combined in a travelling case', were offered as prizes. Sometimes Meissen or Oriental porcelain was offered.

Many sumptuous pieces were made as gifts to the Russian Court (Fig. 1). One such piece used as a table decoration may have found its source of inspiration in the peasant weddings which were celebrated with great splendour at the eighteenth-century courts of Germany and Austria, at which the noblest of princes acted as host. One such celebration took place at the Hofburg on 21 February, 1719. The piece in question is a brandy-holder in the form of an elephant; encircling him on a lower supporting tray of silver are eight peasants, male and female, individually dressed and representative of the eight Austrian provinces. The elephant stands on a porcelain base and the none-too-competent peasant figures hold in their left hands ringed supports for the containers of the brandy.

In the late 1720s, the most ambitious decorative scheme of Vienna porcelain which survives was devised for Count Dubsky in Brünn. A porcelain room now housed in the Österreichisches Museum, Vienna (Fig. 11) has panels in the door and window frames, mirror and picture frames, tables and chairs, chandeliers and fireplace, jars, vases and cups, all of which are porcelain. They are mainly decorated with oriental flowers and landscapes based on Japanese examples, but some of the pieces are painted with the naturalistic German flowers. Thus it would appear that Vienna employed the use of these *Deutsche Blumen* at least five years earlier than Meissen (Fig. 17).

There is a linear quality in Vienna porcelain decoration which appears in the painting of flowers and baroque scroll-work. Loops, palmettes and interlacings abound and there is much lattice-work decoration surrounding perched birds and baskets of flowers.

The enamelled colours employed by 1725, at the latest, were iron red, green, purple, pink, yellow and blue, and this range was hardly increased during the factory's existence. In their soft low key, so different from some of the hard, shouting brilliance of Meissen, they point over the bridge from Baroque to Rococo, but it is only a direction and Vienna porcelain stands firmly rooted in late baroque tradition.

One of the characteristically sombre modes of decoration is known as *Schwarzlot*: black enamel painting with a brush or point (Figs. 6, 14 and 16). This was first used in Europe on pottery and glass by a Nuremberg painter of the latter part of the seventeenth century named Johann Schaper, who executed some very fine miniature landscapes on faience which are celebrated German masterpieces. *Schwarzlot* was used at Vienna to depict *putti*, animals, landscapes, and mythological and hunting scenes. Hunting services, dishes, plates and tureens, were made in this style and are called *Jagd* services.

Independent decorators (*Hausmaler*) worked on such Meissen and Vienna porcelain as they could obtain. '*Jacob Helchis fecit*' appears on a pair of two-handled cups and covers decorated in this manner (Fig. 13), probably decorated by Helchis in the role of a *Hausmaler*, since he cannot be defin-

4

5

6

Fig. 11 **The Porcelain Room,**
*designed for Count Dubsky in
Brünn in the late 1720s.
This ambitious decorative
scheme contains more than
fourteen hundred pieces of
porcelain. Most are adorned with
flowers and landscapes in the
Japanese manner, but some have
naturalistic flowers.
(Österreichisches Museum.)*

Fig. 12 **Wine-cooler,** *Vienna,
c.1740. Polychrome decoration of
flowers and a mouse, height
6¼ ins.
(Victoria and Albert Museum.)*

Fig. 13 **Cup and cover** *by Jacob
Helchis, Vienna, c.1740.
Decorated in* schwarzlot *with
putti and landscapes, heightened
with gilding, and mounted in
silver-gilt. Height 5½ ins.
(British Museum.)*

itely associated with the factory until 1746, after the Du Paquier period. Vienna porcelain was decorated in this style by Viennese and Bohemian *Hausmaler* who greatly influenced the factory style and by artists of the Preissler family.

Schwarzlot painting, especially when further decorated with gilding, is in the baroque tradition of the French furniture of André-Charles Boulle. The bacchantes, satyrs and acanthus leaf mounts of his furniture are in accord with the masks and acanthus applied plastic decorations on Böttger's early porcelain; a style abandoned at Meissen in 1720 and carried on by Du Paquier in his Vienna productions.

The measured gait of the true baroque *Laub und Bandelwerk* (foliage and scroll-work), also appears in softer, more feminine hues of light blue, purple and green; the iron red of the baroque palette still remained (Fig. 15) although not in such a fiery tone as that of Meissen.

Many signed pieces in *Schwarzlot* were painted by Carl Wendelin Anreiter von Zirnfeld, who, in 1737, went to the Doccia factory as an arcanist. His style is that of the engraver. It was said of him that 'there are not many workers in Europe who

produce such fine and beautiful work'.

Purple painting *en camaïeu*, in several shades of one colour, is attributed to Philipp Dannhofer, who was born in Vienna and was one of the outstanding painters of the eighteenth century. He is also notable for genre painting, *chinoiseries* and landscape painting.

Christian Frey, who signed his work with the initials C.F., painted *putti* and his work can be found in the State Hermitage Museum, Leningrad.

We do not know for certain if Helchis was ever at the Vienna factory during the Du Paquier period. A famous gilt hunting service was made, for which he is thought to have been in part responsible. He signed his work, and his style is therefore well known. Possibly his pieces were painted outside the factory. We know that he went to Turin in 1741, and after returning to Vienna he went on to Neudeck, where he became manager in 1747.

The period ends with Du Paquier, unable to withstand the continuing financial burden, offering the factory to the Archduchess Maria Theresa, who took it over in May, 1744, for fifty-five thousand gulden. Du Paquier remained as Director but he retired in the same year and died on 27 December, 1751.

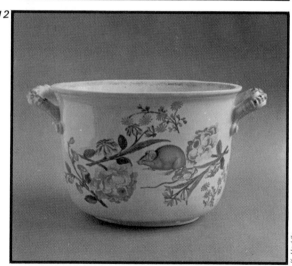

Viennese Porcelain

MUSEUMS AND COLLECTIONS

Viennese porcelain may be seen at the following:

AUSTRIA
Vienna: Österreichisches Museum
GERMANY
Frankfurt: Museum für Kunsthandwerk
Hamburg: Museum für Kunst und Gewerbe
GREAT BRITAIN
London: British Museum
                 Victoria and Albert Museum
Northants: Spencer Collection, Althorp
ITALY
Turin: Museo Civico

U.S.A.
New York: Metropolitan Museum of Art
U.S.S.R.
Leningrad: State Hermitage Museum

FURTHER READING

Continental Porcelain of the Eighteenth Century by Rollo Charles, Toronto, 1964.
German Porcelain and Faience by S. Ducret, London, 1962.
Vienna Porcelain of the Du Paquier Period by J. F. Hayward, London, 1952.
German Porcelain by W. B. Honey, London, 1947.

Fig. 14 *Tureen, Vienna, c.1725–35. Decorated in brownish schwarzlot heightened with gilding. Height 10 ins. This unusually large tureen is decorated with hunting scenes as well as the more usual baroque ornament of Vienna. (Victoria and Albert Museum.)*

Fig. 15 *Tea-caddy, Vienna, c.1725–30. Painted in iron red with chinoiseries in the manner of the engraved designs of Elias Baeck. Height 5½ ins. The delicate colours used on Vienna porcelain, such as this iron red, foreshadow the later subtleties of the Rococo. (Victoria and Albert Museum.)*

Fig. 16 *Bottle, Vienna, c.1725–35. Decorated in schwarzlot heightened with gilding, height 12¼ ins. In best baroque fashion, this handsome bottle is topped by a bust of a Roman emperor. The piece itself is decorated with a combination of Austrian and Japanese elements. (Österreichisches Museum.)*

Fig. 17 *Tankard, the silver lid with the Vienna hallmark of the year 1729. Polychrome decoration of Deutsche Blumen within baroque borders. Height 8 ins. This superb piece is the earliest datable example of Deutsche Blumen decoration – the naturalistic flower style which was later used extensively at Meissen. The high quality of the tankard shows the great proficiency of the Vienna factory even relatively soon after its foundation. (Österreichisches Museum.)*

K. Hoddle

K. Hoddle

Museum Photo

Museum Photo

The Meeting of East and West

Julian Reade

Fig. 1 **Nanban Byōbu**,
Japanese, Momoyama period,
late sixteenth century.
Lacquer, $62\frac{1}{4}$ x $131\frac{1}{2}$ ins. This
beautiful folding screen depicts
the arrival of Portuguese sea
captains and merchants in Japan.
They first came during the 1540s.
(Imperial Collection, Japan.)

Fig. 2 **Mandarin** of the Ch'ing
dynasty (1644–1912).
Water-colour. Mandarins
were Chinese officials who could
achieve any of nine grades of
power. This one is seen, by the
blue button on his cap, to be of
the second grade.
(Victoria and Albert Museum,
London.)

3

Réalités: Charbonnier

4

K. Hoddle

5

多是天工巧　人曉染得色鮮明　方自聖傳老何奇　形曾費葛仙不繼　銀光皎皎固為五色　然成練熟時萬縷　涤色

Museum Photo

European merchants in the sixteenth century found a sharp contrast between the peaceful and sophisticated culture of China and the constant civil wars and corruption in Japan

When, in 1517, the merchant adventurers of Portugal made their first serious expedition to the Chinese coast, they encountered a civilisation far older and more sophisticated than their own. Their behaviour, like that of the Dutch and English who followed over the next hundred years, soon persuaded the Chinese that the majority of Europeans were dangerous barbarians who had to be kept firmly in their place.

The trade that developed shows how little Europe had to offer to a country which had known iron suspension bridges since the seventh century, printed books since the eighth or ninth, and had produced explosives since the tenth. China exported, apart from silk, porcelain, fans and furniture, a reputation for gracious living and civic order. What the Chinese wanted in return was at first not a European product, but spice from Indonesia.

Fire-arms, too, were immediately appreciated, and a flourishing trade developed in European clocks. The West became known in China as a

Historical periods in China and Japan

CHINA
Sung 960–1279
Yuan 1280–1368
Ming 1368–1644
Ch'ing 1644–1912

JAPAN
Heian 784–1185
Kamakura 1185–1392
Muromachi 1392–1573
Momoyama 1573–1615
Edo 1615–1867

Fig. 3 *Temple of the Lamas, Peking.*
China had three major religions: Buddhism, Taoism and Confucianism. This temple was used exclusively for Buddhist ceremonies.

Fig. 4 *Wife of the Mandarin seen in Fig. 2, Ch'ing dynasty. Water-colour.*
In the strict hierarchical system of China, officials of the government needed to maintain the appearance of power in such things as dress. Their wives, as seen here, were also richly and ceremoniously dressed. (Victoria and Albert Museum.)

Fig. 5 *Silk culture and manufacture, the dyeing phase, during the reign of the Emperor K'ang-hsi (1662–1722). Water-colour.*
Silk-making was one of the Chinese industries most important to the relationship of East and West; as well as wanting porcelain, fans and furniture, Europeans had an insatiable desire for the rich silks of China. Here the dyeing process is seen. The skeins of silk are being dyed in huge pots under the shelter, and hung out on bamboo poles to dry in the sun. (Victoria and Albert Museum.)

source of ingenious mechanical devices, but most of them were regarded as little more than amusing toys. Jesuit intellectuals such as Ricci, who settled in China from the end of the sixteenth century, were greatly respected for their genuine contributions to astronomy and the sciences, but even they must have learned as much as they could teach.

Scientific perspective was regarded as odd and unnecessary

Western techniques in the arts, such as the use of scientific perspective and chiaroscuro, were generally regarded as odd and unnecessary, with little to do with the ultimate purposes of art. This attitude was only natural in a nation where aesthetic theory had been almost as precocious as technology. Many centuries had passed since Chinese artists, ensuring spontaneity, had experimented with such methods as throwing ink at the floor or refusing to look at a picture while it was being painted. The Sung emperor, Hui-tsung (1101–25), had felt obliged to order his academicians to change their ways and represent nature as it actually was.

This, in the sixteenth century, was ancient history, but what matters is that the intervening dynastic changes had had no conspicuous effect on the continuity of intellectual development. The extreme views of Hui-tsung and of the painters he had criticised, together, of course, with every kind of intermediate attitude, always remained familiar. The same was true of attitudes to subjects other than painting.

In the sixteenth century, under the late Ming emperors, the traditions of the Sung period were frequently dominant. Hsuan-te (1426–35) had praised one of his court painters because his work was indistinguishable from that of his Sung predecessors. Imitation became a safe way to professional success.

The emperor had to approve standards of craftsmanship in the applied arts

The existence, nonetheless, of a large scholarly class ensured that imaginative work was still done. The amateur intellectuals might be private individuals, or descendants of the royal family kept at state expense but excluded from political office, or members of the bureaucracy which, with an elaborate system of checks and counter-checks against corruption, ruled an enormous area with impressive facility. While competence in the applied arts was guaranteed by the public ownership of numerous factories whose products had to reach standards approved by the emperor, intellectuals could cultivate the inseparable superior arts of poetry, painting and calligraphy in an atmosphere of tranquil experiment.

Around 1600, however, the system began to disintegrate. Emperors, too little interested in government, were surrounded by hordes of eunuch and volunteer eunuch advisers whose rivalries were incompatible with responsible administration. Eventually the Manchu, or Ch'ing, dynasty, from north of the Great Wall, conquered the entire land and introduced the compulsory pigtail as a symbol

of its dominance.

Quite soon, of course, despite the disturbances of the interregnum when many intellectuals died, the Chinese absorbed the Manchus as thoroughly as they had all previous barbarian conquerors. The bureaucracy, with all that it meant for Chinese cultural life, re-established itself; there were merely new men at the top. K'ang-hsi (1662–1722) rebuilt the imperial porcelain factories and studied astronomy, and his grandson Ch'ien-lung (1736–96) was among the most implacably cultivated of all Chinese emperors, with enormous if somewhat indiscriminate tastes for art and learning of every kind. It is difficult to avoid the impression, however, that Chinese art was, during this period, living largely in the past.

Japan, which the Portuguese reached in the 1540s, was a land heavily influenced by Chinese culture, but foreign influences had been adapted and naturalised. At the time, it was divided into a great number of small states, controlled by warlords, each of whom ruled a band of warriors called *samurai*, who were of sometimes fanatical loyalty. Civil war was continuous. There was a nominal emperor in Kyoto, but even he, though respected for his divine ancestry, was effectively subordinate to a chief deputy who was little more than the local warlord. The Imperial Court itself was impoverished, and derived its income from such sources as the sale of titles and antiques.

The cleanliness of the temples contrasted with the sad state of the monks' souls

There were also some powerful Buddhist monasteries, whose peculiar practices horrified the Jesuit missionaries. The monks often formed themselves into private armies, but they also ran schools and were largely responsible for the preservation of Chinese traditions of culture in this chaotic period. Temples such as those of Kyoto and Nara, with their magnificent wooden architecture, rich decorations, and their ingeniously watered gardens, impressed even the Jesuits. One of them noted the contrast between their extreme cleanliness and the sad state of the monks' souls.

The *samurai*, however, inspired the Jesuits' deep respect as their developing *bushido* code, with its emphasis on personal honour and contempt for life, seemed to have much in common with that of contemporary Europe. Women, though freer than in Europe, were kept firmly to heel, divorce being recommended to anyone who found his wife paying as much attention to her religion as to her family.

Though western fire-arms were instantly popular in Japan as in China, the *samurai*'s sword remained an object of enormous significance in his life, and rules of etiquette, as elaborate as the sword-fittings themselves, dictated how he should treat it in public. A different atmosphere is suggested by accounts of the important Zen tea-ceremony then in vogue; a special area of the house and garden was reserved for this, and favoured guests, over a contemplative cup of tea, would admire the kettles and ostentatiously rustic cups which were among the most valuable objects a man could possess.

In the second half of the sixteenth century, a succession of three warlords gradually eliminated their rivals, attacked the independent monasteries,

China and Japan

Fig. 6 *Himeji Castle*, *built in 1609*.
This magnificent castle was built not far from Kyoto which was the ancient capital of Japan.

Fig. 7 *Warlord Nagaro Kagetora* *in council, receiving a report from Marakama Yoshikiyo, Japanese, c.1845.* *(Victoria and Albert Museum.)*

and united the whole of Japan. The emperor survived, but only as a figurehead. Suspect nobles were rendered powerless by such techniques as transferring them and their *samurai* from one province to another; sometimes the migrants exchanged wives as well as estates.

All three warlords were liberal patrons and under their leadership the Japanese arts flourished in an entirely new way. Chinese traditions of restraint lost much of their power. Bright colours and overlays of precious metal were popular, as on the folding screens which were important items of Japanese furniture. Exotic fashions came and went; at one stage, while Christianity was virtually illegal, Japanese officials affected Portuguese dress and rosaries.

The Tokugawa period (1603–1867) saw the

Sakamoto

K. Hodtle

Fig. 8 *Hideyoshi Toyotomi* *(1536–98), Japanese.* *This depicts the supreme warlord of the Momoyama period.* *(Imperial Collection.)*

Fig. 9 *The Art of Music, Ch'ien Lung, Chinese, eighteenth century.* *Mirror painting in lacquer frame.* *(Private Collection.)*

Fig. 10 *The Momokawa tea-house at Edo. Colour woodblock print by Kunishada, Japanese, nineteenth century.* *(Victoria and Albert Museum.)*

Fig. 11 *The Battle of Kawanakajima, between the warlords Takeda Shingen and Uyesugi Kenshin, in the sixteenth century. Colour woodblock print by Kuniyoshi, Japanese, nineteenth century.* *(Victoria and Albert Museum.)*

descendants of Ieyasu, the third of the unifiers, securely established in Edo, the capital (present-day Tokyo), while Osaka became prominent as the commercial centre of Japan. Almost all contact with the outside world was cut off in 1639, and Japan became a closed society. A strict caste system was enforced, with *samurai*, merchants, artisans and peasants as the principal categories; no one could rise above the station to which he was born.

The power of warlords was limited by strict provisions of court attendance, and by compulsory contributions to public works such as the great Tokugawa mausoleums at Nikko. An unintentional result of these measures was the increasing impoverishment of these people, who had once been able to indulge their artistic tastes so lavishly that the government had restricted them.

The Tokugawa themselves were as liberal patrons as they were ruthless dictators. In Edo, many official artists lived on public funds; the Kano family of painters, for instance, with its followers was exceptionally distinguished, but, as so often in such circumstances, their work tended to become repetitive.

Meanwhile, a new class of patron was arising, in the first instance in Osaka. Here the merchants

gained what the *samurai* lost, and attempts by the government to limit their wealth, or inhibit their love of ostentation by harsh sumptuary laws, were uniformly unsuccessful. There is a story of some merchants on a picnic, throwing their litter, covered in gold-leaf, into some running water nearby; poor nobles collected it as it floated downstream. Though the merchants seem to have accepted that they were disqualified by birth from political ambitions, their prosperity was responsible in the eighteenth century for a vast flowering of literature, drama and the applied arts.

Colour-prints are perhaps the most revealing genre of middle-class art, and they are particularly well represented in the West because they were frowned upon by the Japanese authorities, even as late as the twentieth century. The realistic picture they give of Japanese life ranges between the sympathetic and the satirical, but they are, above all, works which have an immediate appeal to the West. As their style owes something to European prints brought into Japan by the Dutch during the centuries of isolation, it is particularly apt that they should themselves have had a notable influence on European painting when they arrived here.

9

Ming Dynasty Porcelain

Anthony Derham

A. C. Cooper

A. C. Cooper

Fig. 1 (Back) **Large dish** of the Cheng-te period (1506–21). Imperial yellow glazed ground, decorated with the outline of a green glazed dragon.
(Front) **Small dish** of the Cheng-te period (1506–21). Plain Imperial yellow glaze, painted with the six-character mark of the Emperor.
(Author's Collection.)

Fig. 2 **Fishbowl** of the Lung-ch'ing period (1567–72). Diameter 29 ins. This massively potted bowl is an example of the larger wares made during the latter part of the Ming dynasty. Infinitely more difficult to produce than thin, delicate pieces, the sides of this bowl are in many places more than an inch thick. The painting is in the best Ming tradition; it depicts five-clawed dragons about to grasp at the flaming pearls on which they feed, and rushing through cloud scrolls above great waves breaking on to rocks. (Author's Collection.)

Fig. 3 **Tou T'sai jar** of the Ch'eng-hua period (1464–87). Although this charming jar has been extensively repaired, it is an excellent example of the earliest type of enamel painting done in China. This was the last major problem to be solved in the potter's art, and the solution, using a 'muffle kiln', was discovered late in the fifteenth century. The jar is one of the now very rare pieces which are painted with the six-character mark of the emperor of the period and accepted as dating from his reign. (Author's Collection.)

Porcelain techniques, developed in China over many centuries, reached perfection in the Ming dynasty when the huge demands of the West for wares of every variety were met

---

Before discussing the characteristics of the ceramic art industry in China during the Ming dynasty, it is essential to put this whole group of wares into context by means of a short historical and social survey.

The Shang dynasty (1766–1122 B.C.), evolving fast from a nomadic, neolithic culture, established a sophisticated farming, ancestor-worshipping civilisation towards 1500 B.C. Of their coarse, sun-dried pottery vessels painted with bold geometric designs, those excavated seem to be predominantly funerary, although among the succeeding Chou dynasty (1027–221 B.C.) burials, a number of obviously secular shapes are found.

Although not a period of economic stability, the first great T'ang emperor, Li Shih-min (called T'ang T'ai-tsung) established the T'ang dynasty in 618 on such a firm foundation that the arts flourished; ceramic shapes and techniques of decoration, often now taken directly from shapes of vessels used by the welcomed near-Eastern trader, for the first time took on a distinctive splendour and freedom.

The potters of the succeeding Sung dynasty (A.D. 960–1279), having discovered the secret of firing a porcelain clay, pandered to the refined tastes of the aesthetic Court by producing a series of wares now usually accepted as the synthesis of the Western collector's vision of Cathay. The emphasis being purely on shape and proportion, these wares were decorated with lightly carved or finely moulded, mainly floral, motifs under the monochrome glazes: the great Kuan and Lung-ch'uan celadons, the ivory Ting yao glazes, the Ch'ing pai wares (the name refers to the colour of the sky after rain, and accurately reflects the state of mind of the patrons of this art).

In 1368, when Chu Yuang-chang (Hung-wu) established the 'brilliant' Ming dynasty at Nanking, his potters had completely mastered the manufacture of a true high-fired porcelain, translucent and with a beautiful resonance. They could execute the most delicately potted stem-cups for the finest wine, or throw massively constructed storage jars. The glaze often cracked along the joints during the firing, showing clearly how the flat base, the lower

---

part of the body, the wide deep shoulder (they would have been potted as bowls) and the neck were made separately, and then 'luted' together (stuck with a porcelain clay watered down to a creamy consistency, called slip) after drying, and before being decorated and glazed. Even though large cracks sometimes appeared in the base during the drying, prior to the firing, this was obviously not considered a defect serious enough to make the vase a 'waster', and that these cracks were simply filled in before the whole vase was fired is a good indication of how highly these large early pieces were valued.

They could execute delicate stem-cups as well as massive storage jars

During the short but culturally important Mongol occupation before the Ming – the Yuan dynasty (1280–1368) – the under-glaze method of painting had been developed. Consisting simply of the painting of the design on to the body after a first firing, this was obviously a major step. The early Ming decorators exploited to the full the possibilities of both the unpredictable iron red (moments of over-oxidisation in the kiln could mean that the colour would either run or turn pale greyish-green) and the costly but instantly appreciated and sought-after wares painted with cobalt blue imported from Burma.

The fourteenth-century examples of both these groups, probably most obviously characterised by the brilliantly precise painting of loosely composed decoration, were potted from finely mixed white clays, which often in the firing burnt a pale orange colour across the predominantly flat or shallowly cut bases, while the glazes tend to be thin and slightly grey in tone. Figure 8 is one of the finest 'text book' examples of fourteenth-century under-glaze blue; it is a storage jar, the construction of which is similar to those mentioned above. The shallowly domed lid was probably shaped like a lotus leaf. Clearly visible in the brush-strokes is the famous 'heaped and piled' effect produced by the slightly uneven grinding of the cobalt.

In early fifteenth-century wares, the clear glazes were often very thick, and though carefully and evenly applied and controlled, this often allowed the blue to 'bleed' or smudge very slightly into them during the firing, giving a depth and richness to the blue very characteristic of this group. Figure 5 shows not only the obvious difference between the early fifteenth-century Chinese porcelain dish and the seventeenth-century Turkish faience dish, but

Ming Porcelain

Fig. 4 *Kuan Yin, the Goddess of Mercy, in meditation, late Ming dynasty (early seventeenth century)*. Blanc de chine porcelain. This fine figure of the Buddhist Bodhisattva, Avalokitesvara, illustrates the extraordinary technical skill of the Ming modellers.
(Author's Collection.)

Fig. 5 (Left) **Dish,** *Chinese, early fifteenth century. Blue and white porcelain, about 14 ins. diameter.*
(Right) **Dish,** *Turkish, early seventeenth century. Blue and white pottery. Diameter about 14 ins. Both found recently in Damascus, these dishes show the importance of Chinese porcelain to near-Eastern pottery design. The Turkish faience dish is a faithful copy of the Chinese piece.*
(Author's Collection.)

Fig. 6 (Behind) **Serving-dish** *of the Wan-li period (1573–1620).* Kraak porselyn.
These early export wares, brought in large quantities to the West by the Dutch East India Company, derived their name from the Portuguese trading ships, the Carracas.
(Left) **'Provincial' dish,** *Chinese, early sixteenth century. Probably intended for the South East Asia market, these dishes were the first mass-produced wares for everyday use.*
(Right) **Ginger-jar** *from the reign of K'ang-hsi (1662–1722) in the Ch'ing Dynasty.*
(Christie, Manson and Woods, London.)

A. C. Cooper

Fig. 7 *Celadon bowl, fifteenth century. Diameter 16½ ins. This magnificent fluted celadon glazed bowl has an applied moulded plaque in the centre of the interior. Bowls of this sort, carrying on the classic Sung tradition of celadon wares, found their greatest success at the Courts of Egypt and Persia, at the rich trading markets of the Malay Archipelago and in the ports of Burma and India. (Christie's.)*

Fig. 8 *Storage jar of the Yuan Dynasty (1280–1368), fourteenth century. Height 12 ins. This heavily potted Kuan jar is a rare example of the fine under- glaze blue painting which was developed during the Mongol occupation before the Ming dynasty. The 'heaped and piled' effect produced by uneven grinding of the cobalt is visible in the brush-strokes. The jar once had a shallowly domed lid, probably shaped like a lotus leaf. (Christie's.)*

illustrates the fact that in Turkey, even at such an early date, Chinese porcelain, which had been traded for several centuries, was considered the ideal and faithfully copied in a less costly ware for the home market.

The tradition which the potters of the classic Sung celadons had established continued into the Ming dynasty; but, whereas the emphasis had earlier been on exquisite proportions and fine potting – they had been admired and, to quote C. P. Fitzgerald, 'venerated as the expression of the artist's percep- tion of truth' – during the fourteenth and fifteenth centuries the celadon wares produced were predom- inantly very heavily potted large plates, serving dishes and great deep bowls (Fig. 7). They also included storage jars and hanging lanterns, boldly carved or decorated with applied pre-moulded designs and thickly covered with a characteristic olive celadon glaze which pooled during the firing into the recesses of carving and around the relief of the applied moulded decoration.

While certainly used at the Chinese Court, these wares found their greatest success not only at the near-Eastern Courts of Egypt and Persia, for which they were perhaps first intended, but also on the rich trading markets of the Malay Archipelago and in the ports along the coasts of Burma and India at which the merchants had to stop during their long sea voyages. In the first early sixteenth-century inventories of the great collections of Chinese porcelains at the Topkapi Saray in Istanbul, the actual generic term for the celadon group was *Martabani*, referring to the port of Martaban in Burma from which these wares were thought to originate.

Poison was supposed to boil if it touched a dish of celadon porcelain

The reason for this great demand was not purely a question of aesthetic appreciation, or one of rarity. Although the origin of the story is lost, poisoned food was supposed to boil if it so much as touched a dish of this celadon porcelain – and it is not difficult to imagine this secret being whispered into any willing ear along the 'silk road'.

Towards the end of the fifteenth century, during the reign of Ch'eng-hua, the Imperial kilns at the now undisputed centre of porcelain manufacture, Ching-te-chen, produced the first porcelain decor- ated with enamel colours. Painted on to a clear glazed vessel which was then refired in a low tem- perature 'muffle kiln', this process was the last major problem in the potter's art to be solved. Figure 3 illustrates a small jar, one of the now very rare pieces which, although painted with the six- character mark of the emperor during whose reign the piece was made (here the characteristically thickly written and crowded mark of Ch'eng-hua) are accepted as actually dating from the period of that mark.

It is as well here to explain an aspect of peculiarly Chinese philosophy regarding the copy versus the fake. Any kiln whose potters and painters were competent enough to make a pot in a popular earlier style so well that it emerged from the kiln in every way as beautiful as the original from which it was taken, would have painted the new piece with the mark of the emperor associated with the period

during which the production of the particular ware reached its (aesthetic and technical) zenith. This was a purely honorific or dedicatory marking, and not until comparatively recently has it taken on a definitely fraudulent intent.

The reigns of the middle to late Ming emperors (Hung-chih to Wan-li), although often unstable in themselves and with strong eunuch corruption and exorbitant taxation, saw a constant increase in the importance of an export trade in porcelain to the countries beyond the established markets of South East Asia, India and the near East. Figure 9 illus- trates the recurrence of a popular exported shape, the ewer. On the bottom left is the heavily potted early fifteenth-century example, perhaps taken from an Islamic metalwork prototype, the smudgy but free style of painting clearly different, under the thick eggshell glaze, from the marked eighteenth- century ewer on the right. Although a faithful copy, the technique is far more precise and controlled, with the 'heaped and piled' effect carefully imitated under a thin glassy glaze. (The bridge and base of the spout have been restored on this ewer, and the dead white of the overpainted repair contrasts with the subtle, deep white of the body, often more clearly seen on a photograph than when the piece is handled.) In the centre is a sixteenth-century ver- sion, the design only very loosely similar, and painted in a washy grey-blue typical of all but the top quality export pieces.

On 6 January, 1515, an Italian in Portuguese ser- vice, Andrea Corsali, wrote to Giuliano de' Medici that 'merchants of the land of China make voyages to Malacca across the Great Gulf (of Siam) to acquire cargoes of spices, and they bring from their own country . . . porcelain'. Although not very long after this specimens arrived in Portugal itself, it was the Dutch who, in 1595, followed the Portuguese routes around the Cape of Good Hope and established themselves at Canton with the declared aim of trading; and it was the Dutch East India Company that first brought quantities of porcelain to the appreciative European market, making porcelain wares objects of relatively expensive everyday use as opposed to the wonderful rarities of fifty years before.

These first imports, the *Kraak porselyns*, as the Dutch called them then and as they are still called, are well illustrated by the large deep serving-dish in Figure 6. They were usually thinly potted, and sand from the saggars in which they were fired was often not properly cleaned off the deep foot rims. This, together with the characteristically

Fig. 9 **Ewers,** *Chinese* (from the left) *early fifteenth, mid-sixteenth and mid-eighteenth centuries. The ewer was a consistently popular form of export ware. (Christie's.)*

9

A. C. Cooper

watered down, deep purplish-blue used in the painting of the later Ming export wares, makes this a distinctive group. The name *Kraak*, rather than referring to the crackled glaze of some pieces, comes from the Portuguese trading ships, the Carracas.

The earlier sixteenth-century 'provincial' dish in Figure 6, a very good example of the first truly mass-produced wares for day-to-day use, shows the diluted blue with which these much cheaper types were painted. Also typical of this class of ware is the very loose calligraphic style with which the predominantly mythical animal and formalised flowering branch subjects were treated.

As widely appreciated as the thinnest and most delicately conceived pieces, but infinitely more difficult to produce, were the colossal fishbowls made for the Court during the latter part of the

dynasty. Figure 2 shows such a bowl; measuring an uneven twenty-nine inches in diameter, the sides are in many places over one inch thick. Dating from the short reign of Lung-ch'ing, it is an example of the very best in Ming painting. On the outside, Imperial five-clawed dragons rush through cloud scrolls above great waves breaking on to rocks, to grasp at the flaming pearls on which they feed. Tradition has it that these bowls were declared impossible to make, until a desperate potter, sure that he would be executed because he could devise no method of firing such vast pieces, flung himself into the burning kiln, and the bowls, having been fired, emerged in every way perfect. Technically, this would be more likely to contain some element of truth were it to refer to an under-glaze red firing, since a burning human body would certainly provide the excess carbon monoxide essential to the production of this colour.

As this is essentially an outline of only the main-stream production of the Ming porcelain industry, the subsidiary tilemakers' wares, the pieces made during the Ming dynasty but following earlier traditions, the Southern Annamese export wares and the monochrome glazes are not discussed here. It must suffice to illustrate as Figure 4 a fine late Ming *blanc de chine* figure of the Buddhist Bodhisattva, Avalo-kitesvara, manifested in Chinese art as the Goddess of Mercy, seated in meditation on an outcrop of rock. The sheer technical skill necessary to model this figure, as to fire the fishbowl, prove that by the end of the dynasty porcelain manufacture was no longer a problem in itself. The kiln managers could then concentrate quietly on developing production techniques to cope with the opening floodgates of European demand. 𝕾

MUSEUMS AND COLLECTIONS

Ming porcelain may be seen at the following:

FORMOSA   Former Imperial Collections, Taiwan
FRANCE
Paris: Musée Guimet
GREAT BRITAIN
London: British Museum
    Percival David Foundation
    Victoria and Albert Museum
Oxford: Ashmolean Museum
IRAN
Teheran: Iran Bastan Museum
JAPAN
Tokyo: Idemitsu Foundation
    Tokyo National Museum
SWEDEN
Stockholm: Östasiatiska Museet
TURKEY
Istanbul: Topkapi Saray Museum
U.S.A.
Cambridge: Fogg Art Museum
Cleveland: Cleveland Museum
Washington: Freer Art Gallery

FURTHER READING

Ming Pottery and Porcelain by Soame Jenyns, London, 1953.
'Fourteenth-Century Blue-and-White' by John Pope in **Freer Gallery of Art Occasional Papers,** Washington, 1952.
Chinese Pottery and Porcelain by R. L. Hobson, New York, 1915.

Lacquered Furniture

Jonathan Harris

R. Todd-White

R. Todd-White

Fig. 1 **Miniature tansu or chest containing drawers**, *Japanese, second half of the eighteenth century. Length 9¾ ins., height 9 ins., depth 4¾ ins. Miniature pieces of furniture were made for the Girls' Festival in the third day of the third moon, a festival created by Tokugawa Ienari as a counterpart to the Boys' Festival. Although it is an eighteenth-century piece, the shape and ornament of this chest are of earlier design. (Phillips and Harris, London.)*

Fig. 2 **Sho-dana or shelf cabinet**, *Japanese, second half of the eighteenth century. Like all Japanese furniture, this cabinet is designed to be used and seen from a low viewpoint in the sparsely furnished houses of Japan. It is of a type never used in China, and has an entirely Japanese delicacy. The shape is probably of seventeenth century origin, and the Karakusa ornament is probably sixteenth century. (Phillips and Harris.)*

Lacquered Furniture

Fig. 3 **Folding chair**, *Chinese,*
c.1600. Carved guri *lacquer.*
(Spink and Son Ltd., London.)

Fig. 5 **Dish**, *Chinese, of the*
K'ang Hsi period (1662–1722).
Porcelain.
This elegant lady is posed against
a cherished possession, a table
with lacquered legs.
(Christie, Manson and Woods,
London.)

Fig. 6 **Cabinet**, *Japanese, third*
quarter of the seventeenth
century. Height 29½ ins.
The highest qualities of the
Japanese artist and craftsman
were brought out in marvellous
cabinets of this sort, which had
a profound influence on European
furniture in succeeding centuries.
Note the unusual refinement
of the gilt-copper mounts.
(Phillips and Harris.)

Fig. 4 **Low table**, *Chinese,*
fifteenth century. Vermilion
carved lacquer.
(Christie's.)

Using a skilled and extremely time-consuming technique, Chinese and Japanese artisans produced lacquer furniture of a quality and beauty rarely seen in Europe

The art of lacquering was probably first used in China in conjunction with furniture-making at the time of the mighty Han empire, around the first century A.D. The craft was placed under the direct patronage of the emperor and imperial workshops were set up in various provinces. Even then, there were specialists in all stages of manufacture, analogous to those of seventeenth-century porcelain-making. There were the artificers of the basic wood shape, the preparers of the cloth base, the applier of the lacquer, the polisher, the gilder, the incisor and the painter.

In Japan, lacquer was probably first made for the embellishment of furniture during the Nara period in the eighth century. Throughout the later periods it was necessary to obtain special permission to possess an article of luxury. Lacquered furniture and utensils were, therefore, made only for the Court or the nobility, and, as Japan was a country of frequent natural and human turbulence, little furniture of quality survives. In China, too, little survives for the same reasons and it appears that apart from the palaces, or the grandest rooms in the houses of the gentry, it was unusual to have all the furniture, or even complete rooms, of lacquer.

Oriental lacquer became known in Europe through Portuguese and Spanish traders

Oriental lacquer was unfamiliar to the West until more recently than porcelain, which began to reach Europe sporadically by the fourteenth century, but it was not until the late sixteenth century, when the mariners of Portugal and Spain plied their commerce with the Far East, that lacquer utensils and the occasional piece of furniture found their way to Western buyers.

Marco Polo, in China for seventeen years during the late thirteenth century, had heard of the fabulous 'gold' accoutrements – saddles, boxes and tables, many of which must have been embellished with gold lacquer – that were sent from Japan to the Imperial Court of China. Both porcelain, prized for its twin virtues of translucence and resonance, and lacquer, another completely strange and magical substance, were paid the compliment of imitation in Europe and were richly mounted in precious metals or gilt-wood. The inventory of Catherine de' Medici, who died in 1589, listed lacquer objects, and Mazarin's inventory of 1653 listed lacquer of identifiably Japanese origin. European furniture certainly began to be influenced by imported lacquer in the early seventeenth century.

For a fuller appreciation of lacquer furniture, it is necessary to describe briefly how it was made. The same basic method of making lacquer is employed all over the East. It has been made in Burma, Siam (much esteemed in the seventeenth century), Korea, and principally in China and

Japan, both with long imperial traditions, reaching perfection in the latter. Discounting later, and less well made imitations, the true art was one of infinite exactitude.

Resin from the *Rhus Vernicifera* (*Urushi-no-ki*) is tapped in the same way as rubber from the tree. The resin is strained, refined and sometimes blended before being put into air-tight jars. The quality differs according to the season of tapping, the soil, the age of the tree and the climatic conditions under which it is grown and also the part of the tree from which the sap is taken. The skilled lacquerer will select the type appropriate to the article on which it is to be used. After the application of one coat of lacquer – and there may be as many as three hundred on a deeply carved finished article – the piece is put to dry in an atmosphere of a particular temperature and humidity. It is then polished and the process repeated. In the case of furniture, the application is on a carcase of soft-wood, expertly dowelled together by the Chinese and Japanese joiners using wood or bamboo pins; neither nails nor screws and little glue were used until the late nineteenth century. The Chinese lacquer screens, so popular in Europe, have leaves made up of two or three planks held together merely with pegs, a tribute to the lasting tensile quality of lacquer. The Oriental craftsman seasoned his material with great care; lacquer furniture lasts extremely well since good lacquer is impervious to water and the base moves very little.

Japanese furniture was designed to be seen and used from a low viewpoint

The style of living varied in China and Japan and this accounts for some of the differences in the furniture of the two countries. The Japanese dwelling with its wooden-posted framework was simple, even austere, divided by sliding paper screens and protected by wooden shutters on the exterior walls. Rooms were very sparsely furnished and occupants sat or knelt on the mats on the floor. Furniture was limited to trunks, both large and small, for storage, writing-boxes, small tables and trays for the tea-ceremony, shelf cabinets and chests. Everything was designed to be seen and used from a low viewpoint.

The *sho-dana* (shelf cabinet) in Figure 2 makes a beautiful small table in a Western house, but was not originally designed for the viewpoint of a man standing or seated on a chair. It is a piece not used in China, and is entirely Japanese in its delicacy. This example dates from the second half of the eighteenth century. It shows a shape that originated probably in the mid-seventeenth century and the *Karakusa* design was probably first used a century earlier. The same could be said of the *tansu*, or chest, in Figure 1. It is in fact a miniature; not designed as would have been the case in England, as an apprentice piece or trade sample, but as an object for the Girls' Festival in the third day of the third Moon, created by Tokugawa Ienari. The festival was a counterpart to the Boys' Festival in the fifth Moon and there would be, among other things, an exhibition of historical dolls and miniature pieces of furniture to celebrate the next generation of motherhood.

Chinese houses would be more familiar to the

A. C. Cooper

European visitor. They possessed stools in abundance (chairs were the prerogative of rank or age) and tables of a greater variety of heights than the Westerner commonly uses for eating, writing and the display of an object or vase of flowers. Some tables, which appear to us uncommonly low, were placed upon the *kang*, a raised, built-in, heated bed, particularly popular in North China, but seldom found in lacquer. Figure 5 shows an elegant lady of the seventeenth century, posed, in much the same fashion as her European counterpart, against a cherished possession, a table with lacquered legs.

The sideboard (*lien san*), with drawers above and cupboard beneath, is rare in lacquer; bookshelves are less rare. The Chinese loved symmetry and order and the casual arrangement of our rooms would have been anathema to them. Pairs of chairs might be arranged on each side of a table, all matching; *armoires* were placed in rooms of state and, in palaces, they were often of large proportions with hat cupboards above.

One type of table peculiar to China was the household altar-table, sometimes made in pairs. Figure 8 shows a magnificent example in dark tobacco brown lacquer from the early years of the seventeenth century. The underlying form is of great beauty and strength. The decoration on the top, with dragons among clouds within a shaped surround, and on the legs and frieze, is not incised but painted gold.

The differences between Chinese and Japanese lacquer furniture are noticeable in the styles of decoration of the two countries. There is a world of

6

R. Todd-White

7

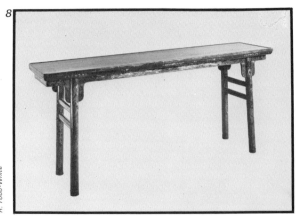

8

R. Todd-White

R. Fortt

Fig. 7 *Cabinet*, *Japanese*, *mid-seventeenth century. Height 27 ins. Of exceptional quality, this cabinet with its hardstone decoration would have cost more in 1650 than now. (Phillips and Harris.)*

9

10

R. Todd-White

R. Todd-White

Fig. 8 *Household altar-table, Chinese, early seventeenth century. Length 6 ft. 3 ins. This magnificent dark tobacco brown and gold altar-table is of a type peculiar to China. (Spink's.)*

Fig. 9 *Cabinet, Chinese, third quarter of the seventeenth century. Height 31¾ ins. This excellent copy of Japanese lacquer emulates the raised gold (taka-makie) work of Japan. (Phillips and Harris.)*

Fig. 10 *Cabinet, Japanese, early eighteenth century. Height 13 ins. This fine example shows why Oriental lacquer-work was so esteemed in Europe for its beauty and intricacy. (Phillips and Harris.)*

difference between even a fine quality, small-size Chinese coromandel screen and the Japanese painted paper partitions of screens. Coromandel lacquer would have been coarse and overwhelming in the small-scale Japanese house. The Chinese have a great sense of the mass of an object and the balancing of masses. They often think in terms of volume, of the filling of the space, rather than the drawing of the line round it. Designs upon ceramics or lacquer furniture are appropriate to the object, and executed with great verve. The top of the remarkable table in Figure 8 has a design of three dragons within a shaped panel, with ten more cavorting round the border. To our eyes the execution of the design in painted gold is remarkable, being done with a certain artistic freedom; precise without being finicky.

Japanese decoration is achieved with great exactitude and labour

The Japanese, however, with their taste and aptitude for incredible precision of finish, do not appreciate such work to the same extent. On the whole they approach design differently; they think in terms of line and the balancing of shapes. The lacquer designs are usually more open than the Chinese, more naturalistic though at the same time more severe. They were not as fond as the Chinese of incising and inlaying different coloured lacquers in another coloured ground. Their designs were built into the lacquer surface by drawing in the materials themselves, gold or silver dust, pieces of

metal and by the carving of laboriously raised surfaces. As so often in the Japanese character, there is a contradiction: a seemingly simple design of some asymmetrically placed blades of grass, achieved, as it were, only by the swift, sure stroke of a brush, is copied with an almost unbelievable exactitude and labour in the long process of lacquer working, achieving exactly the same impression of spontaneity.

In fifteenth-century China, the imperial lacquer workshop was re-established in Peking, and the vermilion lacquers from the reign of Yung-lo and Hsuan-te have retained their contemporary fame. Figure 4 shows a rare survival of a small table from that century; furniture in this style of lacquer is most uncommon, and though the technique evolved ultimately into the carved Cinnabar lacquer of the eighteenth century, the shape of this table could well be found in other techniques in the succeeding four centuries. Very often it is embellished with mother of pearl inlays in a black ground, the shape being borrowed by the Japanese and similarly embellished.

Another very rare survival of carved red lacquer is shown in the magnificent folding chair of about 1600 in Figure 3, which would have been used in a hall or taken outside. It is in so-called *guri* lacquer, in Chinese, *Chien Hwan Hsiang Tsao*, being the description of a kind of grass that the pattern resembles. The thick lacquer is carved with a wedge-shaped tool revealing, rather like geological strata, alternate levels of light and dark red. Examples of this type of lacquer are known from the Yuan dynasty; the Japanese copied it, but as in China the output largely consisted of small boxes.

Mother of pearl inlays picked out with painting in gold (*raden*) have an ancient lineage in lacquer-work and furniture. In the Shosoin at Nara are preserved Chinese T'ang and possibly a few Japanese utensils, chests, musical instruments and cabinets. At this time, the influence of T'ang China was eagerly absorbed, and indeed in the organisation of the traditional Japanese house and in the Gagaku music of the imperial household, we see and hear things essentially unchanged since the eighth century.

The highest quality work was to be seen in the cabinets, so much admired in Europe

The first *raden* lacquers of the Japanese imitated T'ang wares and, by the sixteenth century, the method was again used for the first lacquer wares made expressly for Europeans; utensils, trunks and cabinets. From these, a yet more splendid form of cabinet was developed which, although made by the Japanese to stand on the floor according to their convention, was used differently in Europe. The Japanese had now, by the beauty of their designs and the refinement and development of scores of named techniques, become superior in the art to the Chinese who, even in the sixteenth century, paid vain visits to learn a similar proficiency. It is in these marvellous cabinets that we see displayed, in a manner beautifully suited to European interiors, the highest qualities of the Japanese artist craftsman (Figs. 6 and 7).

Artists of the highest calibre painted for the lacquerer, and their designs were often borrowed by painters. Figure 7 shows a cabinet which might be assigned to the middle years of the seventeenth century. The animals, the pattern around the drawer fronts and on the dividers, the use of hardstones and the quality of the raised gold (*taka makie*), all point to a date around 1650. None of the few cabinets of similar type now in the National Museum of Denmark, formerly in the Royal Cabinet of Curiosities, the collection started around 1635, attain this quality. Few examples of this excellence reached Europe in the ship-loads that arrived in Antwerp from the East which were then much more expensive than they are now.

A great number of exotic pieces were imported into Europe

Because of the historical development of the East India trade, these cabinets would have been more familiar in Continental houses than English ones. When, in 1679, Evelyn remarked of the rich lacquer cabinets at the house of the Portuguese Ambassador, 'I think there were a dosen', he was expressing surprise at the quantity of these rare and exotic pieces.

Seventeenth- and eighteenth-century Europeans distinguished more readily than we do now between the various qualities of lacquer and cabinets, as of course did the Chinese and Japanese. It is noticeable that the finest French furniture of the eighteenth century used the equivalent lacquer of the 1670s or 80s. The front of the great *secrétaire en pente* sold recently in London for a large sum was veneered with lacquer that must have come from a cabinet of the type illustrated in Figure 6.

This piece also shows the refinement of the gilt-copper mounts. Other sorts of Chinese and Japanese lacquer furniture might have them in brass, silver, *pai tung* (pewter) sometimes engraved, or *cloisonné* enamel. A peculiarity is that the Japanese artist worked out his designs and their location in the space without regard for the subsequent application of hinge straps or lock plates. The rich sobriety of the early examples noticed above was also taken over by the Chinese when they paid the Japanese the compliment of copying their wares. Europeans also copied both Chinese and Japanese lacquers, creating some of the most beautiful furniture of the seventeenth and eighteenth centuries.

Quality depended on sufficient time and exacting standards

A very fine cabinet from the first years of the eighteenth century is shown in Figure 10. The ground colour is dark brown, unlike the lustrous black of the previous examples, and a greater variety of colours are used. The design of the lock-plate is more elaborate; the carrying handles are of gilt-copper rather than of iron. In slightly earlier examples of a comparable quality, the flower-heads might have been in hardstone, mother of pearl, *repoussé*, or solid metal. Fine lacquer furniture could be made only when the time of a skilled artist was immaterial, and as long as an extremely exacting standard was satisfied. Unfortunately, demands and standards have changed and furniture of this quality will never be made again.

MUSEUMS AND COLLECTIONS

Oriental lacquer furniture may be seen at the following:

DENMARK
Copenhagen: National Museum

FRANCE
Paris: Musée Guimet

GREAT BRITAIN
London: Victoria and Albert Museum

NETHERLANDS
Amsterdam: Rijksmuseum

U.S.A.
Cleveland: Cleveland Museum of Art
New York: Metropolitan Museum of Art

FURTHER READING

Chinese Art by R. Soame Jenyns and William Watson, London, 1963.
Chinese Domestic Furniture by G. Ecke, reprinted London, 1963.
Japanese Art Lacquer by U. A. Casal, London, 1961.
'Guri Lacquer of the Ming Dynasty' by Sir H. Garner, **Transactions of the Oriental Ceramic Society**, Vol. 31.

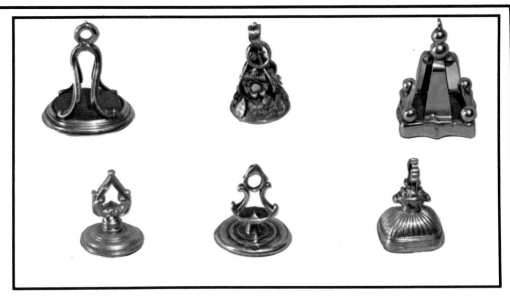

ARTHUR NEGUS
COLLECTORS' ITEM

SEALS

The first seals were made and used by the Greeks and Persians thousands of years ago. Seals were made elsewhere in Europe in the fourteenth century in solid gold, silver-gilt, and with gold or silver loops or handles with seal matrices cut in rich, hard gemstones or engraved in steel; some are in marble or brass, some in glass or ceramics. Although designs are numerous, it is often possible to date a seal. Many bore shields or coats or arms which can be easily identified.

Ordinary English brass during the seventeenth century proved to be too pitted with air-bubbles for seal engraving. Frequently a matrix would be cast in a mixture of iron and steel, engraved with the required device and then hardened by heating followed by sudden cooling.

In Tudor times, the wealthy Englishman revelled in owning a pair of ring seals. The most elaborate style has a bezel or groove to hold a stone revolving in its setting so that more than one device could be cut on it, one heraldic, the other perhaps a portrait of the owner's wife.

Pendant seals incorporated in tiny musical boxes were imported from Switzerland. Sometimes they served as lockets, a hinged box above the seal enclosing a lock of hair or a portrait.

Collecting Hints

Pendant seals have the greatest appeal to the modern collector; they became popular originally when men's breeches acquired a fob pocket for a watch and chain. Early pendant seals have stems fashioned after the baluster outlines of glasses, candlesticks and other small furnishings of the well-to-do late Stuart and early Georgian homes. By the end of the seventeenth century, the matrix

was mounted in a low-domed base.

Flat, gemwork handles, usually chased and burnished and suggesting drawer-handles of the period, are associated with the second quarter of the eighteenth century. From the 1760s, seal-handles were made with narrow, interlacing ribbons of metal variously reeded and moulded by being pressed through the newly developed swage block, and the rim of the matrix mount was shaped to match. Nineteenth-century seals had an attractive, massive simplicity but this soon gave way to elaborately chased seal mounts in complex designs of relief work.

In 1791 the law required gold and silver seals to be assayed, and these are particularly interesting to the collector who looks assiduously for hall-marks.

Names To Look For

James Tassie and his nephew William were famous for their clear-cut seal intaglios of moulded, soft, opaque, white lead glass. In 1776 Tassie charged 1/6d for a seal cast. At the Great Exhibition of 1851, John and Frederick Biden exhibited seals with cornelian, bloodstone, onyx and amethyst. Seals were also produced by factory jewellers in Birmingham and by Matthew Boulton and Edward Thomas.

Prices

These vary considerably, depending on the date of each seal. Early ones are rare and extremely valuable. The collector can, of course, find good examples of later ones for about £20 upwards.

Where To Buy

Search in any good antique shop or market specialising in jewellery and trinkets.

Above: Left to right: Top row: *Fob seal,* c.*1780, gold.* *Fob seal,* c.*1830, with a turquoise set in three-coloured gold.* *Fob seal,* c.*1870, gold.* Bottom row: *Fob seal,* c.*1750, gold.* *Fob seal* by Hester Bateman, c.*1780, silver.* *Locket seal,* c.*1820, gold.*

Below: Left to right: Top row: *Desk seal* of smoky quartz. It is impossible to date this type of seal. *Fob seal,* c.*1835, gold.* *Fob seal,* c.*1860, gold.* Bottom row: *Fob seal,* c.*1810, gold.* *Fob seal,* c.*1870, white onyx in a gold mount.* *Fob seal,* c.*1870–80 in an earlier style, gold.* *Hunting seal,* c.*1820, gold.* This rare item is worth about £165.

Opposite: *Griffin fob seal, probably not English,* c.*1880. Silver and gold.*

Fisher Court Jewellers, Burlington Arcade: R. Todd-White

Fisher Court Jewellers, Burlington Arcade: R. Todd-White

ORNAMENTAL JADE

G. Bernard Hughes

Fig. 1 **Table screen**, Chinese, eighteenth century. White jade with an agate tree, a narrow green jade frame incised with gilt rectangular designs and inlaid with small bats in pink coral, on an ivory stand, height without stand 10 ins., width 7¾ ins.
Table screens were used by scholars as they wrote their scrolls. They protected the unrolled scroll from the splash of ink, and steadied the manuscript.
(Spink and Son Ltd., London.)

For thousands of years, Chinese craftsmen have been shaping jade into useful and ornamental objects of great textural quality and beauty which still delight us today

Some three thousand years ago, the Chinese were shaping pebbles of jade into mystic symbols associated with their religious rituals. Today, jade, or *wu*, is still cherished as being more estimable than jewels, more precious than gold. The Chinese turn a piece of jade about in their hands, revelling in its surface texture, and strike it to enjoy the sonorous ring. This subtle appreciation is virtually unknown by western collectors of jade.

Jade is the conventional name given to two colourful minerals, aggregates of microscopically small crystals, similar externally, and so hard that they cannot be scratched with a steel blade. These semi-precious stones, jadeite and nephrite, are chemically quite distinct substances and both vary in colour from nearly white to very dark green, and from reddish-grey to black. When cut and highly polished they range from the translucent to the almost opaque, and glow with a rich sheen.

Originally, jade was found in the river beds and soil of China itself in the neighbourhood of Peking. For the past seven centuries, jadeite has been obtained mainly from quarries sunk in the peaks of the Kachin country of Upper Burma, near the Chindwin River. It is quarried in the open by the primitive method of fire-setting. Large fires are lit in deep natural cavities of the rock and allowed to burn throughout the day. At nightfall the fires are extinguished; the intense cold of the night then causes the rock to split into portable lumps. Nephrite is quarried principally to the south of Yarkand, towards the borders of Kashmir in the Kun Lun Mountains of Chinese Turkestan.

The very hardness of these minerals is responsible for the rainbow surface-lustre of carved jade, the compactness of its closely inter-woven fibres making the jade carver's craft one of vast effort and painstaking care. Long tedious months could be spent by jade-workers in converting a crude stone or pebble into a work of art.

Ancient jade displays a wider variety of colours than does that quarried in recent centuries, often presenting a combination of three, four or five hues. The more distinct colours a piece displays, the greater its appeal to collectors. Jade carved later than the middle of the Ming period is found in few colours, the more common being milky-white, both semi-transparent and the opaque type termed 'mutton-fat'; white opaque; very light, semi-transparent yellow; semi-transparent or mottled green; opaque grey and black.

The precise dating of jade carved during these periods is difficult, although geologists can analyse the mineral itself and deduce its date and original source. The dates of the first and final workings of individual quarries have been tabulated. Jade worked since the late sixteenth century lacks the patina of age which distinguishes carvings of the previous geometrical and naturalistic periods. Baroque designs for the European market date from after the middle of the sixteenth century.

Treadle-operated cutting machinery was used from this period until the end of the Ch'ien-lung era (1736–95). Jade so worked may be recognised, on close examination, by the almost invisible marks left by the cutting tool. In openwork and lavish carving, the tools leave irregular tell-tale tracks revealing their method of application. Sawing and drilling by treadle power leave surface pittings, usually imperceptible except under a glass. Cavities can never be entirely symmetrical.

Jade attained a rare perfection in the Ming dynasty

Collectors of carved jade are seldom able to acquire examples made earlier than the Ming dynasty (1368–1644), when jade attained a rarely equalled perfection. Carefully balanced shapes, colours and carving make them pure marvels of craftsmanship, yet give an impression of simplicity. Decorations include dragons, cranes, peacocks, lotus flowers, foliage and animals, standing out from the surfaces of flower vases and water dishes in naturalistic relief. Models might be adapted from ancient bronzes – rhomboid, quadrangular or oval – with indented outlines and carving invariably corresponding with that of the period copied.

2

Museum Photo

Fig. 2 *Buffalo*, *Chinese*,
seventeenth century. Green jade,
length about 5 ins.
Buffalos were a popular subject
for carvers; they were considered
to be river gods.
(Victoria and Albert Museum,
London.)

Fig. 3 *Circular table screen,*
one of a pair, Chinese,
eighteenth century. Dark green
spinach jade with lighter green
flecking, diameter 9¾ ins.
Superbly carved on each side in
low relief with flowers and rocks,
butterflies, bats and other
insects, these beautiful screens
would have been placed in
windows as ornaments.
(Spink's.)

Chinese jade carved after the accession of
K'ang-hsi in 1662 was robustly modelled with floral
work and intended solely for decorative purposes.
The Emperor delighted in jade ornaments; his
grandson Ch'ien-lung encouraged jade sculpture in the round. Nobles and rich merchants
naturally followed his example and patronised
the jade-carvers. K'ang-hsi's successor, Yung-cheng
(1723–35), preferred designs of extreme elegance,
with flamboyant craftsmanship, usually lacking the
strength required for practical use. Decorations,
carved in low relief or engraved, are of symbolical
interest, unlike floral patterns. Ch'ien-lung
(1736–95) jade-carvers reached a peak of technical
perfection approaching the miraculous.

Men and animals were carved in the round from
late in the Ming era until early in the nineteenth
century. These pieces were larger and heavier than
formerly, many displaying a marvellous sense of
motion, thus marking the passing of the static
symbolical work. Statuettes and figures in relief in

the main represent illustrious divinities and other
celestial dignitaries. Figures of the Pa-seen, or
Eight Taoist Immortals, supposed to render
assistance to those in distress, were in continual
demand. The majority were carved as single
subjects and exhibited upright on low pedestals of
carved wood. More precious were the groups, each
of the eight figures succeeding the other in the
ascent to the blissful regions, and placed on a
pedestal carved to represent clouds. Pedestals for
supporting decorative jades from the late seventeenth century were carved from single blocks of
eagle-wood (*calambar*) from Ceylon. This rare
wood, highly valued in China, is heavy, close-
grained and pale yellow in hue, with the heart and
isolated elongated patches in intense black.

Animal carvings in jade include monsters from
early Chinese mythology; these were less massive
and more elegant in design than early in the K'ang-
hsi period. For instance, in accordance with
Chinese court etiquette, the fearsome five-clawed

Fig. 4 **Kuan-yin, Goddess of Mercy,** *Ch'ien-lung (1736–95). Green jade with ruby eyes. Although Kuan-yin is often portrayed as a phoenix, she is here seen as a parrot (Peh-ying wu) standing on a rock. (By gracious permission of H.M. The Queen.)*

Fig. 5 **Bowl and cover,** *Chinese, eighteenth century. Palest celadon jade, diameter over rim 6¼ ins. The turned-down rim is carved in open-work with lambrequin panels containing Buddhist emblems of Happy Augury. (Spink's.)*

dragon was restricted to the exclusive use of the emperor and his sons, princes of the first and second ranks; the four-clawed dragon was the prerogative of the princes of the third and fourth ranks; the three-clawed dragon was reserved for the nobility.

Variations of type are numerous, such as hornless dragons, those with one or two horns resembling deer's antlers, and winged dragons. Some dragons have tigers' claws and their bodies covered with scales which resemble those of a carp. Dragons and tigers represent the God of Wealth. The phoenix omen of prosperity and harmony, until early in the eighteenth century was usually perched on a tree; in the Ch'ien-lung period it was largely associated with Kuan-Yin, the Goddess of Mercy, and other immortals.

The horse, one of the signs of the zodiac, was an important Taoist emblem, not widely carved in jade until the Ch'ien-lung period. Group carvings, with riders, are found; others are seen in the 'flying gallop', with four legs outstretched. Other animals included deer, elephants, bears, goats, monkeys, badgers, boars, cats, foxes and the lion or dog of Fo, the latter held to be the defender of law and order and guardian of sacred buildings. Buffalos are considered to be river gods and are usually represented recumbent as though bathing (Fig. 2).

Goldfish found a place in the home of every well-to-do Chinaman. The Emperor Ch'ien-lung apparently possessed a gigantic goldfish bowl of jade, six feet in circumference, cut from a single boulder. Goldfish bowls were usually encircled with carvings of carp, the fabled king of fish capable of changing into a dragon. The Chinese regarded the carp or goldfish as the symbol of vigour and endurance. The carved fish is often shown swimming upstream against the current. Twin fish in a single carving represent happy wedded bliss; goldfish bowls so decorated were very popular as wedding gifts.

Incense burners of three, four or five tiers were used as fumigators in temples and for private use. The lowest tier, supported on three short legs, was a solid bowl in which the incense was burned. Each separate tier, fitting exactly into the one below, was ornately carved and skilfully pierced to permit the emission of the fragrant fumes. The unpierced surfaces of Ch'ien-lung incense burners were carved to display as much symbolism as possible: peaches, bats, lotus flowers, fungi and swastikas were widely used.

Musical jades, resonant carvings associated with the worship of the deities of heaven and earth, had been made for a thousand years before the Ch'ien-lung period, when they were widely reproduced. A single sonorous jade might be placed on the Moon Terrace of a Confucian temple. It was struck with

6

Museum Photo

Fig. 6 *Pouring-vessel and cover, Chinese, eighteenth century. Jade encrusted with gilt metal and precious stones.*
In 1741, a group of expert Indian jade-carvers and jewel-setters came to Peking, where they initiated Chinese craftsmen into the arts of inlaying fine tracery in gold and setting jewels against gold foil. The school they founded was called the Hsi Fan Tsi, *or Indian School of jade-carvers.*
(*Victoria and Albert Museum.*)

a mallet at the end of each verse to assist the choir leader. A set of sixteen stones of different sizes and thicknesses formed the stone chime, a continuation of the custom of the emperor wearing a jade hat with nine strings of jade beads which emitted a range of notes by hitting one another as he walked.

Elaborate sets of equipment for a scholar's table were made. These included the palette, an oval slab of jade with a depression in one end; the ink jar and water-pot; the hand rest; the shallow oblong pen-box; the paperweight, usually a river pebble carved in the form of a mountain with fearsome dragons, lions and mythical monsters; and the table screen (Fig. 1), which was a square tablet of jade carved with an all-over mythical scene, set vertically in a stand. It protected the unrolled scroll from the splash of ink and steadied the manuscript. Similar circular or oblong screens, carved on both sides, were placed in windows as ornaments (Fig. 3).

The Mogul emperors of Hindustan (1526–1707) were fascinated by the splendour of Chinese jade carvings. Imperial workshops devoted solely to this work were established in Delhi, sage-green and white jadeites being imported from Burma. Native jewellers immediately seized upon this

mineral as a perfect background against which to mount precious stones and gems. Jades, resplendently set with rubies, emeralds, lapis lazuli, amethysts and other quartzes, quickly became desirable Mogul luxuries.

Stones were set individually into the solid jade, fixed with gold foil – pure gold beaten into paper-thin sheets – which defined their outlines and created a rich background for their display. Gems and delicate lines of inlaid gold might be set into formal floral patterns. Following the Chinese conquest of Eastern Turkestan, many jewel-encrusted jades were presented to the Imperial Court at Peking as tokens of good will. These superb carvings created a sensation at the Court of Ch'ien-lung, with the result that, in 1741, a group of expert jade-carvers and jewel-setters were attracted to Peking where they established the *Hsi Fan Tsi,* or Indian School of jade-cutters. They initiated Chinese craftsmen into the arts of inlaying fine tracery in gold and setting jewels against gold foil. Within ten years a prosperous trade had been established, the Chinese carvers producing jade which was purely Indian in form and design (Fig. 6). Indo-Chinese jades might be incised with verses in Chinese lauding their divine origin. The finest were inscribed with the square seal of Emperor Ch'ien-lung and retained in the palace. Thus the widespread belief that jewelled jades are invariably of Indian origin is entirely unfounded.

Jewelled jades were also carved and set in China to the commission of the Mogul Court at Delhi, and in the workshops attached to Tibetan and other monasteries in the Buddhist areas of north-eastern India. Religious deities such as Buddha and Tsongkaps, were also carved in the round.

Jades mounted in solid gold or gilt bronze, intended for presents or personal adornment, were made during the Ch'ien-lung period. Also at this time, composite creations representing flowers and fruit were modelled in jade for display on the altars of sacrifice in temples or on tables in homes.

The *Dictionarium Polygraphicum,* 1735, records that jade handles for hunting-knives were imported and that the Turks and Eastern Europeans valued jade-handled sabres. Small articles of eighteenth-century jade include sceptres in shapes adapted from those of a thousand years earlier, household altars, snuff-bottles, ceremonial axes and buckles. ⬧

MUSEUMS AND COLLECTIONS
Chinese jade carvings may be seen at the following:
GREAT BRITAIN
Durham: University of Durham (Museum of Oriental Art)
London: British Museum
Victoria and Albert Museum
Port Sunlight: Lady Lever Art Gallery

FURTHER READING
Outlines of Chinese Symbolism by C. A. S. Williams, revised ed. New York, 1960.
Chinese Jade Carvings by S. Howard Hansford, London, 1950.
Chinese Jade throughout the Ages by S. C. Nott, London, 1936.
Ancient Chinese Jade by Henry H. Wu, Shanghai, 1933.
Early Chinese Jades by Dame Una Pope-Hennessy, London, 1923.
Researches into Chinese Superstitions by Henry S. J. Dore, Shanghai, 1918.

R. Todd-White

Arms for the Samurai

William Allan

Japan's 'age of battles' came to an end in 1600, followed by a time of peace during which Japanese armourers could set aside the restrictions imposed by years of warfare and devote more time to the decorative arts

Fig. 1 **Mask and neck-piece.**
The custom of wearing ferocious masks developed in the eleventh century and persisted until the late seventeenth. After that, masks remained an accepted item of equipment, but were seldom worn; a more conventional form of chin-guard or face-guard took their place.
(Bethnal Green Museum, London.)

The Battle of Sekigahara in 1600 was one of the greatest battles and most complete victories in the history of Japan. It marked the end of the *Sengoku Jidai* ('age of battles') and ushered in two hundred and fifty years of peace in which Japan, secluded from the rest of the world, allowed her social system and all its attendant activities to petrify.

The victor, Tokugawa Ieyasu, had been a noted *samurai*, although his estates were comparatively small; he and his successors chose to rely, for the continuing stability of the regime, on this same caste of dependent warriors. The conse-

quence was that the warrior class grew in numbers and importance, and came in time to rule over the class of farmers and common people with despotic authority. Although there were no longer great wars to fight, the *samurai* kept alive their fighting tradition by continuing to order fine suits of armour and dedicate new sword blades.

Towards the close of this time, known as the Edo period, the *samurai* became less interested in developing ever more elaborate armour, and returned instead to the simpler styles of an earlier age. The more Western influence encroached on the Japanese, the more they retreated into their past. As a result, the history of Japanese arms and armour, however intriguing for the expert, is likely to bring nothing but alarm and confusion to the dilettante.

The first great period of armour making was the Muromachi, which lasted from 1392 to 1573. In this time, the *samurai* emerged as a distinctive class, and took advantage of the innumerable civil wars to extend their privileges and power. Since war was their trade, much of their wealth was spent in equipping themselves suitably. In the early stages of the Muromachi period, armour

2

R. Todd-White

Fig. 2 *Spear.*
Much care was taken in the preparation of spear heads and arrow heads. Unlike European knights, Japanese warriors did not regard the spear as a dispensable item; the spear was as much his own personal weapon as the helmet, or tanto, even though its use was restricted amongst the samurai.
(Bethnal Green Museum.)

and weapons were both designed in the most elaborate manner compatible with fighting efficiency.

The *samurai* wore the *oyoroi* ('great armour'), so-called because it was made up of large segments, in contrast to the *haramaki* ('belly-wrapping') armour which was smaller in scale and lighter in composition. These *oyoroi* suits are ample evidence of the wealth and extravagance of the early Japanese warriors, for the helmets and shoulder-guards were larger and more heavily decorated than anything that came later. By the end of the period, however, the increasing tempo of civil war led to the adoption of the *haramaki* on a wider scale. So the famous decorative armourers of Nara gave place to the more severe designs of the Kozuke and Mutsu schools. The new armour consisted primarily of a scale cuirass, or *do-maru*, similar to that worn by the ordinary foot soldiers. It was close-fitting and divided into seven segments, the whole opening down the back and being held in place by ribbons of coloured silk. The old shoulder-guards were reduced in scale and a spreading neck-guard was added to the helmet.

A tendency towards lighter, simpler armour

The tendency towards lighter, simpler armour was stimulated by the disastrous wars of the Omin era (1467–77) when the capital city was totally destroyed and thousands of *samurai* slain. The high cost of the war led to the gradual recruitment of a new kind of soldier, quite alien to the accepted tradition in Japan. This was the *asigan*, or poor man from the country; these peasants were brought in to replace the *chugen*, or *samurai's* batmen, a class which had suffered particularly during the wars. Since these people were accustomed to shooting with bows and arrows, the bow ceased to form part of the regular equipment of the *samurai*, and became the prerogative of the ordinary soldier, alongside the straight-bladed pike, or *su-yari*.

As the sword became the exclusive weapon of the warrior, so the helmet gained in intricacy and importance. The Myochin and Yoshimishi families were famous for their high-sided helmets, made from a large number of plates, and fitted closely to the head and neck. Another vital factor was the arrival of the Portuguese in 1543; the consequent appearance of the match-lock led to an increase in the thickness of armour, and so to an improved quality of smithwork, as the armourers strove to add strength without too much weight.

The brief Momoyama period (1573–1615) was one of the bloodiest in Japan's history. An armourer's sole preoccupation in this time was to make armour that would combine the maximum protection from all weapons with the minimum constraint to the wearer. For this reason, armour became much simpler in design, and the decoration considered necessary for the *samurai* took the form of badges, crests and flags added to the outside. Many of these devices were large and intricate, and were in themselves fine examples of the armourer's skill. A new type of helmet was developed, the *hineno*, with heavy side-plates and a high, concave peak. These helmets, too, were often heavily or grotesquely ornamented and lacquered.

After the Battle of Sekigahara, the country declined into its long peace under the unpredictable and authoritarian rule of the Tokugawa Shoguns. Both *samurai* and armourers turned their attention to the more decorative aspects of their calling, now that killing ceased to be an expanding trade. There was a conscious revival of archaic patterns: the simple armour of the Momoyama was converted to its new role, covered with rich metal embellishments (*kanomono*) and stencilled and coloured leather. Helmets were increased in size and topped with mythical beasts or horns.

By the end of the seventeenth century, however, the interest in old forms had become more scholarly and less a reaction to the austerity of the 'age of battles'. Low, rounded helmets of classical pattern were revived, ridged and studded, and shorn of the elaborate neck-guard. A great impetus was given to the study of classical armour by the publication in 1709 of the first authoritative history of Japanese armour, by the historian Hakuseki.

Thereafter, two quite separate schools of design developed. One catered for the poorer *samurai*, and produced relatively simple armour, occasionally using embossed designs of the type developed by Kunimichi, one of the greatest of the art metal-workers. The other aimed to make reproductions of classical designs for the richer class of *samurai*, often incorporating pieces from genuinely old suits. Alongside this last fashion, there grew up a taste for ornamental masks, and for armour decorations of russet iron (*okimono*). This remained the pattern of development down to 1867 and the end of Tokugawa rule.

The aspect of Japanese armour which has been most widely studied, and which struck European visitors so forcibly in the last century, is the sword. Although the years of peace had resulted in a shortening of the blade and marked increase in the size and richness of the furniture, they were still weapons 'of a sort to reduce anything to a shambles', according to Sir Rutherford Alcock, first British Head of Mission in 1858. 'I have never seen a more dramatic and picturesque sight', he records, 'than these warriors, all clad in chain armour, with their steel headpieces, long two-handled swords and Japanese lanterns'.

By the end of the nineteenth century, a number of English visitors had written on this subject, and set about tracing and collecting examples of fine workmanship. Charles Gilbertson wrote: 'I look upon a well-finished Japanese blade as a marvel of mechanical skill and perfect workmanship, as delightful to contemplate as the grinding and polishing of a speculum or large telescope lens'. Alfred Dobrée went even further in declaring that 'in their best form they represent the highest development of artistic metal-working'. The reason for this high standard was that Japanese swordsmiths were rated as artists rather than mere artisans. In each province, separate dynasties of smiths grew up, forming rival schools of sword-making which continued for hundreds of years. The earliest forms of sword were already in use by the eighth century, and in the hundred years following, the sword achieved the style which it has retained ever since. From the time of the divinely inspired Yasutsuna, through the era of the great sword-makers of the fourteenth century, to the revival in the nineteenth under Masahide, the

十八番弓

Fig. 3 *Order of putting on armour,* *one of the series* Kojitsu Sosho *by Yoroi Chakuyo Shidai,* c.1910. *(Victoria and Albert Museum, London.)*

Fig. 4 *Armour* *made for Lord Doi in 1800 by Muneto, master of the Miochuri School, out of pieces made by six of his predecessors from the thirteenth to the sixteenth centuries. (Bethnal Green Museum.)*

Fig. 5 *Samurai helmet* *of a pattern common from the mid-fourteenth century. (Bethnal Green Museum.)*

Fig. 6 *Matchlock pistol* *bearing the badge of the Hosokawa family in gold overlay, the stock of red lacquer. (Bethnal Green Museum.)*

Fig. 7 *Sword furniture* *of the Goto School. (Bethnal Green Museum.)*

R. Todd-White

K. Hoddle

R. Todd-White

R. Todd-White

8

K. Hoddle

Fig. 8 *Joust sword* (detail), 1682.
(*Victoria and Albert Museum.*)

pattern of the sword remained constant. Many of the weapons that Japanese officers carried in the war against Russia in 1904 had been carried in countless battles by ancestors five hundred years previously.

The sword came in this way to acquire an almost religious quality. Certainly, the business of forging a sword was a quasi-religious ceremony, and smiths led a monastic life, shunning excesses of every kind and donning special robes for the ritual of forging a blade. Swords were also thought to possess magic qualities, for they were compounded of the five elements: *sui, kwa, moku, kin* and *do* (water, fire, wood, metal and earth). The metal from which they were forged came from deposits of magnetic iron ore and ferruginous sand, and was 'cemented' into steel. Iron and steel plates were welded together, folded, and welded again often as many as eighteen times before being drawn into the final shape. This marrying of hard and soft metals, to produce a hard edge and softer blade, is the main point of difference between Japanese and European swords.

Most of the smiths used characteristic designs to decorate the *yakiba*, or blade-edge, and they are of great importance in reckoning the age and value of a sword. Styles varied between the jagged *uma no ha* ('horse's tooth'), and the careful stepping of the *saka ashi*, or 'road up the mountains'. The blades were often decorated with *harimono* (engraved figures), although this form was less popular in the Kyoto period (prior to 1615) than in the later Shinto period. The blade itself was handsomely mounted in the handle (*kodzuka*) and fitted with an elaborately decorated guard (*tsuba*).

After the beginning of the Edo peace, sword furniture became more obtrusive in its decoration, and by the end of the eighteenth century was condemned by many swordsmiths as decadent. Those *samurai* who wished to emphasise their displeasure at this trend, inscribed the guard with some improving text. One typical line was 'even in midsummer a drawn sword brings a cool breeze into a large house'.

MUSEUMS AND COLLECTIONS

Japanese arms and armour may be seen at the following:

GREAT BRITAIN
Birmingham: Birmingham City Museum and Art Gallery
London: Bethnal Green Museum
JAPAN
Tokyo: National Museum
U.S.A.
Los Angeles: Municipal Art Gallery
New York: Metropolitan Museum of Art

FURTHER READING

A Short History of Japanese Armour by H. Russell Robinson, London, 1965.
Japanese Pole Arms by R. M. Knutsen, London, 1963.
The Arts of the Japanese Sword by Basil Robinson, London, 1961.
Les Gardes de Sabre Japonaises by F. Poncetton, Paris, 1924.

Basil Gray

CHINA AND JAPAN
IN THE EIGHTEENTH CENTURY

2

3

4

5

Historical periods

CHINA
Sung 960–1279
Yuan 1280–1368
Ming 1368–1644
Ch'ing 1644–1912

JAPAN
Heian 784–1185
Kamakura
1185–1392
Muromachi
1392–1573
Momoyama
1573–1615
Edo 1615–1867

6

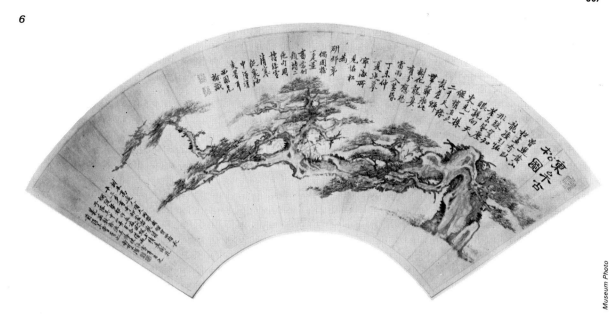

Museum Photo

Fig. 1 (Frontispiece) *Detail from a twelve-fold screen painting by Shen Nan-pin (active c.1725–80), Chinese, 1750. Painted with peacocks, loquats and flowers in colours on silk, in a style which Shen Nan-pin made popular in both China and Japan.* (British Museum, London.)

Fig. 2 *Pomegranates and apples in a dish Chinese, c.1690. Coloured wood-cut, 11 x 13⅛ ins.* (British Museum.)

Fig. 3 *Lady on a rustic seat by Leng Mei (c.1710–50), Chinese early eighteenth century. Colour on silk.*
This mannered painting is the counterpart of a rococo chinoiserie picture in Europe. (British Museum.)

Fig. 4 *A lady perfuming her dress over a brazier by Yu Chih-ting (1647–1705), Chinese, 1684. Ink and light colours on paper, 32 x 21⅔ ins. This charming composition is in the traditional pai-miao technique of fine line with light shading.* (British Museum.)

Fig. 5 *A Chinese Beauty by Mori Tessan (1775–1841), Maruyama school, Japanese, 1804. 39⅞ x 17¾ ins. Painting in colour on silk. There was a strong artistic link between China and Japan.* (British Museum.)

Fig. 6 *An old pine tree from an album of twelve leaves of fan paintings by Kao Feng-han (1683–1748), Chinese, 1722–25. Ink and light colour, 7 x 21 ins.* (British Museum.)

The Ch'ing state in eighteenth-century China had entered into a steady decline while the Japanese feudal rulers were providing the basis for a new and more dynamic society which included patronage of the arts

At first sight there appears to be considerable similarity in the basic situations of the two Far Eastern countries in the eighteenth century. Both were subject to authoritarian regimes which favoured paternalistic Confucian principles and which tended to suppress intellectual deviations intermittently but harshly. Partly in response to this situation, in both countries the kind of painting favoured in circles in touch with the scholarly classes was the *Wen-jenhua* in Chinese, or *Bunjin-ga* in Japanese. While this approach demanded complete personal integrity from the painter and 'freedom of spirit', it was backward-looking, in that its limits were drawn in reference to the accepted standards of the old masters of the Yuan and Ming dynasties. This resemblance between the two countries was, however, superficial and conceals wide differences. These may be briefly summarised by noting that the Ch'ing state in China was already in the eighteenth century entering on a steady decline, due to the fossilisation of its basic ideas; whereas the Japanese Tokugawa regime, while equally doomed, concealed and sought to contain the rising new life from the urban societies and the many centres of provincial life. The feudal rulers in Japan provided the basis for a new and more dynamic society, as well as the patronage required by some independent artists and by crafts like pottery, lacquer-work and *cloisonné* enamel-work.

At the time, however, China looked much the more impressive cultural society. She had an ancient bureaucratic tradition and a long-established scholar-official class, although this had become largely estranged from the foreign, conquering Manchus. The strong emperors K'ang-hsi, Yung-cheng and Ch'ien-lung managed to maintain an efficient administration by their policy of using Chinese officials whenever possible to

mitigate the foreign appearance of Manchu rule. During the eighteenth century the entirely Manchu army was serving outside China in a series of successful campaigns which enlarged her frontiers and influence over wide areas of Turkestan, the north-west, Tibet and the south, as well as in Formosa. The Chinese were proud of the victories of their rulers, which were celebrated by the Emperor Ch'ien-lung in several series of engravings of which the first was prepared in Paris by French engravers during the years 1767–74, recording the subjugation of Turkestan.

The personal control of the emperor was maintained through the bond-servant system, by which the descendants of Chinese captured during the early Manchu conquests in the north remained servants of the ruling house. The able and ambitious ones were promoted to key positions such as the Censors of Salt administration and the Textile Commissioners in charge of the production of woven silks for the use of the imperial bureaux and for official robes and patents. Many of these families increased their influence and status by supplying concubines to the Court.

As has often been the case with foreign conquerors, the Manchu rulers were lovers and patrons of Chinese culture. The imperial house did much for the editing and printing of the classics of poetry and history and the compilation of encyclopedias, including one of painters and paintings. They were also interested in antiquities and curiosities. K'ang-hsi, on his periodic tours of the provinces, was regularly offered presents of rare objects.

Ch'ien-lung was more methodical in his collecting and used his position to bring together the huge collection of paintings by old masters as well as contemporary hands, the greater part of which is preserved in the Palace collections in Taiwan (Formosa). He also assembled the now well-known collections of porcelain from Sung to Ming, and bronzes and jades. All these were methodically catalogued and inspected and the Emperor recorded his appreciation in poems which were added to the painting-scrolls and even engraved on some specially prized porcelains. Owing to his long reign and increasing preoccupation with his art collections, Ch'ien-lung may be regarded as the greatest collector of any period or country.

The system of personal control through bond-servants was successful so long as the Emperor was vigorous and attentive to detail. The corruption which had accompanied the power of the eunuch officials under the Ming dynasty disappeared with their exclusion from high office. Nevertheless there was tension between the official bureaucracy nominated by the old system of examination in the classics, and those families of personal favourites with hereditary claims as imperial bond-servants. The literary inquisition, always on the watch for secret partiality towards the fallen Ming house, provided opportunities for the settling of private scores of jealousy and rivalry. A denounced official might lose a part or a whole of his salary and have his goods requisitioned. The sense of community of interest and culture of the intelligentsia-official class was under constant strain.

Album leaves and fans bore paintings, poems and inscriptions

But the close connection between the arts of calligraphy, painting and poetry remained the prevailing tradition. This is illustrated by the ink-scroll by Cheng-hsieh (1693–1765) of chrysanthemum, orchid and bamboo, dated 1755 and now in the British Museum. The brush-strokes of the characters mingle with the free delineation of the flowers and rocks in a free pattern of accented ink.

Such paintings, which were exchanged among friends and often bore poems or inscriptions recording the occasion of their making, are the most characteristic relics of this Chinese society. The favourite form is the album leaf or the fan, essentially intimate and personal. A painter whose free brush-work was admired in these circles was Kao Feng-han (1683–1748), an unsuccessful official who could thus devote more of his time to painting. In the British Museum is an album of twelve fans dating from his early years, 1722–25. They vary considerably in style, but are not, as was the work of the more orthodox painters, specifically based on different old masters. He liked to wander in the country and afterwards record some particular tree or blossom. When rheumatism disabled his right arm he painted with his left in a free and personal style.

Other aspects of the interest of the period are reflected in painting of a different technique and intention. K'ang-hsi displayed considerable interest in Western art; he employed Chiao Ping-chen to illustrate a traditional series of views of the culture of rice and silk, in forty-six designs to be reproduced in woodcut form with autograph poems by the emperor himself. This book, which appeared in 1696, shows a modified view of Western perspective. When he celebrated his jubilee in 1713 by a special progress through Manchuria to Jehol, he asked an Italian priest, Father Matteo Ripa (1682–1746) to engrave thirty-six illustrations. These had been drawn by Shen Yu, a court painter, and depicted views among the palaces which K'ang-hsi had built there during the previous decade. The Emperor was so delighted with this technique that he got Ripa to engrave a great map of China in fifty sheets from the survey made by the Jesuits for him. K'ang-hsi liked to talk with Christian missionaries, and he was deeply interested in scientific discovery and its application.

Yu Chih-ting (1647–1705) excelled in figure drawing in a semi-western manner. His charming composition in the traditional *pai-miao* technique of fine line with light shading, of a lady perfuming her dress over a censer under a basket (1684), rivals a study from the hand of a European master. A few years later another court artist, Leng Mei, produced a less artless, more mannered painting on silk of a lady on a rustic seat with a four-volume book beside her, which is the Chinese counterpart of a rococo *chinoiserie* picture. These paintings, however, were not then known in Europe, although some Yung-cheng enamelled porcelain was actually decorated with French *chinoiserie* figures. Sophistication could go no further.

What did travel to Europe at this time were some of the colourful woodcut prints, originally intended as illustrations to painting manuals, which provided the craftsmen of the West with useful motifs for the decoration of objects in the Chinese taste. As for centuries past, porcelain remained in the eighteenth century a chief export from China. This trade was on a vast scale and highly organised. The great imperial kilns at Ching-te-chen also produced work in the native taste. The factories established by K'ang-hsi within the Forbidden City before 1683 made a wide range of luxury products to a high standard of craftsmanship. These products included work in jade, ivory and lacquer.

Whereas in China it was the Court which interested itself in Western art and science, in Japan it was the new class of city merchants which was hungry for information from the West. This could only be transmitted in books after the exclusion of the Christian missionaries, the proscription of the religion in 1637 and the strict control of all foreign contacts, even through the only licensed port on the island of Deshima in Nagasaki harbour. Contact with the Dutch East India Company personnel was only through the accredited interpreters, the *Rangakusha*, who made themselves conversant with Dutch scientific studies in such subjects as anatomy, surgery, botany and astronomy.

Nearby on the mainland was the area carefully demarcated in 1688 for sole access by the Chinese traders from the continent. By this date imports of Chinese porcelain had been resumed, while from 1700 China was importing from Japan large quantities of copper in an attempt to remedy the severe currency shortage. After 1710, very little Japanese porcelain was exported to Holland and the West, and the heyday of the export of both blue and white and of enamelled wares was the second half of the seventeenth century. It was through Nagasaki alone that Chinese cultural influence could penetrate to Japan. The Shogunate encouraged orthodox Confucian studies but was suspicious of other Chinese books, in particular because of the Chinese tolerance of Christianity.

Although China retained in Japan its age-long primacy as the source of learning and the arts, there was no longer in the eighteenth century the close contact that had been so fruitful in the seventeenth, and which was especially reinforced by the arrival of refugees irreconcilable to Manchu rule. New influence in art was then limited to the import of woodcut painting books like the 'Mustard Seed Garden', which was copied in Japan in a Japanese edition of 1748. In 1731–33 a Chinese professional painter named Shen Nan-pin had spent two years at Nagasaki and instructed some Japanese in his

7

Fig. 7 ***The Dutch Factory on the Island of Deshima***, *Nagasaki School, Japanese, c.1700. Detail from a makimono (lateral scroll painting on paper), height 12½ ins.*
After the exclusion of the Christian missionaries from Japan in 1637, there was strict control of all foreign contacts, even through the only licensed port on the Island of Deshima in Nagasaki harbour. Contact with the Dutch East India Company personnel was allowed only through accredited interpreters called rangakusha, *who made themselves conversant with Dutch scientific studies in such subjects as anatomy, surgery, botany and astronomy. This scroll shows one of these interpreters being entertained by the Dutch merchants.*
(British Museum.)

realistic style of bird and flower painting. He carried on a tradition which had been current in China since the T'ang period (618–906), in that he was prepared to execute commands for such decorative objects as screens – a practice despised and ignored by the scholars who wrote about Ming and Ch'ing painting. In China the screen usually consisted of twelve narrow panels of silk which were mounted on a folding frame and which formed a single composition. Very few have survived and the British Museum is fortunate in having one by Shen Nan-pin dated 1750, some years after his return from Nagasaki. It shows the kind of style which he introduced there and which fell in with the strong contemporary feeling for realism in Japan.

This tendency is apparent in the work of the famous painter Okyo and of the Maruyama school which he founded. It took the form of a naturalistic treatment of figures and landscape. The link with China is amusingly demonstrated by the rather later work by his pupil Mori Tessan (1775–1841) of a Chinese beauty, dated 1804. Close observation of nature had been a growing influence in Japanese painting since the seventeenth century, as is seen in the sketches of flowers and birds by Ogata Korin (1650–1716). When he worked in full colour and on the scale of screen painting, he sacrificed detail and relief to a superb sense of decorative patterning carried out in soft-edged but brilliant colour-wash on a gold ground. His leading follower in the mid-century, Watanabe Shiko (1683–1755), retained greater sharpness of definition in his finished work without losing either the original freshness of his flower studies or the decorative brilliance of the gold-ground screen.

The existence of this tradition of sensitive and decorative work alongside that of the older Kano and Tosa schools demonstrates the value to Japan of the diversity made possible by the structure of her society, each feudal lord being a possible source of local patronage, as opposed to the monolithic structure of the Chinese centralised state. Moreover in the cities new patrons were arising in the merchant class who supported the *kabuki* stage and the *ukiyo-e* painters and print-makers. Their strongly

nationalistic line contrasts with the Chinese scholarly tradition and with the work of the then dominant Zen sect of the Buddhist faith inspired by the treasured masterpieces of Chinese old masters in the safe keeping of the temples. The most lively literary movement in early Tokugawa Japan (1615–1868) was that of the *haiku*, or seventeen-syllable poem, in the hands of the master Basho (1644–94), who flourished in the expansive climate of the new capital, Edo.

Forty years after Basho's death, in about 1735, Buson sat at the feet of another *haiku* master, Hajin, and combined an understanding of classical T'ang poetry with the epigrammatic style of *haiku*. Later, he found his natural gift for painting, which he fused in the new art form *haiga*, in which Chinese *Wen-jen* (literary) style of painting could be combined with Japanese subject matter associated with the *haiku* poem. A kindred spirit was Ikeno Taiga (1723–76), who absorbed all he could of the Chinese literary tradition, but combined with it an independence of spirit, due to his skill in calligraphy.

These two artists illustrate the liberating effect which this same scholarly style could have in the more sensitive conditions of Japan. In 1771 Ikeno Taiga and Buson combined in a joint work, the *Juben Jui* (Ten advantages of life in a mountain hut and Ten pleasures in the views from it), illustrating the work of a Chinese poet, Li Li-wang. The twenty album leaves are only eighteen centimetres square and the designs are executed in the combination of ink and light colours which was generally employed by the Chinese scholar-painter. As in these, the poem illustrated is written in the sky, and the whole is carried out in the *Nanga* (the southern literary style) but with a lightness and sense of beauty and wit which is peculiarly Japanese. Indeed, it has been well said that the *bunjin-ga* art of Japan was seldom pure and unmixed with the decorative or the naturalistic. But Buson's late work is extraordinarily free and economical. His controlled casualness at this time, about 1780, is well seen in a composition sketched on four small sliding door-panels, a kind of minor work most characteristic of the austerity of Japanese decor.

Ch'ing Dynasty Porcelain

John Cushion

Fig. 1 **Reign marks (nien hao)** *from the Ch'ing dynasty. Above, that of K'ang-hsi (1662–1722); below, that of Ch'ien-lung (1736–95). During this dynasty, many pieces of porcelain were marked with the personal mark of the reigning emperor, invariably painted in under-glaze blue, and consisting of six characters. The seal mark, shown here below the reign mark, is rarely seen during these reigns.*

Fig. 2 **Kettle**, Yung-chêng (1723–35). The handle and spout are modelled in the form of dragons under a yellow glaze. Height 5⅛ ins.
(Victoria and Albert Museum, London.)

Fig. 3 **Plate**, K'ang-hsi period. Painted in under-glaze blue with pine branches, a lady and a ch'i-lin (Chinese unicorn, symbolic of Perfect Good). Diameter 10⅜ ins.
(Victoria and Albert Museum.)

Fig. 4 **Vase**, K'ang-hsi period. Mirror-black (wu chin) decorated with gilding. Height 18 ins.
(Victoria and Albert Museum.)

Fig. 5 **Vase**, K'ang-hsi period. Covered with translucent apple green over a crazed glaze. Height 4⅜ ins.
(Victoria and Albert Museum.)

With the appointment of a new director in 1682, Chinese porcelain reached an unprecedented perfection in quality which was to continue throughout the eighteenth century

By the time of the collapse of the Ming dynasty in 1644 the Chinese had built up a prolific export business with Europe. While tea, spices and silks formed the bulk of such trade, the manufacture of porcelain specifically for the European market had reached such proportions that many wares were being sold in Amsterdam at public auctions.

Weakened by internal unrest and strife, China was taken over by its more powerful neighbours, the Tartars from Manchuria. For the purpose of porcelain study, the years between the decline of the Ming dynasty and the settlement of the succeeding Ch'ing are referred to as the period of Transition, dating from approximately 1620, following the death of the Emperor Wan-li, until about 1682, when the Emperor K'ang-hsi appointed Ts'ang Ting-hsuan as director of the Imperial factory. During these years the production of porcelain in the city of Ching-te-chen in the southern province of Kiang-si, which had been the centre of this industry since at least the tenth century, suffered considerably. Throughout most of the Transition period the Dutch were prevented from continuing their activities and turned to Japan as an alternative source of porcelain, a move that is clearly reflected in the style of decoration seen on much of their own tin-glazed earthenware made at about this time.

It was from the time of the newly-appointed director in 1682 that Chinese porcelain attained unprecedented perfection in quality and proportions, a situation which was to continue throughout the eighteenth century until its decline on both counts after the death of the Emperor Ch'ien-lung in 1795.

It was in 1712 that Father D'Entrecolles' first letter was written detailing the production of porcelain at Ching-te-chen, where he lived and worked as a Jesuit missionary. He described the

6

7

8

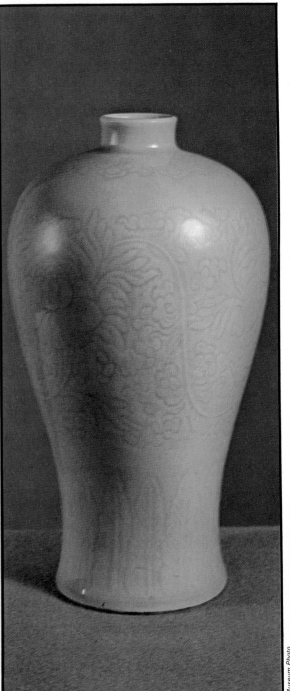

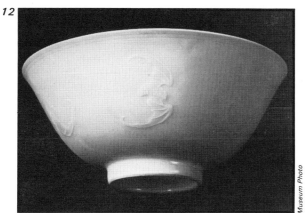

Fig. 6 **Vase,** K'ang-hsi period. Painted with the Flowers of the Seasons, the plum, tree peony, lotus and chrysanthemum in colours of the famille verte on a black ground, famille noire. Height 18⅛ ins. (Victoria and Albert Museum.)

Fig. 7 **Plate,** Yung-cheng period. Painted in the enamel colours of the famille rose, the entire back of the plate also in rose-pink enamel. Diameter 7⅞ ins. (Victoria and Albert Museum.)

Fig. 8 **Vase,** Yung-cheng. In the mei p'ing form for holding a spray of plum-blossom, decorated with incised flowers and foliage under a celadon glaze. Height 9¼ ins. (Victoria and Albert Museum.)

Fig. 9 **Plate,** K'ang-hsi period. Painted in under-glaze blue with the flowering plum and cracking ice symbolic of the Chinese New Year. Diameter 10½ ins. (Victoria and Albert Museum.)

Fig. 10 **Water-pot** for the scholar's writing-table, in the form of a mouse, K'ang-hsi period. Decorated with enamel colours on the biscuit. Height 3⅛ ins. (Victoria and Albert Museum.)

Fig. 11 **Wine-pot** in the form of a peach, late K'ang-hsi. Decorated mainly in coral-red enamel. Height 5 ins. This type of pot, which was filled through a cone-shaped hole in the base, became popular at the Rockingham factory in Yorkshire and was known as a 'Cadogan' pot. (Victoria and Albert Museum.)

Fig. 12 **Bowl,** Yung-cheng. White porcelain painted in white slip with designs of bats, the reign mark written on the base in under-glaze blue. Diameter 5⅞ ins. Best seen against a strong light, this 'secret decoration' (an hua) symbolises the Five Blessings – longevity, riches, serenity, the cultivation of virtue and the completion of a life's work. (Victoria and Albert Museum.)

preparation of china clay and china stone as being strenuous and laborious tasks which gave the workers little time for the practising of Christianity. The production of porcelain on such a scale can be better appreciated when he relates that 'a piece of porcelain has passed through the hands of seventy workmen'. Even the painting of a single subject was shared by several hands: 'another traces flowers, which a third paints'. Such methods are hard to reconcile with the results.

During the reign of K'ang-hsi (1662–1722) the porcelain decorated in under-glaze blue for the European market was produced in ever-increasing quantities. These pieces were usually of a far superior quality to those previously exported during the late years of the Ming dynasty. Such perfection may be seen on the plate in Figure 3, which is unmarked. The porcelain is pure, fine-grained and white, the glaze slightly tinted to a bluish green, and the rich blue of pure cobalt unsurpassed. Wares made during K'ang-hsi's reign rarely bear his reign mark, those of the Ming Emperors Hsuan-te (1426–35) or Ch'eng-hua (1464–87) being more frequently seen and hence very unreliable guides.

The ch'i-lin, depicted on this plate together with pine-branches and the figure of a lady, is the Chinese equivalent to the European unicorn. It is a composite animal (ch'i, male; lin, female). The creature has the head of a dragon, the hooves of a deer and a flowing, bushy tail; it breathes fire but is emblematic of Perfect Good. This animal should not be confused with the more common Buddhist lion, or 'Dog of Fo'.

Figure 9 illustrates a more popular style of decoration seen on K'ang-hsi blue and white porcelain – the flowering plum (Prunus mume). The subject is symbolic of the Chinese New Year, which occurs in the early spring, hence the blossoming of the plum and the cracking of the ice in the background. This subject is probably the most commonly imitated of all Chinese blue and white. Jars of poor commercial quality especially made for the marketing of preserves, such as ginger, have been produced until the present time. During the reign of Yung-cheng (1723–35) there was a decline in the production of wares decorated in blue. There are nevertheless some excellent copies of wares of the Hsuan-te, Ch'eng-hua, and Chia-ching reigns, nearly all accurately marked with the nien-hao of Yung-cheng. It was at this time that more successful attempts were made to imitate the manner in which the dense early blue often piled up on the surface of the glaze in the form of black specks. Such later reproductions are usually much too slick and lack the vigour and seeming carelessness of the earlier painting.

From the time of K'ang-hsi many wares were made in China for the home market with monochrome glazes. The lustrous mirror-black vase in Figure 4 is a particularly fine example of this technique. Mirror-black, or wu chin, was, according to D'Entrecolles, a novelty in 1722. Such wares were certainly continued into the reign of Yung-cheng, in whose reign some of the finest monochrome glazes were introduced. The colour was produced by mixing iron and manganese and necessitated many coatings of the coloured glaze to ensure a depth of colour. This enamel colour invariably tends to show either a brown or a purple hue, rather than the bright, sticky-looking, perfect black of nineteenth-century imitations.

Fig. 13 *Bottle*, Yung-cheng mark
and period. Modelled in relief
with a dragon and covered with a
pale lavender glaze.
Height 9⅝ ins.
*Monochrome glazes, free from
crazing, were especially popular
during the reign of Yung-cheng.
(Victoria and Albert Museum.)*

Fig. 14 ***Kuan-ti, God of War***
*impressed with the signature of
Ho Chao-tsung in seal characters,
made at Te-hua in the Fukien
Province, eighteenth century.
Blanc de Chine porcelain.
Height 11¾ ins.
(Victoria and Albert Museum.)*

13

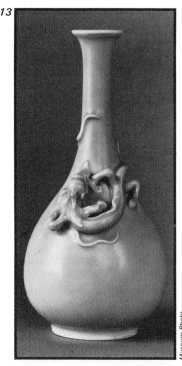

Museum Photo

14

Museum Photo

The simple vase in Figure 5 shows a much
sought-after apple green colour (*p'ing kuo ch'ing*).
The translucent coating of emerald green is applied
over a white glaze which has been deliberately
crazed by applying a glaze which contracts on
cooling at a different rate to the body. Colouring
matter is then rubbed into the cracks to emphasise
this look of antiquity. Many beautiful mono-
chromes of this type were produced during the
reign of K'ang-hsi, especially several fine yellows
and greens, all with the same translucency.

The large coloured vase in Figure 6 illustrates a
type of K'ang-hsi decoration that was especially
sought by all the major collectors of Chinese
porcelain during the nineteenth century. The con-
fusing term 'enamel on the biscuit' merely
indicates that the coloured enamels were applied
as glazes directly on to the surface of the once-fired
porcelain, instead of being fused on to a previously
applied clear glaze. This example shows the
colours of the *famille verte*; green, yellow and
aubergine-purple formed the limited palette,
together with line-drawing in black. In this
instance the entire ground surrounding the flower
painting has been enamelled black in the manner of
famille noire. Wares of the period have a wash of
translucent green over a brownish black. In later
wares decorated in *famille rose*, the green is mixed
with the black before application. This four-sided
vase illustrates the Flowers of the Seasons: the
plum, tree peony, lotus and chrysanthemum.
Other varieties were used to represent the Flowers
of the Months.

The water-pot in Figure 10 is a further instance of
enamel on the biscuit in the palette of the *famille
verte*. Many such wares were made for the scholar's
table, including water-droppers, palettes or slabs
for mixing their inks; seals, boxes, paper-weights,
stands for holding scroll-pictures, and small
vases for a single bloom.

The vessel in Figure 11 was almost certainly made
in the late years of the Emperor K'ang-hsi. This
peach-shaped wine-pot is filled through a deep,
cone-like hole in the base. It is a form that became
popular at the English factory of Rockingham in
Yorkshire, where it was made in a white earthenware with a brownish purple treacle-like glaze. This
shape became known in England as a 'Cadogan' pot.

Figure 12 shows a fine example of Yung-cheng
white porcelain. White being the colour used at the
Chinese Court, such pieces were comparatively
uncommon. This bowl is decorated with designs of
bats painted in an opaque white clay. Such patterns
are best seen by transmitted light and are referred
to as '*an hua*', or 'secret decoration'. Bats were often
used to symbolise the Five Blessings – longevity,
riches, serenity, the cultivation of virtue and the
completion of a life's work. The vase in Figure 8 is
also of the Yung-cheng period and is in the form of
the popular, narrow-necked *mei p'ing*, a shape
intended for a single spray of plum-blossom (*mei*).
This same shape appears in the wares of the earlier
Sung dynasty (960–1279), when it was decorated
in a variety of styles. This example is in imitation of
the famous Sung celadon glazes. The incised
decoration, which can be clearly seen through the
translucent, pale green glaze, shows a neatness and
fastidiousness that is lacking in the freer and more
vigorous decoration on the earlier wares.

Blue, purple and lavender monochrome glazes
were especially popular during Yung-cheng's reign.

Such colours show a purity of tone and are free from
crazing. The bottle in Figure 13 is covered with a
pale lavender glaze and has a finely modelled
dragon encircling the neck. This gives a pleasing
variety of tone where the depth of the deeper glaze
emphasises the form of the creature. Similar detail
of modelling can be seen under the strong yellow
glaze of the kettle in Figure 2. Here, the dragon
(*lung*) has been amusingly elongated to form the
handle. Although the five-clawed dragon is an
emblem of the Emperor, it does not signify that all
pieces so decorated were made for the Court.

It was probably during the late years of the reign
of K'ang-hsi that the rose-crimson enamel derived
from gold was first introduced into China from
Europe. By mixing this enamel with white a variety
of pinks to deep rose colours were now obtainable,
resulting in the palette of the *famille rose*. Wares
painted in these colours are seen at their best in the
reign of Yung-cheng (Fig. 7). In the succeeding
reign of Ch'ien-lung (1736–95) the whole ground
tends to become too busy with overcrowded decoration and complex borders. The majority of the
wares mentioned continued to be made throughout
the later years of the Ch'ing dynasty and only the
recognition of genuine marks and the appreciation
of fine quality porcelain can help determine the
correct period of manufacture. It is not unusual to
find pieces of nineteenth-century Chinese
porcelain with the reign marks of contemporary
Emperors, and checking is always advisable.

The white figure of Kuan-ti, the God of War
(Fig. 14) was made at Te-hua in the southern
province of Fukien. Such beautiful white porcelain
is commonly called 'blanc de Chine'. There seems
little likelihood of such porcelain having been
made prior to 1650. Buddhist figures appear to
have been among the most popular productions.

It was the more modest pieces made in Fukien
that were imitated by such European factories as
Meissen, Saint Cloud and Bow. *Blanc de Chine*
rarely had any enamel decoration applied in
China. Where such colours are seen, they are
almost certain to have been added in Holland or
Germany.

MUSEUMS AND COLLECTIONS

Chinese porcelain of the Ch'ing dynasty may be
seen at the following:

FRANCE
Paris: Musée Guimet
GREAT BRITAIN
Cambridge: Fitzwilliam Museum
London: British Museum
     Percival David Foundation
     Victoria and Albert Museum
Oxford: Ashmolean Museum
U.S.A.
Boston: Museum of Fine Arts
New York: Metropolitan Museum of Art
Washington D.C: Freer Gallery of Art

FURTHER READING

Oriental Blue and White by Sir Harry Garner,
London, 1970.
World Ceramics ed. by R. J. Charleston, London,
1968.
Later Chinese Porcelain by Soame Jenyns,
London, 1965.
**Ceramic Art of China and Other Countries of the
Far East** by W. B. Honey, London, 1945.

Netsuke and Inro

Nicolas Wolfers

Netsuke and inro were designed for everyday use but the craftsmen of Tokugawa Japan fashioned them as works of art

The *netsuke* provided an easy way for the Japanese wearing a kimono, which has no pockets, to carry at his girdle such objects as an *inro* (seal-case), later often used for medicines, a purse, a tinder-box, a drinking gourd, or a tobacco-pouch (Fig. 9). The *netsuke* (pronounced *nĕtskĭ*) was a toggle on the girdle from which, at the end of two cords, with its several compartments held together by the *ojime* (sliding bead), hung the *inro*.

The kind of *netsuke* used would depend on the rank and needs of the wearer, and sometimes more than one would be worn at a time. *Samurai* (members of the warrior class) did not smoke in public as this would have been beneath their dignity. Their *netsuke* were usually finely carved for use with the lacquered *inro*, which perhaps contained the family seal, some pills or a herbal remedy. A large *netsuke* would be worn to support heavy objects or to match the figure of a large man such as a *sumo* wrestler. Gamblers often wore *netsuke* of skulls or snakes to bring them luck (Fig. 2). In the Tokugawa hierarchy the merchant ranked beneath the *samurai*, artisan and peasant; members of the merchant class were therefore quite happy to be seen carrying at their side pipes in cases, tobacco-pouches and all the paraphernalia of smoking. Some *netsuke* were even designed to serve as ashtrays *(sui-gara-ake)* as well as toggles.

The origin of the *netsuke* is obscure, as are the dates of its development as an art form. Although now considered among the finest and most characteristic of Japan's minor arts, early *netsuke* were merely shells, gourds or tree roots; the word *netsuke* is a compound of *ne* (a root), and *tsuke* (to fasten). There are few illustrations of *netsuke* in use until the eighteenth century and it is hard to identify seventeenth-century examples with any certainty. Not many were signed before the mid-eighteenth century. Some authorities believe that use was first made of *netsuke* in the late sixteenth century, though toggles were certainly worn in China before that date.

Until the Meiji restoration and the Revolution of 1868 there were a large number of ceremonies at which the *inro* could be worn to advantage. The Japanese lacquerer practised his trade to perfection so that even in China his work was highly praised. The Chinese Emperor K'ang-hsi (1662–1722) attributed the superior quality of Japanese lacquer to the damper climate, which allowed it to dry more slowly and a harder finish to be achieved. The particular qualities of the Japanese *rhus verniciferus*, the tree from which the lacquer gum comes, also contributed to the high standard of Japanese lacquer-work.

Smoking was a major factor in the development of the *netsuke*. Though tobacco was introduced by the Portuguese in the sixteenth century, the habit only slowly became fashionable. In the seventeenth century, tobacco-boxes or pouches became a prerequisite for successful merchants and fashionable men of all but the *samurai* class. More and better *netsuke* were demanded. Gradually the *netsuke* ceased to be a purely utilitarian object to

Fig. 1 **Brown lacquer inro** *with gold and shell inlay depicting water fowl rising from a bed of rushes, mid-nineteenth century. Cornelian* ojime *(sliding) bead. Ivory* netsuke *depicting a man and boy scattering beans at New Year.* (Victoria and Albert Museum, London.)

2

R. Todd-White

4

R. Todd-White

3

be worn, worn out and discarded.

The Portuguese brought not only tobacco and trade, but also the Christian faith, which proved so popular that the Shogun felt his position to be threatened. In 1614 an edict was promulgated banning Christianity. In 1639, after a two-year rebellion, Japan was closed completely to the Portuguese. The handful of Dutch allowed to trade from the island of Deshima off Nagasaki were virtually Japan's only contact with the outside world until the coming of Commodore Perry's 'black ships' in 1853. The fables, fashions and fancies of the unique and inward-looking society which developed during Japan's seclusion were mirrored in the subjects chosen by the makers of *netsuke*.

Folklore, religion and the legendary history of China and Japan provided some of the most popular early subjects. There were often many stories about a single character and many versions of one story. The great artist and *netsuke*-maker Hogen Shuzan loved to carve figures from the *Sankaikyo* (a classical legend of the Mountain and the Ocean) or from the *Ressenden* (Lives of the *Rishi*). *Rishi*, or *Sennin*, were popular figures in Buddhist and Taoist mythology; resting for thousands of years from the cycle of transmigration, they would emerge from solitude in the mountains to perform miracles. The crane, a symbol of longevity, was depicted as a messenger or as a tireless mount. Shiei, one of the Taoist Immortals, rode to heaven on a large carp, a symbol of perseverance. Kinko, another Immortal, was translated on his carp either to the heavens or to the realm of fishes, depending on the version of the story. Gama *Sennin* (Fig. 3), a frequent subject, is portrayed with a toad into which his astral body is once said to have strayed. The *Ho-o* bird and the

Fig. 2 (Left) **Cow and calf,** netsuke *by Tomotada, late eighteenth century. Carved ivory. This maker is best known for his recumbent oxen made of ivory.*
(Right) **Skull and snake netsuke,** *unsigned, mid-nineteenth century.*
(British Museum, London.)

Fig. 3 **Gama Sennin.** *Ivory netsuke, c.1800. This Immortal is portrayed with a toad into which his astral body was said to have strayed. (British Museum.)*

Fig. 4 **Baku,** netsuke, *unsigned, c.1800. This popular mythical beast, which ate nightmares, is a rare subject in netsuke. (Victoria and Albert Museum.)*

Hamlyn Group Library

Fig. 5 **Goshisho,** *a Chinese general (c.500 B.C.), with heavy kettle and writing-brush, winning his place as the King of Wu's counsellor.* Netsuke. *(D. J. K. Wright Ltd., London.)*

Fig. 6 **Shojo** *(a drunken sprite) sleeping off the after-effects of* sake, netsuke *signed by Ikkwan, mid-nineteenth century. (Victoria and Albert Museum.)*

Fig. 7 **Uzume,** *Goddess of Fun and Folly, fondling the nose of a* Konoha Tengu, okimono *made by Umpo for the western market, mid-nineteenth century. (British Museum.)*

Fig. 8 **Octopus and Kappa,** netsuke. *Octopuses were thought to be lascivious and are usually shown making advances to mermaids. The Kappa was less expansive. (British Museum.)*

Fig. 9 **Flirting at the waterfall** *by Suzuki Harunobu, eighteenth century. Woodcut. Detail showing a tobacco pouch held in place by a* netsuke. *(British Museum.)*

Fig. 10 **Karasu Tengu,** netsuke *by Shumin. (Victoria and Albert Museum.)*

11

12

Kirin were sacred hybrids. Born of the conjunction of two stars or of a cow and a dragon, the *Kirin* symbolises elegance, virtue and, in Japan today, a popular make of beer.

The *Baku* (Fig. 4), another popular mythical beast though not a sacred one, is a surprisingly rare subject in *netsuke*. Its function is to eat nightmares. The *Kappa*, with its strange tonsure, is more common but less benevolent (Fig. 8). Sometimes shown with a turtle-shell back, sometimes only with scales, it is a creature of the rivers with a taste for the entrails of children and young women, whom it first abuses before drowning and eating. It also has a taste for cucumbers, but the more usual way of appeasing it is to bow low in Japanese style. Being a well-mannered monster it will bow low in reply and spill from the top of its head the precious liquid from which comes its strength and aggression.

The *Karasu Tengu* (crow sprite) is more frequently seen than the long-nosed *Konoha Tengu* (Fig. 7). Many wooden *netsuke* depict a crow sprite hatching (Fig. 10), a subject which not only appealed to the imagination but could be carved in a robust shape for everyday use.

The *Shojo* (a drunken sprite) is an example of the wit of the *netsuke*-carver (Fig. 6). The creature is a pun on *Shojo* (young girl) and *Shojo* (orangutang, an animal of Borneo and Sumatra, with long reddish-brown hair, which was reputed to have a liking for alcohol). The *netsuke* therefore showed a long-haired girl inordinately fond of *sake*, either holding out an empty cup or, as portrayed by the great carver Ikkwan, sleeping off the after-effects.

Netsuke of the zodiac animals, symbolising different periods of time, were outstandingly popular. The rat, ox, tiger, hare, dragon, serpent, horse, goat, monkey, cock, dog and boar were each assigned a year and an hour of the day.

Gradually there was a change in fashion from subjects drawn from Chinese mythology and history to native Japanese subjects; and later to natural subjects, for example animals, plants and fruit, which were so popular in the nineteenth century. The researches of such men as Motoori (1730–1801) into Japan's early Imperial history gave new vigour to Shintoism, a religion combining the worship of nature with fanatical loyalty to the reigning dynasty. Shintoism in turn invigorated the opposition to Tokugawa which culminated in the Meiji restoration. Instead of *Sennin*, Confucian paragons, heroes of the Han dynasty or figures like Goshisho (Fig. 5), there were Uzume (Fig. 7), Goddess of Fun and Folly, and the Treasure Ship of the Seven Gods of Good Luck (Fig. 11). In addition, there were Buddhist subjects such as Emma-O, King of Hell and Judge of the Dead, and very often Daruma, the founder of Zen, was represented.

Daruma in particular is a good example of the scant respect the *netsuke*-carver accorded even to semi-sacred and religious subjects. Since tradition had it that his nine years of silent, seated meditation had withered his legs, he is often made in the form of a self-righting doll. There were ghosts, goblins (*bakemono*) and demons (*oni*), usually getting the better of Shoki, the demon-queller, and in the first half of the nineteenth century a profusion of natural subjects, each with some symbolism or story.

There were also *netsuke* of musical instruments like the *koto*, *biwa* and *samisen*; of dances like the New Year Lion Dance or the peasants' *bon odori*;

Fig. 11 *The Treasure Ship of the Seven Gods of Good Luck,* netsuke, *signed by Masahiro, nineteenth century.*
The cargo of this mythical ship included the Inexhaustible Purse, the Hammer of Chaos, the Hat of Invisibility and the Lucky Raincoat to ward off evil. Hotei was the most popular god; he could sleep in the snow and predict the future, loved children but hated washing.
(Victoria and Albert Museum.)

13

R. Todd-White

Fig. 12 *Inro of five compartments signed in gold characters by the Kajikawa family (active c.1750– c.1850), early nineteenth century. Lacquer with gold and mother of pearl inlay. The* netsuke *is a miniature mask from the classical* No *theatre. (Spink and Sons, London.)*

Fig. 13 *Dutchman with cockerel, unsigned* netsuke, *eighteenth century. (D. J. K. Wright Ltd.)*

of ceremonies like the *cha-no-yu* (tea ceremony); of sports like *sumo* wrestling and *judo*; of games like *kakurembo* (hide-and-seek), or *go*; and in particular there were miniature masks from the classical *No* plays (Fig. 12). Deme Yeiman of Edo and his descendants were mask-carvers by profession and noted for this form of *netsuke*. There were courtiers and monkey showmen (*sarumawashi*), acrobats, blind masseurs (*amma*) and nightwatchmen. Household articles were depicted and mechanical objects such as tinder-boxes or the Dutch traders' compasses and matchlock guns. Nor were the Dutchmen themselves neglected (Fig. 13).

There was great variety in the forms and materials of *netsuke*: the early seal forms, the miniature masks, the *sashi* (rod) form, the *hyotan* (gourd), the coloured dolls called 'Nara-ningyo' (a form originated by Hogen Shuzan), the *ichiraku* (woven wire) form, the simple hunters' trophies or the clever trick *netsuke* of goblins with sliding necks, skulls with moving jaws and loose seeds rattling in a lotus pod. Delicate scenes were carved in clamshells or figures inside a walnut, but the most common forms were the compact statuette or *katabori* group of figures, designed for everyday use, and the *manju*, a disc in the shape of a rice-cake.

A variation on the *manju* was the *kagamibuta* (mirror lid) *netsuke*, a decorated metal disc set in ivory or wood. Metalworkers were most active in this form in the second half of the nineteenth century when *samurai* no longer required their traditional output of swords and sword fittings.

The majority of *netsuke* were made of wood or ivory. Shuzan and other carvers of the early period preferred *hinoki* (Japanese cypress), but it was too light a wood to wear well. Boxwood was most frequently used because of its hardness and fine grain, but *netsuke* of cherry, ebony and other woods are also found. In ivory there is a wide variation in quality; Kwaigyoku Masatsugu was one carver who insisted on using only the best. In Iwami province by the sea, marine ivory was very popular: the tusk of the walrus, the horn of the narwhal and the tooth of the sperm whale. Staghorn was quite a common material while metal, bone, amber, crystal, jet, hornbill, mother of pearl and porcelain were among materials used occasionally. Sometimes *netsuke* were lacquered and painted; sometimes materials were combined. Shibayama and his school are famous for inlay.

Inro were mainly of lacquered wood, since porcelain and other materials were too heavy or too fragile for everyday use. In general, they were made in oblong box forms, with four or five neatly interlocking compartments (Fig. 1). *Inro* in the shape of a tortoise, cicada or some other animal are unusual. There is considerable variety in the kinds of lacquer and the methods in which they were applied for decoration. Blue and green are very rare colours, black, gold and red being the most common. The Kajikawa family and Zeshin are perhaps the most famous names in *inro* (Fig. 12).

Not enough is known about the lives of the makers of *inro* and *netsuke*. Since the signing of works became general only in the nineteenth century, the hand of a master must usually be deduced from the known facts about his materials, forms, style and the quality of the workmanship. A signature may mean no more than that a work is by a pupil or in the style of a master. Kwaigyoku Masatsugu used several signatures.

Moreover there are many forgeries and false signatures; even an expert may not always be able to date and identify a work with certainty. At best, he may be able to show that a particular claim for a piece's authenticity is unsubstantiated. Over two thousand signatures of *netsuke*-makers are recorded, four times as many as for makers of *inro*, the skill of the lacquerer being more difficult to acquire. Some of the greatest makers of *inro*, such as Zeshin (1806–91) also produced a few *netsuke*.

Some makers of *netsuke* and *inro* became especially known for one subject, which was so popular that it was widely copied within their lifetime: Tomotada for the recumbent ox (Fig. 2), the first Masanao for the *fukura suzume* (inflated sparrow), Ikkwan of Nagoya for the sleeping *Shojo*, and later for the rat.

Most of the makers of *netsuke* and *inro* naturally lived in the large towns of Osaka, Kyoto and Edo, where they could best make a livelihood from their carving. By 1750 Edo's population was about one million. Another important centre was Nagoya, close to the forests of Gifu, whose output seems in consequence to have consisted entirely of wooden *netsuke*. Issai and other fine carvers came from other small centres.

After the ending of Japan's seclusion and with the Meiji restoration, the production of *netsuke* and *inro* declined. Many of the patrons from the ruling classes were dispossessed, the *samurai* lost their status, and Western-style clothes with pockets came into fashion. The smoking of cigarettes, also in fashion at this time, was another factor.

The demand for *netsuke* came instead from the influx of foreign collectors and tourists looking for something typically Japanese. *Okimono* (ornaments) were turned out in large numbers, sometimes finely carved but without the simple beauty of the genuine *netsuke* (Fig. 7). The *himotoshi* (cordholes) were either missing or bored in the wrong place for wearing so that the carving showed to its best advantage. However, at this time also, a few perceptive foreigners built up the great collections of *netsuke* and *inro* which have led to these art forms being so appreciated in the West.

MUSEUMS AND COLLECTIONS

Japanese *netsuke* may be seen at the following:

FRANCE
Paris: Musée d'Ennery (Sundays only)

GREAT BRITAIN
Cambridge: Fitzwilliam Museum
London: British Museum
              Victoria and Albert Museum
Oxford: Ashmolean Museum
              Pitt Rivers Museum

JAPAN
Tokyo: National Museum

U.S.A.
Boston: Museum of Fine Arts
Washington
D.C: Freer Gallery of Art

FURTHER READING

The Netsuke Handbook by Ueda Reikichi, translated and adapted by R. Bushell, Tokyo, 1961.
The Netsuke of Japan by Egerton Ryerson, London, 1958.
The Art of the Netsuke Carver by Frederick Meinertzhagen, London, 1956.

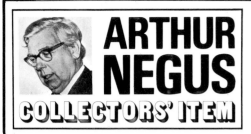

ARTHUR NEGUS
COLLECTORS' ITEM

Sac Frères, London W.1. R. Todd-White

Sac Frères, London W.1. R. Todd-White

AMBER

Amber is one of the oldest and most beautiful substances in the world. Sometimes classed as a semi-precious stone, it is not really a mineral at all but a fossilised resin originating from the giant conifer trees which flourished in various parts of the world during the Oligocene era, some fifty million years ago. These trees were very large indeed, sometimes thirty feet or more in diameter, and in consequence their natural production of resin was considerable. With the eventual decay of the pine forests, the lumps of resin underwent chemical changes and were subjected to extreme pressures. In due course, the sea covered the land where the forests had been; the resin became completely fossilised and was washed up on many beaches in varied shapes and colours and covered by a rock-like crust. This crust was cut away and the piece was polished to shine in bright and lovely colours, sometimes quite clear and sometimes opaque.

Many beautiful things have been made in amber over the centuries, including necklaces, rings, bracelets and pendants. Many carvings were also produced. These last were superb pieces of craftsmanship; the Chinese were the finest artists of all in this field. With many of these delicate pieces one mistake could ruin the work of months or years.

A number of copies of amber have been, and are still being, produced, and it is sometimes a little difficult for the would-be collector to tell the real from the fake, However, one of its chief characteristics is the weight — it is very light indeed. It is also always warm to the touch, in contrast to such stones as jade and cornelian. It should pick up small pieces of tissue-paper when rubbed on a sleeve or cloth, but this is not a final test as many other substances do the same thing. Amber emits quite a strong negative electricity. This fact makes it a fine electrical insulator and it is used today in electronics where high voltages need reinforced insulators.

Sac Frères, London W.1. R. Todd-White

Prices
Prices range between about £4 for a Victorian amber ring to £100 and more for fine pieces of antique amber.

Above left: **Seal,** *made from part of a Persian hookah pipe, c.1750. £100.*
Above right: **English paste ring** *containing a piece of Burmese amber, c.1840. £35.*
Prayer necklace *made for the Persian market from Baltic amber, made up of ninety-nine beads, one for each martyr of the* Muslim faith, c.1820. £50.
Centre: **Carved figure** *from Konigsburg, East Prussia, where trade in amber was carried on until the time of the First World War, c.1790. £85.*
Opposite: **Chinese carving** *of a man riding a donkey, c.1736 (Ch'ien-lung period). £150.*

Sac Frères, London W. 1. R. Todd-White

The Porcelain of Japan

Michael Eveleigh

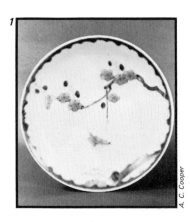

Fig. 1 **Dish**, *Japanese, mid-seventeenth century. Blue and white. Painted in a typically free style of brushwork, this dish shows the blurred effect due to the fluxing of the cobalt blue with the glaze.*
(Author's Collection.)

Fig. 2 **Buddhistic Lion,** *Kakiemon, second half of the seventeenth century the base with typical octopus scroll decoration in association with peony flowers.*
(Christie, Manson and Woods Ltd., London.)

Fig. 3 **Baluster jar,** *early Kakiemon, c.1670. Decorated with enamel colours. This early piece is painted boldly with a typical river and mountain landscape.*
(Christie's.)

Fig. 4 **'Coloured Arita' plate,** *first half of the eighteenth century. Decorated in enamel colours in a style inspired by Chinese famille verte. Pieces of this sort were made at both the Kakiemon and the Arita kilns, using a similar palette.*
(Author's Collection.)

Although the first Japanese porcelains were directly inspired by Chinese ceramics, in a short time they acquired a distinctly Japanese character

Although China had begun producing true high-fired porcelain in the fourteenth century, it was not until the early seventeenth century that the technique was mastered in feudal Japan. Prior to this date, all porcelain had been imported from China. It is probable that the Tokugawa Shogunate, wishing to be free of the Chinese porcelain merchants, abducted potters from Korea. (Attacks were made on Korea in 1592 and again in 1597.) Part of the spoils of war were the 'potter communities' that were brought back to Japan and settled near Arita. But it was not until 1616 that a Korean, Rhee Sambae (in Japanese, Risampie) found porcellaneous clay at Tegundani in Arita, thus making him the father of Japanese porcelain. The kilns, techniques and styles of this proto-Japanese porcelain clearly show a strong Korean affinity and can often be mistaken for Korean by those who are not familiar with the originals.

A popular misconception is that the name 'Imari' indicates a kiln or factory. The name derives from the port of Imari whence the wares were shipped, just as 'Nanking' has become a generic name for the Chinese export blue and white shipped from that port. The name 'Imari' has been adopted to describe the palette of under-glaze blue and over-glaze iron red and gilt of the Arita export wares. The bulk of seventeenth-century Japanese porcelain is blue and white, and a characteristic feature is that, due to fluxing of the cobalt with the glaze, the blue decoration bleeds into the surrounding area causing a blurred effect (Fig. 1). It was basically to overcome this fault that the early workmen painted iron red and gold on to the glaze to conceal the blurred edges.

European influence began to be felt as early as 1542 with the arrival of the Portuguese and, a little later, of Saint Francis Xavier who preached Catholic Christianity to great effect. So much so, in fact, that the Shogunate, realising the disturbing effect it was having, ordered the expulsion of the missionaries. The Protestant Dutch, lacking missionary zeal but with good commercial instincts, were allowed to establish their warehouses on the island of Deshima, and became the only group of Europeans to carry on trade with the Japanese.

A curious feature of early Japanese porcelains is the spur marks, usually three, five or seven in number. These are marks made by the small supports used in the kilns during firing. China ceased using such spurs in the tenth or eleventh century but the practice persisted in Korea into the fifteenth and sixteenth centuries. As skill improved and purer cobalt became available, so the decoration became more controlled. Simple flowers gave way to elaborate panels enclosed by octopus scroll borders (in fact, a dissolved foliage scroll). The decorative repertoire is drawn basically from folk history and culture, and includes the 'Three Friends' motif: the plum, bamboo and pine; birds and tigers also often occur. Pieces expressly made for export were often copied from wooden models supplied by the Dutch traders and include covered jars, tankards (some especially designed for silver mounting in Europe) and large dishes, most famous of which are those bearing the 'V.O.C.' monogram of the Dutch East India Company (Vereenigde Oostindische Compagnie).

Pieces for the home market were at this date still usually made in imitation of the ware imported from China. Among these the pieces enamelled in the typical late Ming style were the most popular and it is interesting that this group is still among the most collected today. Having established a successful industry producing good quality blue and white, the kiln masters turned their attention to perfecting the technique of enamelling in colours on porcelain. Three basic types exist: coloured Imari, Kakiemon and Kutani.

The history of Kakiemon has been gleaned from the records of the family. According to tradition, Sakaida Kizai-emon, an Arita potter, made an ornament in the form of twin persimmons (*kaki*) for his feudal lord, the *daimyo* Nabeshima, who was so pleased with its artistry that he conferred on him the honorific name of Kaki-emon. Sakaida adopted this as his family name, marking his lord's favour. He worked as a foreman under a merchant named Toshima Tokuyemon, who is thought to have acquired the secret of enamelling in colours from a Chinese enameller at Nagasaki; after some false starts they mastered the art and began one of the most important ceramic productions.

In the early stage the white-glazed pieces were brought from the factories to the Kakiemon workshops for enamelling, although eventually they acquired their own kiln. Their highly distinctive designs and colour schemes made such an impact on the European market that, within a few years of the first pieces being imported, all the major porcelain factories in Europe produced pieces in direct imitation. The body of these wares is generally milky white with a matt surface showing a slightly greasy-looking sheen, while the poorer quality pieces have a coarse, almost gritty texture.

On the best pieces the enamelled designs are delicately and sensitively executed with occasional black outlines which hint at, rather than define, the decoration. The earlier pieces use a thick bright turquoise and a vibrant iron red, imitating the fiery orange-red of ripe persimmons. This colour scheme must have been taken from the Chinese Swatow porcelains imported during the sixteenth and seventeenth centuries. The additional colours which distinguish the Kakiemon enamel palette are a striking azure blue, soft orange, transparent primrose yellow, lavender blue and grass green. The use of a brownish purple occurs only on rather later pieces.

All the early Kakiemon pieces were intended for the personal use of the *daimyo* and his Court, and the decorative themes reflect a strictly Japanese taste. The first-phase work of the Kakiemons (roughly 1640–70) is confined to boldly painted designs of landscapes (Fig. 3); flowers and shrubs growing from rockwork; and birds on branches. Unlike so many decorative techniques, the Kakiemon group became more refined as time went on and, while the seventeenth-century pieces had decorations which covered large areas of the piece, in the eighteenth century the decoration

2

3

4

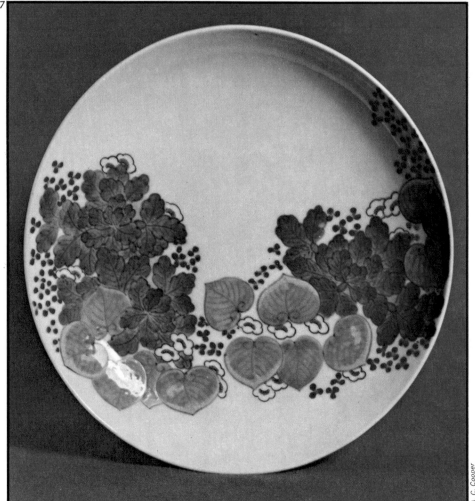

becomes sparser. It is this group that shows, more than any other, the water-colour quality of the enamelling. Marks rarely appear before the eighteenth century, and those most commonly found are the *fuku* (happiness) and *kin* (gold) marks. A wide variety of shapes occur, ranging from covered baluster jars, deep, covered food bowls, ewers and bottles, to human and animal figures (Fig. 2). The influence of European designs and shapes can be seen on pieces which date from the early eighteenth century onwards, and there are a number of pieces executed exclusively for the European market.

Any successful innovation has its copyists and the neighbouring kilns at Arita soon adapted their Imari palette by adding pale yellow and green enamel to foliage, thus giving a new liveliness to their pieces; before long, something approaching the Kakiemon palette developed alongside the old Imari palette.

The problem of identification or classification of these wares as distinct from the true Kakiemon pieces is so difficult that some scholars prefer to think only in terms of 'coloured Arita' (Fig. 4), thereby avoiding any separate classification. Among the rarest coloured Imari pieces are those early pieces with designs exclusively for the Japanese market, like the *Kabuki* plate in Figure 5 which has, in addition to the Imari colours, yellow, turquoise and aubergine over-glaze enamels.

While the decoration of most Kakiemon wares was of purely Japanese inspiration, the Kutani wares represent a different tradition, being directly derived from the late Ming coloured pieces. Of all Japanese porcelains, these Kutani wares are the most highly prized, but they are also perhaps the most difficult to date. So far no positive kiln-site or reliable literary records have been traced. The early porcelains are always referred to as *Ko*-Kutani (old Kutani), to distinguish them from the *Ao*-Kutani (new Kutani) stonewares of the nineteenth-century revival wares.

Rich, harmonious colours and free, impressionistic decoration

The body of *Ko*-Kutani pieces is generally whitish grey, the glaze milky white with a subtle, velvety softness to the touch. The enamels are always rich and harmonious, varying from brilliant transparency to subdued opacity. The palette includes a thick, vivid green, egg yellow, aubergine, Prussian blue and an iron red which ranges from cherry red to warm brown. The decoration is nearly always executed in the boldly free and impressionistic manner of the late Ming wares which inspired them (Fig. 8), frequently with birds and insects amid flowering trees and shrubs. Animals rarely feature in these decorations and the figures particularly are Chinese in conception. The true *Ko*-Kutani pieces were probably made during the last half of the seventeenth century and were again for the exclusive use of the *daimyo* and his Court. In 1816 Yoshidaya Denyemon revived the manufacture of Kutani wares, either on the original site or close to it. These kilns continued to operate until their closure between 1863 and 1869, caused by a general depression. These *Ao*-Kutani wares somehow lack the vitality of their earlier counterparts; the designs are stiff and the use of colour smudgy, even

Japanese Porcelain

Fig. 5 **Dish**, *Imari, mid-seventeenth century. Decorated in under-glaze blue and over-glaze enamels with a* Kabuki *theatre scene. (Private Collection.)*

Fig. 6 **Small hexagonal wine-cup**, *Nabeshima, early eighteenth century. (Author's Collection.)*

Fig. 7 **Dish**, *Nabeshima, early eighteenth century. Decorated in under-glaze blue and over-glaze enamels with toadflax flowers. (Sotheby and Co., London.)*

A. C. Cooper

Fig. 8 **Dish**, *Ko-Kutani, first half of the seventeenth century. Decorated in bold enamels with the 'three friends' – plum, bamboo and pine. (Christie's.)*

Fig. 9 **Dish**, *Nabeshima, second half of the eighteenth century. Painted in blue and white with water gushing through a weir. (Sotheby's.)*

Fig. 10 **Figure**, *Imari, late seventeenth century. A type of figure originally made at the Kakiemon kilns. (Christie's.)*

when directly copying the earlier examples. The most typical of these *yoshidaya* (revival wares) are those with heavy enamelling, green or yellow grounds and with the decoration outlined in black. These pieces frequently bear a two-character mark never seen on *Ko*-Kutani wares.

It does not seem that the volume of *Ko*-Kutani pieces claimed as genuine could have come from a small factory with a short life of about thirty years. The Arita pieces in *Ko*-Kutani style still use the same type of enamel but usually overdo the original designs and so change their essential character. It is possible that the craftsmen who worked at the early Kutani kilns moved to Arita when their own factory ceased in the late seventeenth century, and this could explain the large volume of *Ko*-Kutani style wares coming from Arita.

The kilns were moved to preserve intact the secret skills of the potters and enamellers

Of all porcelain made in Japan, the most exclusive was that produced for the *daimyo* Nabeshima. The Nabeshima family records, more reliable than usual, state that a kiln was started in 1628 to produce fine porcelains 'like the Chinese'. The first kiln lasted on the same site until about 1665 or 1660, and the wares it produced seem to have been of little significance. It is probably at the second site, until about 1675, that coloured Nabeshima was produced, and the general wares were of noticeably higher quality. These moves were occasioned by the need to preserve intact the secret skills of the potters and enamellers. It was on the final site that the finest Nabeshima pieces were produced, achieving a unique degree of technical excellence. All the pieces were made for the exclusive use of the *daimyo* Nabeshima, his family and friends, and any piece of less than perfect quality was ordered to be destroyed.

Unlike the other kilns at Arita, those of the Nabeshima family were protected from industrial uncertainty and the potters had a status superior to their counterparts working in the other kilns. There was a deliberate policy to recruit the very best artists, enamellers and potters for this kiln and, having succeeded in getting them to join the Nabeshima workshops, steps were taken to ensure that they stayed there. If for any reason a workman should leave, he was obliged to keep all that he had learnt to himself, and he was forbidden to join another kiln or set up on his own as a potter or enameller. One of the notable successes of these kilns was the mastery of painting in under-glaze blue. A high degree of skill was required and achieved, and there is a complete absence of fuzziness of the outlines of the under-glaze decoration. The colour of the blue is thin and soft (Fig. 6), lending itself admirably as a base for over-glaze enamelling in colours which achieved a high degree of excellence.

The decoration is always executed in a naturalistic manner, though some compositions are very formal. Naturalistic plum-blossom floats on formalised water, or naturalistic trees cascade on to water that resembles fish scales (Fig. 9). Whatever the subject used, be it flowers (Fig. 7), shrubs or birds, a certain balance between formality and naturalism was sought. The underside is always in a simple

style, with formal flower sprays, or bundles of money joined with elaborate tassels, and a simple comb or cog-wheel pattern round the disproportionately high foot. Particularly apparent in the dishes which use designs derived from textile patterns is the technique of *tou ts'ai* enamelling copied from the Chinese.

Last of the main producers of porcelain in Japan are the kilns on Hirado, which are thought to have started in the late sixteenth century under the Koreans brought there by the *daimyo* Hideyoshi. Porcellaneous clay was found on the island and production commenced.

These early wares were mostly blue and white, and show the strong influence of a Korean heritage, but it was not until the late eighteenth century and early nineteenth century that the Hirado wares achieved recognition. They are made of the finest white porcelain and painted in a soft, slightly violet toned cobalt blue with miniaturist landscapes. These wares are mostly faceted bottles or flasks with narrow necks, although some other vases and utensils have animals or insects moulded on to the sides. The aesthetically fine earlier wares are regrettably eclipsed in sheer virtuosity by the later nineteenth-century wares which achieve a staggering mastery of the medium. Vases and incense-burners of elaborate construction have large areas of reticulated panelling and appear so frail that it seems a miracle that they even survived the kiln firings, let alone the long journeys to Europe.

While it was in feudal Japan that these first porcelain factories flourished, the appreciation of the medium is still very much present in today's affluent islands, and the porcelain produced for both home and export markets still show a definitively original concept of handling and decoration.

MUSEUMS AND COLLECTIONS
Japanese porcelain may be seen at the following:

GREAT BRITAIN
London: British Museum
                Hampton Court Palace
                Victoria and Albert Museum
Oxford: Ashmolean Museum

JAPAN
Tokyo: National Museum

U.S.A.
Boston: Boston Museum of Fine Arts
Cambridge: Fogg Art Museum
Cleveland: Museum of Art

NETHERLANDS
Amsterdam: Rijksmuseum
Leyden: Rijksmuseum voor Volkenkunde

FURTHER READING

Japanese Porcelain by Soame Jenyns, London, 1965.
Porcelain and the Dutch East India Company, 1602–1682 and **The Japanese Porcelain Trade of the Dutch East India Company after 1683** by T. Volker, vols. 11 and 13 published by the Rijksmuseum voor Volkenkunde, Leyden, 1954 and 1959.

JAPANESE WOOD-BLOCK PRINTS

Jack Hillier

The Asia Society

Sperryn's Ltd.

Sperryn's Ltd.

One of the best-known and most popular forms of Oriental art, the Japanese woodcut, reached the peak of its perfection in the eighteenth century with such artists as Harunobu, Kiyonaga and Utamaro

Among collectors, the term 'Japanese print' has come to mean the broadsheets of one particular school of artists, the painters of *Ukiyo-e*. Less specifically, the words could apply to any form of graphic art, and looking at them first in their more general sense will help to situate the print in relation to the art and literature of Japan.

At first and until comparatively recent times, the wood-block was the sole method of printing; metal-engraving, etching and lithography were methods learned only after contact with the West. In the absence of movable type, the texts of books were also cut on wood-blocks. As the medium was in use from the eighth century onwards, by the eighteenth century there was a tradition of skill in wood-block cutting unrivalled elsewhere in the world, not excluding China where the medium was older and as universally used.

As a result of changes in social conditions and the consequent emergence of a new class of literate commoner, wood-block book-illustration became increasingly common in the seventeenth century. The illustration of the more popular (and often erotic) literature led to the evolution of the style that came to be known as *Ukiyo-e*. Literally, this term means 'pictures of the floating world', but there are underlying meanings of the fashionable and topical, and a concern with low life. In the latter part of the century, Moronobu (1618–1703), generally thought of as the founder of the school, began to illustrate books and albums in a bold, rhythmic line and mass, eminently appropriate to the woodcut medium. These set the pattern in style and content for the generations of *Ukiyo-e* artists that were to follow.

The medium was a reproductive one. As with wood-engraving in Europe, the artist supplied a design that a skilled craftsman then cut on the block.

Portraits of contemporary beauties were in great demand

By the beginning of the eighteenth century, the *Ukiyo-e* woodcut was firmly established and already had an acknowledged repertoire of subjects. Pictures of the great courtesans and their attendants were the most popular. Known as *bijin-ga* (pictures of beauties) and the exact counterpart of the modern pin-up, they were idealised portraits in which the superb *kimono* and brocaded sashes were as much a feature as the conventionally out-lined faces. In the first decades of the century, the Kaigetsudo group of artists designed some of the grandest of these prints (Fig. 3), which today are amongst the rarest and most valuable of works. The courtesan print became the stock-in-trade of

Fig. 1 *The poet Teika* by Torii Kiyomasu, c.1750. Detail of a hand-coloured ink-print, 22⅞ x 11¾ ins. The Torii family are known for their prints of the popular theatre. (Mr. and Mrs. Richard P. Gale Collection, Mound, Minnesota.)

Fig. 2 *The actor Ichikawa Dansaburo III* in a scene from a play performed in 1772, by Katsukawa Shunsho, c.1772. 12⅛ x 5⅝ ins. Shunsho and his school were widely acknowledged portrayers of the Kabuki actors. (Formerly Mellor Collection.)

Fig. 3 *Beauty playing with a cat* by Kaigetsudo Dohan, c.1715. Hand-coloured ink-print, 22½ x 11½ ins. The Kaigetsudo group designed some of the grandest of the bijin-ga, prints corresponding to the modern pin-ups. (Formerly Mellor Collection.)

Fig. 4 *The actor Iwai Sagenda* in a play scene with a child, by Torii Kiyonobu, c.1705. Hand-coloured ink-print, 11 x 6 ins. (Art Institute of Chicago.)

Fig. 5 *Echigo Store in Suruga Street, Edo* (now Tokyo), a perspective picture by Okumura Masanobu, c.1740. Hand-coloured ink-print, 17¼ x 25⅛ ins. Masonobu introduced the uki-e, or western-type perspective picture. (Formerly Mellor Collection.)

every *Ukiyo-e* artist, even when his speciality was in another field.

Next in demand were prints of actors. It was natural that *Kabuki*, the popular, as opposed to the classical, drama, was recorded by the 'people's print'. The favourite actors were admired by theatre-goers with the same fervour that enthusiasts accord to pop-stars today. There was a tremendous demand for pictures of performers in the plays currently showing in the numerous Edo theatres, and certain families of artists devoted themselves to this type of print. Earliest in the period under review were members of the Torii family, of whom Kiyonobu (Fig. 4) and Kiyomasu (Fig. 1) were the greatest. They were the founders of a line whose descendants even today record the theatre with something of the same style.

Apart from these two great classes of print, there were others that depicted the everyday life of Edo, with particular emphasis on the sights of the town. The most fascinating were the 'world within a world', the Yoshiwara, an area of licensed brothels,

were called 'lacquer-pictures' (*urushi-e*), in which areas such as the details of dress were lacquered and sprinkled with brass-dust.

Early in the 1740s, wood-blocks for additional colours were introduced. For about the first twenty years, the colour-blocks were limited to two, normally pink and green, though other combinations were sometimes used. Such prints are known as '*benizuri-e*' (pink-printed pictures). Colour-printing of a most refined kind had been practised in China in the seventeenth century and very occasionally in Japan before 1740 for book-illustration, but the Japanese so rapidly reached a high degree of technical mastery in the medium that the delay in introducing more general colour-printing is unaccountable.

The use of the colour had subtle reactions on the artists' designs and on the block-cutters' interpretation. The massive brush-strokes which had been reproduced so boldly in the ink-prints had to be pared down to the kind of line that would not conflict with the coloured areas. The outcome was

6

Museum Photo

Fig. 6 ***The printer's shop*** *by Utagawa Kunisada (1785–1864), signed Toyokuni, nineteenth century.*

The various stages of making a colour-print are here fancifully represented as being carried out by women. In the foreground at the right, the wood-cutting tools are being sharpened on a stone over a tub of water. Behind, an engraver is preparing the black outline for the print, and to her left another is cutting the large colour areas. In the centre front, the paper is being prepared, and, at the left, peeled off and hung up to dry.
(Victoria and Albert Museum, London.)

other centres of night-life, and famous landmarks such as the Nihon-bashi and the Ryogoku Bridge over the Sumida River.

Perhaps the most universal genius of the print in the first half of the century was Okumura Masanobu, who designed prints of many kinds and introduced novel forms, such as the narrow pillar-print (*hashira-e*) and the *uki-e*, a sort of perspective picture probably deriving from prints brought into the country by Dutch traders (Fig. 5).

Hand-coloured and lacquered prints soon came into fashion

At first the prints were in black outline only, and to us today the uncoloured Kaigetsudo beauty and the Kiyonobu actor, with their bold arabesques of sweeping lines, are among the greatest artistic triumphs of the Japanese print. But the Edo commoner's taste was for something more colourful, and some of the ink-prints were soon being enlivened with touches of lead oxide called *tan* (prints hand-touched with *tan* being called *tan-e*). Later, more colour was applied, sometimes so heavily as almost to obscure the woodcut line. The process of hand-decoration went still further in what

some of the most exquisitely patterned colour-prints of the world. Okumura Masanobu and Ishikawa Toyonobu were among a number of artists who made the utmost of the deceptively simple elements of the pink and green print. The finesse and subtlety of such prints makes the word 'primitive' used for artists before 1765 a complete misnomer.

1765 was the year that full colour-printing was firstly widely employed. The culmination of a gradual increase in the number of colour-blocks since about 1760 coincided with the issue of certain amateur-inspired calendars for 1765. The principal designer of these landmark prints was Suzuki Harunobu (*c*.1718–1770), and in his short career he designed many delightful prints which, in their playful exquisiteness (akin to the Rococo fantasies of his contemporaries in France), and in the complexity of their designs, mark the most distant point reached from the grand simplicity of Moronobu (Fig. 7).

The reaction came in the relative naturalism of the prints of Koryusai, Shigemasa and Kiyonaga (Fig. 9). Their subject-matter was normally the kind of genre common to Harunobu's prints, but the figures are restored to a more natural amplitude and are often depicted out of doors with touches of con-

Fig. 7 **Rain in May** (Satsuki) by
Suzuki Harunobu (died 1770),
c.1769. Polychrome print,
11 x 8 ins.
During his short career, Suzuki
Harunobu designed many
delightful prints. He was the
principal creator of the landmark
prints of the late 1760s, which
first used full colour-printing
with all its complexity.
(Philadelphia Museum of Art.)

Fig. 8 **Segawa Kikunojo III** in
the role of a woman with a long
sword, by Ippitsusai Buncho,
c.1770. Polychrome print,
12 x 5½ ins.
Along with Katsukawa Shunsho
and his school (Fig. 2), Buncho
produced some of the great
masterpieces of the theatrical
print.
(R. G. Sawers Collection.)

vincing landscape. Katsukawa Shunsho and his
school and Ippitsusai Buncho were now the
acknowledged portrayers of *Kabuki* actors and
produced masterpieces of the theatrical print
(Figs. 2 and 8). Among earlier western historians,
Kiyonaga's prints were looked upon as the culmination of the Japanese print, but nowadays the
tendency is to look to the artists from the end of the
eighteenth century, and to find the greatest *Ukiyo-e*
artist to be Utamaro, and other almost equally
significant figures in Sharaku, Toyokuni, Choki and
Eishi.

Utamaro prints have the originality and virtuosity of an outstanding master

Utamaro is unquestionably one of the great
masters of the figure-print. Even in the 1790s, a
decade above all remarkable for an amazing outpouring of splendid prints from a dozen masters, his
originality and daring innovation were outstanding.
His so-called 'large heads', the close-up of a girl's
head in which monumentality is achieved by the
placing of the superbly coiffured hair, the sparingly
outlined features and the patterned colour of the
neck of her *kimono*; the prints of two or of three

figures in compositions of immense virtuosity
(Fig. 10); and the single, elongated figure – all have
the mark of a very great master.

Sharaku brought to the actor-print a new
intensity, and his 'large heads' on mica ground
are now among the most prized of Japanese prints.
His period of activity was limited, for reasons that
have never been discovered, to the years 1794/5,
and all his prints are of extreme rarity. The same
can be said of the dozen or so finest prints of another
great artist of surprising, Modigliani-like modernity
– Choki. Eishi, who brought a refinement to his
drawings, even to those of courtesans, possibly
explained by his gentle birth, was less adventurous
and exciting than the foregoing, but in certain
prints with a yellow ground and others on mica, he
achieved a matchless elegance. Toyokuni, eclectic
and plagiarist, truly came into his own in the mid-
1790s and if he were known by one set of prints
alone, the *Portraits of Actors on the Stage*, his
reputation would probably stand higher than it
does.

Most eighteenth-century prints are scarce today,
especially those in fine state with unfaded colour.
The original owners often pasted them on to screen
or wall, or hung them up like paintings. The
colours – vegetable dyes for the most part – are

9

R. Todd-White

10

R. Todd-White

Fig. 9 **Shell gatherers** *from a set of Five Festivals by Torii Kiyonaga, c.1786. Polychrome print, 10 x 7 ins.*
Reacting to the exquisiteness and complexity of artists such as Suzuki Harunobu (Fig. 7), Kiyonaga depicted genre scenes with great naturalism, often incorporating touches of convincing landscape. His work has been regarded by some historians as the zenith of the Japanese print.
(R. G. Sawers Collection.)

Fig. 10 **Two girls stretching the spotted cloth called Kanoko,** *from the series* Women's Crafts *by Kitagawa Utamaro, c.1797. 14½ x 9½ ins.*
Now considered the Ukiyo-e *(pictures of the floating world) artist par excellence, Utamaro is outstanding for his originality and daring inventiveness even in a decade remarkable for its outpouring of splendid work. His compositions show immense virtuosity; note the unusual close-up placing of the two figures in this superb print.*
(R. G. Sawers Collection.)

fugitive, and prints exposed for any length of time become mere shadows of what artist and publisher intended. Japan has, more than most countries, been visited by earthquakes, fires and floods, and the last war also took its toll. The prints were rarely issued in very large editions – although we have little evidence, it is thought that between two and five hundred would have been normal – and today many are known only in unique impressions, while others have disappeared altogether.

The number of collectors constantly grows, partly because of the now accepted part the

Japanese print played in the development of modern western art, and partly because of a growing realisation of the wealth of untried aesthetic experiences offered by the Far Eastern art. The Japanese print was the expression of a vigorous, intelligent people, shut off from all but the most tenuous contact with the outside world. The medium was one they had perfected and which they used with astonishing skill and resource. The result is a work of art with an exotic apartness that in some way enhances the powerful line, the harmonious composition and the sheer decorativeness.

HINTS FOR COLLECTORS

The commoner formats of the prints are as follows:
Kakemono-e (hanging-picture size): 23 by 12 inches.
Hashira-e (pillar-picture, for hanging on pillars): about 28 by 4½ inches.
Oban (large size): about 10 by 15 inches.
Hosoban (narrow size): about 12½ by 5½ inches.
Chuban (medium size): about 11 by 8 inches.

FURTHER READING

Harunobu and His Age by D. B. Waterhouse, London, 1964.
Masters of the Japanese Print by Richard Lane, London and New York, 1962.
Japanese Colour Prints by R. L. Binyon and J. J. O'Brien Sexton, London, 1960.
Chats on Japanese Prints by Arthur Davison Ficke, Rutland, Va. and Tokyo, 1958.

MUSEUMS AND COLLECTIONS

Japanese prints may be seen at the following:

EIRE
Dublin: Chester Beatty Library
FRANCE
Paris: Musée Guimet
GREAT BRITAIN
Bristol: City Art Gallery
Cambridge: Fitzwilliam Museum
London: British Museum
Victoria and Albert Museum
Manchester: Whitworth Art Gallery
Oxford: Ashmolean Museum
JAPAN
Tokyo: National Museum
U.S.A.
Boston: Museum of Fine Arts
Chicago: Art Institute of Chicago

THE VOGUE FOR ORIENTAL ART IN EUROPE

William Gaunt

Fig. 1 **The Peacock Room,** *originally the dining-room at 49 Prince's Gate, London, painted by J. McN. Whistler (1834–1903) for F. R. Leyland, 1876–77. The painting is Whistler's* Rose and Silver: La Princesse du Pays de la Porcelaine, *1864. (Smithsonian Institution. Freer Gallery of Art, Washington D.C.)*

2

Museum Photo

4

K. Hoddle

3

Giraudon

Fig. 2 **Ming vase**, *Chinese, fourteenth century. Porcelain. Victorian collectors of 'blue and white' were first attracted by Ch'ing wares. As interest grew, it extended to the Ming period. (Victoria and Albert Museum, London. Eumorfopoulos Collection.)*

Fig. 3 **Emile Zola** *by Edouard Manet (1832–83), 1867–68. Oil on canvas.*
This portrait with the Utamaro print on the wall shows the fashion in France for Japanese art. (Musée du Louvre, Paris.)

The importation of Japanese prints and Chinese blue and white wares aroused in Europeans of the nineteenth century an unprecedented passion for all things oriental

A new enthusiasm for the art of the Far East grew up about the same time in Paris and London, not long after the middle of the nineteenth century. Two main focuses of interest were the blue and white porcelain of China and the Japanese prints of the *ukiyo-e* school of popular genre. 'Blue and white', the beautiful, characteristic ceramic product of the Ming dynasty, which lasted from the fourteenth century to the seventeenth, was still produced in the eighteenth century when the Ch'ing dynasty ruled. It had been known to Europe for a considerable time and had long been collected with enthusiasm.

Blue and white export porcelain was part of the flourishing maritime trade carried on by the Dutch East India Company. The popularity of the wares brought to the Netherlands by Dutch ships had made it a commercial proposition to imitate them; hence the rise to prosperity and prestige of the town of Delft as a centre of ceramic production.

European influences in return affected the decorative style of Chinese wares intended for export. During the fifteenth century, export wares differed only slightly from the imperial (home) types, the quality being frequently as high. From the sixteenth century onwards, there was usually a marked difference between home and export types,

5

Museum Photo

Fig. 4 **Kyoto Bridge by Moonlight,** *one of the* Hundred Famous Views of Yedo *by Utagawa Hiroshige, c.1855. Colour print. See Figure 5. (Victoria and Albert Museum.)*

Fig. 5 **Nocturne in Blue and Gold: Old Battersea Bridge** *by James McNeill Whistler, first exhibited in 1877. Oil on canvas. How far Whistler was influenced by the many Japanese prints he collected may be estimated by a comparison of this painting with the print in Figure 4. (Tate Gallery, London.)*

although there were always certain examples that could be either. It may be noted that wares intended for Japan differed from those intended for Europe and those for the Middle East. But in the first half of the nineteenth century other forms of design claimed more attention in Europe: the neo-Classicism of Wedgwood, decoration in the form of romantic topography and imitative versions of the richness of Sèvres.

The change of attitude that once more brought 'blue and white' into favour was part of the revived interest in the Far East and its products that followed the agreement of Japan in 1853 to reopen trade and other connections with the West after the long period of self-imposed isolation. The change was also symptomatic of a reaction in the West against the drabness of brown in paintings covered with yellow varnish, and the clutter of undis-

tinguished objects in the average nineteenth-century interior. Appreciation of oriental artefacts became an aesthetic discovery, in the first place by artists, and it was not exclusively concerned with Chinese porcelain; eyes became attuned to finding fresh inspiration in the art of the Far East generally. They delighted equally in a Chinese bowl and a Japanese colour print, and collected both together.

The print in colour from wood-blocks was the greater novelty. The work of the graphic masters of Japan during the eighteenth and nineteenth centuries produced for home consumption during the period of isolation was a surprising phenomenon to Europeans. Such pictures of 'the passing world' (*ukiyo-e*), of geishas, actors, landscapes and flowers, were perhaps no more highly regarded in Japan than was a poster in the West. The fact that a volume of Hokusai's woodcuts arrived in Paris in the late 1850s as part of the packing of Japanese goods, seems to reflect this low esteem. But the French painter-etcher Félix Bracquemond, who acquired the woodcuts, was able to recognise the genius of Hokusai. He gave an initial push to the vogue that soon acquired momentum. Bracquemond's friends in the Parisian world of art and letters shared his admiration. The oriental shop opened in the rue de Rivoli in 1862 by Monsieur and Madame de Soye, *La Porte Chinoise*, became a centre for collectors. Its customers included such painters as Degas and Manet and such connoisseurs as Baudelaire and the brothers De Goncourt.

The place of Far Eastern art in the French interior of the second half of the nineteenth century is vividly shown in paintings. Zola has his Utamaro print on the wall behind him in the portrait by Manet (Fig. 3). There are suggestions of the Japanese taste in the background of Renoir's portrait of Madame Charpentier and her children. The prints painted by Van Gogh as a background to his portrait of the dealer Tanguy are evidence of the market that he found for them.

In London in the 1860s two architects, William Burges and E. W. Godwin (the latter described by Max Beerbohm as 'first of the aesthetes'), were pioneers in the appreciation of Japanese art. In 1862 Godwin, newly established in Portland Square, Bristol, gained a local reputation for eccentricity by a simple scheme of interior decoration, followed later by Whistler, which consisted in painting the walls of his rooms in plain colours, hanging up a few Japanese prints, laying Persian rugs on bare floors and severely restricting the choice of furniture.

1862 was the year of the second International Exhibition in London, at which Japanese art came as a revelation to many visitors. Objects from it were acquired by the firm of Farmer and Rogers, whose Oriental Warehouse in Regent Street could be regarded as the London equivalent of the De Soyes' shop in Paris. The Warehouse supplied the two remarkable artist-collectors James McNeill Whistler and Dante Gabriel Rossetti. According to the dealer Murray Marks, of whom they were also customers, Whistler, fresh from Paris, passed on to Rossetti his enthusiasm for 'blue and white' and the Japanese printmakers. This seems likely enough, although Rossetti went independently to the Farmer and Rogers Warehouse, where he met its manager, Lasenby Liberty (later Sir Arthur Liberty), founder in 1875 of the famous shop that prospered on oriental imports.

Rossetti, in turn, parted with the pieces of

porcelain he had bought from Liberty to Whistler, and also introduced Whistler to their London source. They competed in friendly fashion in the acquisition of Japanese screens, fans and prints, and especially Chinese 'blue', aided and abetted by their henchman, Charles Augustus Howell, past master in the art of buying and selling, and with the advice of Murray Marks. Marks (1840–1918) was a dealer of flair and energy, an enthusiast equally for Chinese porcelain (his personal taste inclining to Ming porcelain of the Wan-li period, 1573–1620) and renaissance bronzes. He conducted business for many years from 395 Oxford Street, behind the Queen Anne front that Norman Shaw designed for him, frequently replenishing his stock of 'blue and white' from Dutch sources at modest prices.

Marks' trade-card was eloquent of both his specialisation and his clientele. Designed by Rossetti and printed from six wood-blocks, the card represents a Chinese ginger-jar with the characteristic prunus blossom pattern (always referred to by Rossetti as 'hawthorn'). The lettering was supposedly contributed by William Morris and a background of gold stars by Whistler. It would seem that Whistler and Rossetti especially favoured the Ch'ing dynasty pieces of the K'ang-hsi (1662–1722), Yung-cheng (1723–35) and Ch'ien-lung (1736–95) periods, export examples of these being perhaps the most readily available. But the motives of the two artists in collecting were quite distinct. Rossetti, in the 1860s leading a widower's careless life at 16 Cheyne Walk, collected indiscriminately

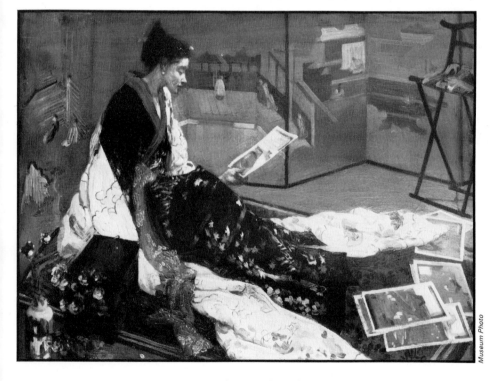

Fig. 6 *Caprice in Purple and
Gold. No. 2 – The Golden
Screen by J. McN. Whistler,
1864. Oil on panel.*
*This delightful painting contains
the various forms of* japonaiserie
*which were favoured by the
cultivated taste of the time. Note
the screen, the kimono worn by
the model and the series of prints
by Hiroshige, one of which she is
studying.*
(Freer Gallery of Art.)

anything old and unusual that took his fancy – embroideries, old musical instruments, dresses of archaic fashion, antique chests – all, including his oriental finds, in picturesque disorder. 'Blue and white' was an additional curiosity, one motive for collecting it being the fun of friendly competition with Whistler.

For Whistler, on the other hand, the oriental porcelain and prints stood for the purest and highest standards of art and were to be treated with corresponding respect. The example of Godwin, as well as of oriental custom, caused him to set out his treasures with the most scrupulous regard for

spacing and harmony with their surroundings.

Both Whistler and Rossetti influenced other collectors, infecting friends and patrons with their enthusiasm. The surgeon and amateur painter Sir Henry Thompson was one such friend of Rossetti, and for him also Marks became a trusted adviser in the collection of 'blue and white'. An exhibition of his collection at 395 Oxford Street, in 1878, was a celebrated occasion attended by the cream of London society and marked by 'the very *recherché* supper . . . served by Scott's on wonderful Blue and White dishes which formed extraordinary foils of colour to rich pastries, glowing lobsters . . .'. A rarity of the period is the catalogue of Sir Henry Thompson's collection of three hundred and thirty-nine pieces, prepared for him by Marks in 1878; twenty of the etched illustrations were made after Whistler's beautiful water-colours.

Whistler's patron, the Liverpool shipping magnate Francis Leyland, also became an ardent collector of 'blue and white'. In order to set off his pieces to advantage, he had the dining-room of his house, 49 Prince's Gate, specially designed with Whistler's painting *La Princesse du Pays de la Porcelaine* as the centrepiece. The room (now in the Freer Gallery, Washington), was decorated in the owner's absence and – much to his wrath – with Whistler's peacock designs (Fig. 1). Brilliant as the designs were, it was Marks' opinion that the original effect of the porcelain on walnut shelves against a background of unpainted leather was much preferable.

The dispersal of many of Rossetti's acquisitions after the collapse of his health, and of Whistler's possessions after his bankruptcy in 1879, increased the number of admirers of oriental art by again bringing many examples on the market and was a factor in the making of the popular cult of Aestheticism in the following decade. Marks bought for £700 what remained of Rossetti's collection after the artist's death in 1882. By that time, he was regarded as a main authority and was instrumental in building up many other collections, notably that of the Australian-born millionaire George Salting, who was to bequeath his to the British nation.

What was not granted to the nineteenth-century collector, knowing only the wares of the K'ang-hsi and the other later periods which had been exported to the West, was the ability to survey and appreciate the 'blue and white' development as a whole. As a present-day expert, Mr. Adrian Joseph, has pointed out, an understanding of the comparative merits of various wares depends on a study of all of them. The connoisseurship of R. L. Hobson in the 1920s first drew notice to the quality of early Ming. The specimens of imperial Ming porcelain found in China by Sir Percival David, and brought back to England by him, encouraged collectors of this century, such as George Eumorfopoulos and S. D. Winkworth, to turn to the earlier products of the Ming centuries. The vision and the legacies of these devotees have been vastly beneficial to the great museum collections of Britain.

The export record of Japanese colour-prints in the later years of the nineteenth century was one of decline due to the import and use of inferior inks and the dilution of contemporary Japanese effort by European influence. There are, nonetheless, fine examples by Utamaro and other of the earlier nineteenth-century masters, once in Whistler's collection, in the British Museum and the galleries of the University of Glasgow.

R. Todd-White

JAPANESE IVORY CARVINGS

Neil Davey

Richly carved and inlaid with
rare materials, the ivories of Japan
are as much prized throughout
the world today as they once were
in their country of origin

Fig. 1 **Handara Sonja,** *Japanese,
nineteenth century. Walrus ivory,
height 10¾ ins.*
*A disciple of Buddha, Handara
Sonja is depicted standing on a
rock and holding an alms-bowl
out of which is crawling a dragon.*
(Sotheby and Co., London.)

Fig. 2 **Mounted samurai in full
armour,** *Japanese, nineteenth
century. Ivory, height 8½ ins.*
(Sotheby's.)

Fig. 3 **Peasant,** *Japanese,
nineteenth century. Ivory,
height 9¾ ins.*
*This beautifully observed
figure is walking along looking at
a branch of maple leaves.*
(Sotheby's.)

Ivory was first introduced into Japan during the
latter part of the seventeenth century by traders
eager to sell this formerly unknown material to
the Japanese. The novelty of ivory was due to the
fact that elephants were not indigenous to that
country. From an early date, Japanese carvers
managed to acquire small bits of ivory which were
usually the left-overs from the finely carved pieces
made in China, where elephants still existed in a
few areas. Ivory was much sought after in China and
was used for cups and other special gifts presented
to the Emperor, to visiting dignitaries or between
friends. It was not until Japan was opened up to
traders from the West in the middle of the last
century that the large tusks were imported and used
for the creation of nearly all the Japanese
ivory-carvings found in the rest of the world today.

Unlike the Chinese, the Japanese did not place a
high value on ivory and, at the beginning, this
material was used mainly for utilitarian objects such
as *netsuke, inro* and chopsticks. This early neglect
of a material much prized by other countries is no
doubt due to the fact that the Japanese carvers were
at first only able to obtain rejects from China. In
view of this, one should not be surprised to find that
religious statues and highly prized gifts were made
of porcelain or gilt and lacquered wood instead
of ivory. Ivory carvings from Japan are conspicuous
by their absence from the majority of museums.

The craftsmen used several kinds of ivory
besides elephant tusks and one frequently comes
across walrus ivory, distinguishable from elephant
ivory by the somewhat cancerous-looking patch
in the centre of the base or sometimes forming part
of the carving (Fig. 4). Stagshorn, also, should not
be confused with elephant ivory; it is distinguishable by tiny black flecks on a rather porous surface.
Although rare, whale teeth, hippopotamus tusks,
boar and narwhal tusks are often found to be the
materials of some of the later pieces (Fig. 6).
Narwhal tusks are perhaps the most sought after
of the three. When purchasing a carving today, it
is extremely important to make sure that one is not
simply acquiring a well-carved piece of plastic. The
imitated ivory is unbelievably close to the genuine
article, but careful examination of the surface
always reveals the truth. Plastic will not have black
flecks, minute cross-hatching, white streaks nor any
other distinguishable marks, and will normally be
lighter in weight.

These horns and tusks were intricately or boldly
carved in varying degrees of relief showing the
carver's very acute powers of observation. The
accurate and frequently humorous rendering of
human expressions, the movement and grace of

4

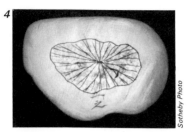

Fig. 4 **Cross-section** *of a piece
of walrus ivory, forming the base
of a carved figure.
(Sotheby's.)*

5

6

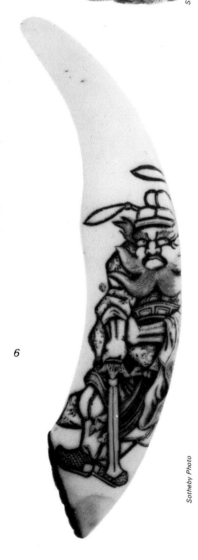

Sotheby Photo

7

Sotheby Photo

8

R. Todd-White

animals (Fig. 5) and the delicacy of plants is difficult to equate with anything done in Europe during the last century, and some carvings, for instance of fruit, flowers and birds' feathers, were often coloured to give a naturalistic impression. The carvings were also lacquered, gilt or inlaid with pieces of horn, pearl, shell and coloured ivory to add a rich decoration to the plain surface. This type of inlay was much in demand among Western clients at that time. The Japanese even mounted some of their more elaborate pieces in silver and one must here mention the Shibayama family who particularly excelled in fine inlays and gave their name to this style of decoration (Fig. 7).

Few individual craftsmen of *okimono* (small decorative carvings) are known, since carving ivory was considered to be artisans' work. However, one must here mention the nineteenth-century artist Ishikawa Komei (also known as Mitsuaki), who is especially notable for his well-modelled animals. Even some of the top *netsuke* artists, such as Kwaiyokusai, Chikuysai Tomochika (the third in a line of *netsuke* carvers with that surname) and Asahi Kyokuzan, who should be mentioned for his naturalistic rendering of skulls, turned their hand to ivory *okimono*.

Netsuke play a large part in the history of ivory carvings since some of the earliest *netsuke* are to be found in this material. These toggles were very much part of Japanese clothing for both men and women, since they had no pockets and suspended a number of things from the sash around their kimono. *Sagemono* is the collective Japanese name for these items, which comprised tobacco-pouches, pipes, small ash-trays, purses, writing-utensils and medicine- and seal-boxes. Although *netsuke* are still being made today for export purposes, the arrival in 1853 in Japan of the American Commander Perry and the opening up of the trade routes to Africa and the West were to change the use of ivory from the utilitarian to the decorative. First of all, European dress was gradually adopted and *netsuke* became increasingly a collector's item. The later the *netsuke*, the

more delicate and less useful they tend to be.

Furthermore, with the arrival of many tradesmen and even tourists, the Japanese discovered that there was an ever increasing demand for ivory figures, boxes of all sizes, vases and other useful or purely decorative pieces. There started a widespread output of these objects, which still goes on today. The Tokyo Art School is one of the best-known sources for figures of deities, fishermen, beautiful women, mythical creatures and other pieces, and this school of carvers produced a particularly high standard of work, examples of which can be seen in great numbers all over the West. Until the last few years, the Japanese have not really given these works of art their rightful acknowledgement, and it must be hoped that one day museums all over the world will give people a chance to enjoy that particularly Japanese gift for observing life. One may well say that these acute powers of observation can also be attributed to Chinese craftsmen; but the difference lies in that the Japanese render people, animals and plants in their own most lively way. To this should be added a great sense of humour, which is lacking in Chinese ivory carvings. The rich decoration of gold lacquer and inlaid materials is also essentially Japanese and has not been mastered so well by the craftsmen of any other country. There is no doubt that we owe a great debt to Commander Perry for, if he had not opened up the trade routes to Japan when he did, the art of carving ivory might well have stopped with the use of *netsuke* and many of us would not today be the possessors of such fine works of art.

MUSEUMS AND COLLECTIONS
Japanese ivories of the nineteenth century may be seen at the following:
GREAT BRITAIN
Cambridge:	Fitzwilliam Museum
Isle of Arran:	Brodick Castle
London:	British Museum
	Victoria and Albert Museum
Oxford:	Ashmolean Museum

R. Todd-White

Fig. 5 **Netsuke,** *in the form of a rat nibbling a candle, Japanese, late nineteenth century. Ivory. (Sotheby's.)*

Fig. 6 **Netsuke,** *showing the figure of Shoki the demon-chaser, Japanese, nineteenth century. Boar tusk.*
Whale teeth and hippopotamus, narwhal and boar tusks were used for some later pieces. (Sotheby's.)

Fig. 7 **Elephant,** *Japanese, late nineteenth century. Ivory inlaid in Shibayama style with pearl, horn and coloured ivory, height 15 ins. (Sotheby's.)*

Fig. 8 **Okimono** *of a huntsman and a child, Japanese, nineteenth century. Ivory engraved and stained for effect, height 5¼ ins. The huntsman is shown in typical hunting-dress, carrying a deer. (Sotheby's.)*

Fig. 9 **Farmer with a boy,** *Tokyo Art School, nineteenth century. Ivory, height 13¾ ins. This unusually large figure is holding a sheaf of corn. (Sotheby's.)*

Fig. 10 **Vase,** *one of a pair, Japanese, nineteenth century. Elephant ivory decorated in Shibayama style with inlaid pearl, horn and coloured ivory and enriched with gold lacquer, height 12½ ins. (Sotheby's.)*

R. Todd-White

Melvin Grey

Fig. 1 **Sword-blade,** showing hamon *(edge pattern) and signature, on the tang, of Taikei Naotane, Suishinshi School, nineteenth century. Steel. This sword is in the Bizen style, one of the many in which the versatile Naotane worked. (Private Collection.)*

on Dale

Metalwork in Nineteenth-Century Japan

*. 2 **Horse,** *signed by*
omitsu, late nineteenth
tury. Red and brown bronze,
eyes in gilt copper and
kudo (an alloy of copper with
nall proportion of gold).
is is a fine piece intended
the European market
her than the Japanese.
J. K. Wright Collection.)

*. 3 **Sword-furniture,***
anese, nineteenth century.
*p: **kodzuka** (small knife fitted*
o the side of the scabbard),
ned 'Tomei'. Millet-sprays on a
kudo ground. Bottom:
dzuka signed 'Iganokami
netsune'. Dragonfly and
terfly on a shakudo ground.
*ntre: **tsuba** (hand-guard) with*
Seven Gods of Good Luck
the treasure ship
karamono. Shakudo, gold,
er and copper details. Left:
hikashira (metal ornaments at
top and bottom of the two-
ndled hilt) with bats and lotus
ves. Shibuichi (a metal alloy)
l gold inlay. Right:
hikashira with dragons. Silver
l gold.
J. K. Wright Collection.)

Rooted in the manufacture of the sword — 'the soul of the Samurai' — the tradition of Japanese metalwork was one of the most exacting and artistic in the world

The nineteenth century was probably the most cataclysmic in the whole of Japanese history. In 1836 the Japanese embarked on their third century of *sakoku* (closed country), which meant almost complete isolation from the rest of the civilised world. Living under the despotic rule of the Tokugawa Shoguns, Japan was a feudal state in the way that parts of Europe had been some seven hundred years previously. By the end of the nineteenth century, Japan had fought and won a major war with China, distinctly her superior in size and manpower.

It is not surprising that this switch from feudalism to modern westernised living brought great changes to all aspects of Japanese culture. The arts in particular had flourished in an atmosphere of quiet progression within strict traditions, uninfluenced from outside.

These traditions were more strictly adhered to in the various arts of working in metal than in any other artistic area. From the Heian period (794–1185) to the end of Edo-Tokugawa in 1867, the greatest artistic endeavour went into working in iron and steel, and specifically into the perfection of the Japanese sword, called the 'soul of the Samurai'. It was the weapon upon which the ebb and flow of political ambition in the struggle for power depended. From the Kamakura period (1185–1337) through the Muromachi to the end of the Momoyama period in 1616, this struggle for power was unceasing.

The feudal era officially ended in 1867 with the restoration of the young Emperor, later known as Meiji, to the throne, but in fact it did not completely end until the Satsuma Rebellion (1876–77), when the remaining clans holding on to the old way of life were finally overthrown. At this time, an important edict was published which forbade the *samurai* and other classes of civilians to wear swords, thus depriving of their means of livelihood thousands of craftsmen engaged in various skills connected with the sword.

The bronze horse shown in Figure 2 is a fine example of late nineteenth-century workmanship, intended for the European market rather than the Japanese. After 1877 this kind of work was produced by artists who had hitherto specialised in making fittings for the sword until the demand for these virtually ceased. The needs of the new 'foreign devils' were not as exacting aesthetically or in standards of workmanship as those of the true Japanese taste in sword-furniture. From the strict limitations of working on the metal plate of a *tsuba* (sword-guard), the artist-craftsman now found himself free to work in three dimensions and on a much larger scale.

The ancient craft of casting in bronze was traditionally confined to work for temples, mostly religious figures and great bells. The schools of *ikebana* (flower arrangement) also used bronze vessels and other decorative adjuncts in practising their art, particularly in the nineteenth century. The use of bronze had been restricted to these areas until the sword metalworkers, who were skilled in making alloys, turned to it. Often their products are decorated with the purely Japanese combinations of metal, *shakudo, shibuichi, sentoku* and others, which until then had been used only on sword-furniture and in the decoration of armour. The results of this change were not always very satisfactory. Much of the work produced was of inferior quality, and was made only to satisfy the increasing demand of European tourists who were now able to visit the newly 'discovered' and exotic land of Japan.

To class the sword-blade as the finest work in metal ever produced in Japan implies that a weapon can be a work of art. The finest sword-blades have been regarded as works of art in steel by the Japanese for centuries. In Japan, many blades from the early periods are designated national treasures. The reason for a weapon's being regarded in this dual and paradoxical role is bound up in the unique construction of the Japanese sword. Its status as a work of art lies in the extreme subtleties of structure in the surface of the steel, and the way in which these fit into the shape of the blade.

The two most obvious signs of this construction are the *jihada* and the *hamon*. The *jihada* (surface steel) is formed by the repeated folding and welding of the original block from which the sword is to be made. When this is drawn out into the final shape of the blade, it will have been laminated into about a quarter of a million layers of steel. When finally polished, these will show on the surface as a delicate pattern, not unlike the grain of wood. The *hamon* (edge pattern) is the most immediately striking effect and is unique to the Japanese sword. This is the pattern of the hardened cutting-edge, and it

Fig. 4 **Tsuba**, *inscribed 'Somin'
nineteenth century.
Shibuichi (a metal alloy) with
details in gold, silver, copper and
shakudo (an alloy of copper with
a small proportion of gold).
On this humorous hand-guard,
an oni (demon) falls back in
fright on seeing a kakimono
painting depicting the
ferocious Shoki, the demon-
chaser.
(D. J. K. Wright Ltd.,
London W.1.)*

Fig. 5 **Suit of armour**, *mostly of
early nineteenth-century
workmanship, but mounted in
the style of the sixteenth
century. The main portions are
of iron, lacquered smooth in brick
red, laced in dark blue. The
russet iron face mask is signed by
Myochin Muneyasu (active
1833–38). The iron helmet is
signed by Nagasone Masanori
(active 1673–80).
The religious convictions of the
original owner of this
extraordinary suit are inscribed
in gold lacquer on the
breastplate, and it seems likely
that he was a priest of the militant
Nichiren sect.
(J. Anderson Collection.)*

Fig. 6 **Helmet**, *with protruding
rivet heads, nineteenth century,
the low rounded bowl made
c.1750. Iron, mounted with
shakudo, silver, gold and copper,
laced with green silk.
(J. Anderson Collection.)*

reveals itself as a milky-white area running the entire length of the edge of the blade. The breadth and shape of this depends on the tradition of the school and the skill of the swordsmith. The steel of this area is extremely hard and will take a very sharp edge.

The nineteenth-century swordsmith inherited the secrets of a craft going back well over a thousand years. Japanese sword-making is divided into periods. The *shin-shinto* (very new sword) period started in 1781 and lasted until 1868. Before that was the *shinto* (new sword) period. This distinction dated from 1596; before that date, all swords were *koto* (old swords). Some nineteenth-century sword-smiths referred to their ancestry in the way they signed their work. Yokoyama Sukenaga (d.1851) often included in his signature the phrase '*Tomonari goju-roku dai-no-mago*' ('fifty-sixth in descent from Tomonari', a famous swordsmith in the Heian period).

Of the many swordsmiths of this period, Taikei Naotane represents the most famous. When Suishinshi Masahide, founder of the influential Suishinshi school, died in 1825, Naotane took charge of the school and maintained its prosperity. He was an active and versatile man and made blades with great success in the styles of several earlier schools. He followed the teachings of his master Masahide and revived the methods of the *koto* schools of Bizen, Yamashiro, Yamato and Soshu provinces. The blade by him illustrated in Figure 1 is made in the Bizen style and displays a distinctive *hamon* typical of his masterly technique. The illustration also shows the tang of the blade which fits into the hilt of the sword and is where the swordsmith puts his signature and other inscriptions suiting his versatility. Naotane signed his work with one of at least twenty-six recorded variations of his name and titles, usually adding a *kakihan* (personal seal).

Japanese armour, which is most distinctive in appearance, and is comparatively light and flexible, might easily be thought too fragile to withstand a blow from the extremely sharp Japanese sword. The answer is that Japanese armour developed in that way because of this very sharpness of the blade it had to combat. The armour is in effect laminated so that a blow is slowed down rather than immediately stopped, which would produce far greater damage.

The fine example of armour illustrated in Figure 5 is mostly of early nineteenth-century workmanship, although it is mounted entirely in the style of the sixteenth century. All the main portions of the armour, helmet, cuirass, sleeves, thigh-guards and shin-guards are iron, lacquered brick red. The russet iron face-mask is signed beneath the chin 'Myochin Muneyasu', an armourer working in the period 1833–38, in whose workshops the armour, with the exception of the helmet, was almost certainly made. The striking helmet is of an earlier period and is signed Nagasone Masanori, who worked in 1673–80. It imitates the folded cloth of a cap worn by a priest of the Nichiren sect of Buddhism and is entirely made of iron. The religious convictions of the original owner are well displayed by the gold lacquered inscriptions on the breast-plate. This is the centre portion of the *mandala*, sacred to the Nichiren sect, the centre column of which is the invocation '*namu mioho renge-kiyo*' ('Hail lotus of the good law'). The Nichiren sect

was a particularly militant body and it is possible that the armour belonged to a priest.

The *kabuto* (helmet) illustrated in Figure 6 has a russet iron bowl composed of sixteen plates with large round rivet heads protruding from the surface. The bowl was made in about 1750 and was mounted in its present form in the early nineteenth century. The neck-guard is composed of small lamellae lacquered in strips which are held vertically by green silk lacing. The whole helmet is finely mounted with *shakudo* – an alloy of copper with a small proportion of gold – and with gilt copper. The front of the helmet is decorated with a pair of silver-on-copper horns and a peony blossom in silvered and gilt copper. All the metal decorations are finely engraved and chiselled and are small masterpieces of the metalworker's art. Copper was a metal much used by the sword- and armour-furniture makers; the surface is always patinated to one of several rich semi-matt colours, never polished to a bright surface.

On a Japanese sword, the furniture – the metal fittings with which it is mounted – can be very

4

complex (Fig. 3). In the most simple traditional form they comprise the fittings of the *katana*, the long fighting-sword of the *samurai*. These are the *tsuba* (hand-guard); *fuchikashira* (metal ornaments at the top and bottom of the two-handed hilt), and the *kodzuka* (small knife fitted into the side of the scabbard). Although all these objects may be extremely decorative and finely wrought in varied metals, their presence on the sword is strictly functional, for strength and protection.

By the nineteenth century, the decoration of sword-fittings had reached its peak; nevertheless many imitations of earlier and more simple forms in plain iron were still made.

The last great master of sword-furniture was Kano Natsuo (1828–98). Much of his work on *tsuba* uses an iron ground upon which other metals are superimposed in relief or inlaid into the iron. The superb colour and surface texture of his metal grounds together with his delicate modelling make his work more akin to painting in some instances.

The subject-matter upon which the artist could draw was unlimited, ranging through historical events and battles, mythology and folklore to everyday objects. Subjects were often treated humorously as shown on the *tsuba* illustrated in Figure 4 in which an *oni* (demon) falls back in fright on seeing a *kakimono* painting depicting the ferocious Shoki, the demon-chaser.

After 1876 and the ban on wearing swords, not only the craftsmen but also untold thousands of *samurai*, who had formed the private armies of the feudal barons, were without a means of livelihood. Each had owned at least two swords (the *samurai* were known as 'two-sworded men'). In the hard times which followed, these swords were offered for sale, together with many other long-cherished treasures, to the new race of tourists which invaded Japan. It was at this time that the great private collections in Europe were formed, some of which contained several thousand items. Much of this material has gone into museums, but so enormous was this influx of Japanese works of art that there are still good pieces to be found on the open market.

These pieces constitute a unique art form of great beauty, and were in everyday use less than one hundred years ago.

6

Melvin Grey

FURTHER READING

Japanese Armour by L. J. Anderson, London, 1968.

The Arts of the Japanese Sword by B. W. Robinson, London, 1961.

The Samurai Sword by J. M. Yumoto, London, 1958.

MUSEUMS AND COLLECTIONS

Nineteenth-century Japanese metalwork, arms and armour may be seen at the following:

GREAT BRITAIN

Birmingham:	City Museum and Art Gallery
Edenbridge, Kent:	Chiddingstone Castle
Edinburgh:	Royal Scottish Museum
Liverpool:	City of Liverpool Museums
London:	Bethnal Green Museum
	British Museum
Maidstone:	Museum and Art Gallery
Manchester:	Whitworth Art Gallery

ITALY

Venice:	Museo Orientale

JAPAN

Tokyo:	Tokyo National Museum

U.S.A.

Chicago:	Field Museum of National History
New York:	Metropolitan Museum of Art

Melvin Grey

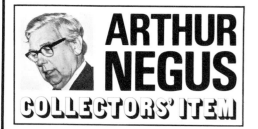

ARTHUR NEGUS
COLLECTORS' ITEM

CHESS PIECES

The origins of chess can be deduced from the name of the final move – checkmate. 'Sheikh Mat' was the Arabic for 'the Sheik is dead', and it is fair to assume that the game was introduced to the West by crusaders and merchants returning from the Levant.

Early chess pieces were extremely fine, made of ivory or horn and ornamented with gold and precious stones. By the end of the seventeenth century chess had become popular throughout Europe, and many different kinds of pieces were made. Ivory, ebony or wooden pieces have always been the most common, although there was a vogue in the early eighteenth century – revived recently – for sets cast in bronze, pewter or lead. Pink and white alabaster sets were also made, although the fashion for these was restricted to southern Europe. In Britain, sets were made in the eighteenth century by various porcelain factories, including Rockingham and Wedgwood. One of the most interesting aspects of collecting chess pieces is their historical connection. From the sixteenth century onwards sets were made to commemorate the victories of famous commanders such as Tilly and Turenne in the wars of the seventeenth century, and Charles XII of Sweden, Frederick the Great and Napoleon, thereafter.

Prices

Prices range from about £5 for nineteenth-century pieces, to £250 or more for a complete set of eighteenth-century Italian pieces. Pieces from India and the Middle East can be very costly to buy, especially if the carving is of unusual intricacy.

Baumkotter Antiques: A. C. Cooper

Top: *Left to right: Eighteenth-century Indian carved ivory pawn, £250 the set; nineteenth-century Minton knight, £850 the set; eighteenth-century Italian ivory pawn, £250 the set; eighteenth-century Chinese ivory king, £120 the set; Burmese king, nineteenth century, £180 the set; bishop from Indian ivory Juggernaut set, £1000; eighteenth-century Italian king, £250 the set.*

Bottom: *Left to right: Indian ivory king, nineteenth century, £350 the set; rare eighteenth-century Burmese king, £250 the set; green knight from an East India Company set, c.1830, £100 the set; red Staunton knight, c.1870, £150 the set; piece from an early nineteenth-century German set, £220 the set; pearwood knight from a 'Bears of Berne' set, c.1880, £65 the set; castle from a late eighteenth-century Indian set, £220 the set.*

Opposite: *Left to right: Eighteenth-century German Queen, £45 the set; red king from Canton, c.1840, £150 the set; bishop from Kashmir, c.1780, £120 the set; king carved from bone in Dieppe at the end of the eighteenth century, £200 the set.*

Baumkotter Antiques, London W.8: A. C. Cooper

B. W. Robinson

JAPANESE COLOUR PRINTS

Hokusai and Hiroshige were the most famous of the scores of printmakers who depicted with skill and often genius the life and scenery of Japan in the nineteenth century

Sixty or seventy years ago, when the collecting of Japanese colour-prints was still in its first heyday, the nineteenth century was generally described by the pundits as a period of decadence and crudity. One might be permitted to wax ecstatic over Hokusai and Hiroshige, but it was unfashionable to be stirred by Kuniyoshi's *Last Stand of the Kusunoki Clan*. Yet things have changed, and not only in matters of Japanese art. High Victorian and Art Nouveau productions are studied and appreciated, and the Pre-Raphaelites are no longer despised and outcast. So in the world of the Japanese print the pendulum has swung. Hokusai, Hiroshige and Kuniyoshi have come before the public in centenary exhibitions since the War, and people are bolder and more honest in admitting to what they really like.

Eighteenth-century Japanese prints are almost exclusively concerned with women and the theatre, and the tradition of portraying these two ever popular subjects was carried over into the nineteenth century by Utamaro and Toyokuni respectively. Utamaro died in 1806, however, and the tradition of *bijin-gwa* (pictures of beautiful women) passed to Yeizan and Yeisen. Theatrical prints, meanwhile, were turned out in vast quantities by numerous artists of the Utagawa School, of which Toyokuni was the head.

But great changes were on the way, and, as the new century opened, three artists who were to transform the appearance and enormously expand the range of the Japanese print were on the scene.

In the year 1800 Hokusai (1760–1849) was already forty, but his eighteenth-century work is comparatively conventional, and he made his major and most characteristic contribution to Japanese pictorial art in the last fifty years of his long life. In the hands of Hokusai and Hiroshige (1797–1858), landscape was raised to one of the principal subjects of the colour-print, and Kuniyoshi (1798–1861) did the same for legendary and historical themes. One other artist who was beginning to achieve success in the early years of the nineteenth century was Kunisada (1786–1864). Toyokuni's senior pupil. In a working life of almost sixty years, he produced thousands of prints, the great majority of them theatrical pot-boilers; he followed any line that seemed to be popular or profitable, designing a few remarkable landscapes under Hiroshige's inspiration and some heroic prints in imitation of Kuniyoshi.

By 1825, Hokusai was in the middle of his first great series, the *Thirty-six Views of Mount Fuji*, and had already brought out the first ten volumes of the immortal *Mangwa*, that inexhaustible encyclopedia of Japanese life, folklore, religion and humour. This was his greatest period so far as prints are concerned; the *Bridges* and *Waterfalls* were undertaken before the *Thirty-six Views* were complete, and these led up to his masterpiece, the

Fig. 1 *Moonlight boating under Suyehiro Bridge* by Gakutei, c.1830.
Gakutei left a delightful set of views such as this around Osaka's harbour area, Tempozan.
(Victoria and Albert Museum, London.)

**Fig. 2 *Clearing weather at Yenoshima,* one of the Eight Views of Famous Places *by Toyokuni II, c.1835.*
Applicable to any locality, the classical 'eight views' (hakkei) were Autumn Moon, Lingering Snow, Sunset Sky, Vesper Bell, Returning Boats, Clearing Weather, Night Rain and Homing Geese.
(Victoria and Albert Museum.)

Fig. 3 *Gyokkirin Roshungi,* from the Hundred and Eight Chinese Heroes, *by Kuniyoshi, c.1827.
The semi-historical Chinese romance Shui-hu-ch'uan *was immensely popular in Japan under its Japanese name* Suikoden, *in Bakin's translation. It relates the adventures of a gang of a hundred and eight brigands. With this series, the artist Kuniyoshi at last gained the recognition he had been seeking since he first showed his artistic bent in 1818.*
(Private Collection.)

3

Fig. 4 **The Kegon Waterfall at Nikko** by Yeisen, c.1845.
Nikko has some of the finest scenery in Japan, and it is famous for its waterfalls. There, also, are the magnificent tombs of the Tokugawa Shoguns. Yeisen is best known for his prints of sultry beauties of the Yoshiwara (gay quarter).
(Private Collection.)

Fig. 5 **Mount Fuji from the Sumida River embankment,** *one of the* Views of Fuji from Edo, *by Kuniyoshi, c.1842 Kuniyoshi often experimented with European artistic ideas, as is evident here in the large tree in the left foreground, a device found in the work of many European landscape artists. Note also the fine printing in the background.*
(Private Collection.)

Imagery of the Poets, a rare set of ten large, upright prints, dating from about 1830. Hiroshige had not quite found his form by 1825; for this one has to wait for the *Great Tokaido* of 1833–34. But he had already published some heroic diptychs in the manner of Shuntei or the early Kuniyoshi and some designs of mothers and children that seem to have been inspired by Yeizan, and he had certainly begun to experiment with landscape. Kuniyoshi, too, was still struggling for recognition at this time. As early as 1818 he had given an indication of his future bent with a triptych of Tomomori's ghost threatening Yoshitsune and his men in their ship (a subject to which he returned more than once in later life). But he did not really find his feet until the series of the *Hundred and Eight Chinese Heroes (Suikoden)* began to appear in 1827 (Fig. 3). Kunisada meanwhile was established as head of the Utagawa School (Toyokuni died in 1825) and continued turning out numerous competent, but generally undistinguished, actor-prints and book-illustrations.

The 1830s was perhaps the finest decade of the nineteenth-century Japanese print. Hokusai began it, as we have seen, with his masterly *Imagery of the Poets*, although after that he seems not to have

designed any more prints, spending the remaining years of his life in painting. Hiroshige's *Tokaido* of 1833–34 (Fig. 10) was the first of a splendid succession of landscape series, among which the *Eight Views of Lake Biwa* (*Omi Hakkei*) is perhaps the greatest of all. There are several fine sets of Edo views (Fig. 9), and one of the stations of the Kisokaido highway in which he collaborated with Yeisen. Yeisen's life and art were largely devoted to the sultry beauties of the Yoshiwara (gay quarter) but in this set he shows a brilliant turn for landscape. He also produced a fine set of the *Waterfalls of Nikko* (Fig. 4).

Hokusai and Hiroshige are usually bracketed together as the two outstanding landscape masters of the popular school. But no two men could be more different in their personalities or in the character of their work: Hokusai, the Bohemian *par excellence*, with his highly individual and almost arbitrary vision of both nature and mankind, and Hiroshige, sociable, gentle and humorous, who was content to be a vehicle of nature's beauties and a sympathetic observer of the human condition. The 1830s also saw Kuniyoshi rising to his full stature with heroic scenes and portraits of great dramatic power, and

A. C. Cooper

set of landscapes, the *Eight Views of Famous Places* (*Meisho Hakkei*) (Fig. 2).

In the 1840s Hiroshige, Kuniyoshi and Kunisada stand head and shoulders above all their fellows, and they co-operated on a number of occasions, Hiroshige supplying landscape backgrounds to the figure subjects of the other two. Kuniyoshi and Kunisada were by this time training a considerable number of pupils, whose signed work is sometimes permitted to appear on the same sheet as that of their master. Thus, in a series of about 1845, devoted to the sixty-odd provinces of Japan, the main designs are the work of Kuniyoshi and Kunisada, but each print has a small inset panel signed by a pupil. All this seems to argue an atmosphere of good nature and co-operation among the leading artists of the day. In the second rank, Yoshitora and Sadahide, pupils of Kuniyoshi and Kunisada respectively, are outstanding. Yoshitora's best work, indeed, is almost indistinguishable from that of his master.

Prints of actors and courtesans were banned absolutely

The 1840s was also a period of strict censorship. Prints had been subject to some form of censorship since the latter years of the eighteenth century, and the round *kiwame* (approved) seal is found on many of them. But in 1842 the authorities, who give the impression of having been reluctant to miss any opportunity of harassing the common people, introduced a stricter system. Prints of actors and courtesans were banned absolutely, and all designs had to be submitted to one of a roster of censors, who affixed his personal seal to the drawing before it was engraved. Between 1842 and 1846, prints bear one such seal, and from 1847 to 1857, two. Additional date-seals giving the year and month of publication were introduced in 1852. This strict censorship is often said to have given a great fillip to Hiroshige's landscapes and Kuniyoshi's heroes, both of which were looked upon with official favour; but it was not long (less than five years) before theatrical prints reappeared in as large numbers as ever before the 1842 edict, and all bearing censors' seals. The edict does, however, seem to have been more dutifully observed in the case of prints of courtesans, their place being taken by numerous series depicting ordinary women and girls in various everyday domestic occupations and amusements. In 1844 Kunisada took his late master's name, calling himself Toyokuni II, and so signed his prints for the rest of his life.

The 1830s were brilliant, the 1840s prolific and almost over-ripe, but in the 1850s the Japanese print definitely entered upon its decadence. Hiroshige, Kuniyoshi and Kunisada were all in late middle age, and all three had been unflaggingly prolific. As a result, Hiroshige seldom touches the heights of the 1833–34 *Tokaido* or the *Omi Hakkei* (most of his prints after 1850 are of vertical format); Kuniyoshi is sometimes reduced to repeating heroic scenes he had treated more effectively in earlier life; while the unabated flow of Kunisada's theatrical prints may be searched in vain for the occasional flash of brilliance of which he had formerly been capable. Their innumerable pupils were busily engaged in turning out second-rate imitations of their respective masters' work. Beside this, Japan

Fig. 6 *Surimono* (greetings-card), *depicting a lady in seventeenth-century costume, by Kunisada, c.1835.*
Often commissioned for some family occasion, these cards were much used at the New Year.
(*Victoria and Albert Museum.*)

Fig. 7 *Part of a Triptych of the destruction of Chinese warships by the Japanese off Korea in 1894 by Kiyochika, 1894–95.*
(*Victoria and Albert Museum.*)

Fig. 8 *Yoshitsune's ship in the haunted bay of Daimotsu, one of the series* A Hundred Phases of the Moon, *by Yoshitoshi.*
In 1185, Yoshitsune annihilated the Taira clan at the sea-battle of Dan-no-ura, and the ghosts of the slain Taira are said to have later attempted to sink his ship.
(*Victoria and Albert Museum.*)

some very remarkable landscapes in which he experiments with European ideas (Fig. 5); to the same period belongs his best-known series on the life of the Buddhist saint Nichiren, in which landscape and heroics are nicely blended. Kunisada also designed a few landscapes at this time, and heroic compositions too, but his main production continued to be in the theatrical field.

The same decade is also remarkable for the flowering of the *surimono*, a small, almost square, sheet of comparatively thick paper, exquisitely printed with metallic colours, *gaufrage* (embossing), and every refinement of the printer's craft (Fig. 6). These were often specially commissioned to be used as greetings-cards to mark the New Year or any other festive occasion, and the most notable examples were the work of Hokusai and his pupils, especially Hokkei, and of other artists who came under his influence, such as Gakutei. This latter was an artist of great talent and delicacy of execution; his set of *Views of Tempozan* (Osaka) is one of the most distinguished in the whole range of *ukiyo-e* landscape (Fig. 1). Toyokuni II, whose claim to the great name was later brushed aside by Kunisada, also deserves great credit for a beautiful

Fig. 9 **Winter snow on the
Sumida River,** one of the Views
of Edo in the Four Seasons by
Hiroshige, 1835–40.
Hiroshige designed numerous
sets of prints illustrating views in
and around Edo.
(Victoria and Albert Museum.)

Fig. 10 **Hara,** the thirteenth
post-station on the Tokaido Road,
by Hiroshige, 1833–34.
This great highway linked the
cities of Edo (now Tokyo) and
Kyoto; Mount Fuji was a
prominent landmark in the early
stages of the journey.
(Victoria and Albert Museum.)

was thrown into turmoil by the arrival of
Commodore Perry and his U.S. Naval squadron;
change and revolution were in the air, and the old
ideas and standards were crumbling. In 1858
Hiroshige died of cholera.

The 1860s and 1870s were an even more depress-
ing period. Kuniyoshi died in 1861, and Kunisada in
1864. Aniline colours imported from Europe make
the prints of these years increasingly and sometimes
almost unbearably harsh and discordant. The
numerous prints of 'southern barbarians', as the
Western visitors were called, and of their new-
fangled contraptions such as umbrellas and brass
bands, are often amusing, but of little or no
aesthetic merit. The style of Hiroshige was kept
precariously alive by Hiroshige II and III;
Kunisada's successor in the theatrical field was the
strident Kunichika; and battle-scenes of incredible
and blood-drenched complexity were still being
produced by Kuniyoshi's numerous pupils (all of
whose names begin 'Yoshi-'), but among them
Yoshitoshi is the only one who shows real originality
and promise. Kyosai, who had sat at Kuniyoshi's
feet as a small boy, had immense talent and vigour,
but his paintings are much better and more
numerous than his prints. Perhaps the only really
outstanding print-designer in the 1870s was
Kiyochika, who was beginning his career with a
number of striking landscapes incorporating
European ideas of perspective and chiaroscuro.

But in the 1880s and '90s the glaring aniline
colours were being brought under control. Much of
the early strength was lost, and especially in prints
of women by such artists as Gekko and Toshikata
the effect is merely pretty. But Yoshitoshi, who had
evolved a very individual and effective style of
drawing, was producing some notable work,
especially in his fine series A Hundred Phases
of the Moon (Fig. 8), and Kiyochika developed
remarkable talent in the field of historical illustrations in the closing years of the nineteenth century.
Shoson (who later changed his name to Koson)
showed great skill as a sympathetic portrayer of
birds and animals, but most of his work belongs to
the early years of the present century. The heroic
triptych returned to favour in the Sino-Japanese War
of 1894 and in the Russo-Japanese War of 1904–5.
Kiyochika and other artists found plenty of subjects

for such compositions in the stirring events of these
two great struggles from which Japan emerged as a
great power in the modern world (Fig. 7).

Looking back over the nineteenth-century
achievements of the Japanese print, it is possible to
recognise an enormous expansion both in range of
subject and in volume of production during its first
half. The opening up of the country during its third
quarter had the effect of robbing the prints of all the
appeal of subject, colour and composition by which
they were formerly distinguished. But in the last
quarter a certain revival of quality was achieved.
Fifty years ago it was thought eccentric to collect
Kuniyoshi, but today the works of such as
Kiyochika and Yoshitoshi are eagerly sought after,
and command very respectable prices. For many
people nineteenth-century prints have more appeal
and interest than those of the earlier periods; they
are easier to appreciate, easier to come by, and,
apart from a few 'star' pieces like Hokusai's Wave,
considerably cheaper; and also for those who are
prepared to temper pure aesthetics with a lively
interest in the subject-matter – Japanese history
and legend, folklore, humour, and topography –
they are more rewarding.

FURTHER READING
Master Prints of Japan by Harold P. Stern, New
York, 1969.
Kuniyoshi by B. W. Robinson, London, 1961.
Japanese Masters of the Colour Print by
J. Hillier, London, 1954.
Japanese Colour Prints by E. F. Strange, London,
reprint 1931.
Japanese Colour Prints by L. Binyon and J. J.
O'Brien Sexton, London, 1923.

MUSEUMS AND COLLECTIONS
Japanese prints of the nineteenth century may be
seen at the following:
GREAT BRITAIN
London: British Museum
             Victoria and Albert Museum
JAPAN
Tokyo: National Museum
U.S.A.
Boston: Boston Museum of Fine Arts
New York: Metropolitan Museum of Art

The Porcelain of China & Japan

Michael Eveleigh

A. C. Cooper

With the exception of some wares produced for domestic use, the porcelain industries of the Orient suffered greatly from the influx of Europeans to China and, more especially, Japan

It was during the last half of the eighteenth century in China, during the reign of the Emperor Ch'ien-lung (1736–95), that the vogue for 'china' assumed vast proportions. It became something of a status-symbol for the gentry of Europe to have large dinner-services, especially if a coat of arms was emblazoned on them in full colour. This trade was almost exclusively handled by the East India Companies. Services of two hundred pieces upwards were ordered to ensure the safe arrival of a service large enough to use for the grand style of entertaining that prevailed.

In England the growing impetus of the Industrial Revolution brought with it a new, moneyed class who wanted to display their affluence by using *famille rose* porcelain on their tables. The East India Company withdrew as importers of china in 1801, leaving the field open to smaller operators who were less familiar with the customs of the Chinese and therefore less able to exact from them the standards required in Europe.

These changes in Europe almost coincided with the abdication of the Emperor Ch'ien-lung and the ascent to the Imperial Throne in 1796 of Chia-ch'ing, who reigned until 1821. During this period the traditions of the Ch'ien-lung period were continued, but the lack of stability, both at the kilns and among the new importers, brought about a steady decline in the quality of most export wares. There are, however, many pieces which show skill in both potting and decoration (Fig. 1).

By far the most important wares produced in China in the nineteenth century were those

Fig. 1 **Vase and cover,** *one of a pair, Canton, Chia-ch'ing mark and period (1796–1821). Painted in* famille rose *enamels, height 20 ins. (Christie, Manson and Woods, London.)*

intended for the Chinese themselves. The growth of smaller private kilns beside the Imperial kilns brought the more luxurious porcelains within the reach of both the Mandarinate and the Chinese leisured classes. Almost without exception, these porcelains were either painted in under-glaze blue or enamelled in colours in the 'Chinese taste'. Instead of the typical *chinoiserie* decorations, these other wares were sparsely decorated with subjects which could be of appeal only to the Chinese – simply sprays of peonies, orchids or lilies, with an insect or bird hovering nearby. These wares echo their eighteenth-century precursors both in quality and in style, even though they lack the final brilliance which is so highly regarded by some collectors. It must be remembered that it was only the weakening of the Manchu Empire by

lishments – 'the hall of brilliant colours' (Fig. 3), or 'Cloudy fragrance hall'.

Closely akin to these pieces are those which bear commendation or felicitation marks. These marks were generally inscribed on pieces intended as gifts, and the marks were intended to praise the object as worthy of acceptance. Such marks as 'of unique value', 'a gem among precious vessels of rare stones' and 'a fine vessel for the rich and honourable' frequently occur, as well as simple dedications of 'happiness', 'honour' or 'long life' to the recipient.

Throughout the nineteenth century, a wide variety of porcelains were produced for home consumption, and often types produced in the eighteenth century which did not find general favour or acceptance recur with a new liveliness.

There are, for instance, the so-called 'palace

Fig. 2 **Oviform vase**, *Hirado, mid-nineteenth century. Painted with under-glaze blue and pink with finches and plum blossom, height 10 ins. (Author's Collection.)*

Fig. 3 **Bowl**, *Chinese, mid-nineteenth century. Painted in* famille rose *enamels with panels, with the iron red mark of the 'brilliant colours hall', diameter 5¾ ins. Pieces marked in this fanciful way were intended for use only in palace rooms, pavilions or retreats. (Author's Collection.)*

Fig. 4 **Moon flask**, *one of a pair, Chinese, mid-nineteenth century. Painted in* famille rose *enamels with Hsi Wang-mu, the Taoist Fairy Queen, with the iron red mark of the 'brilliant colours hall', height 10½ ins. (Private Collection.)*

the Europeans that brought the total decline of the Chinese ceramic industry.

A curious feature of most nineteenth-century Chinese porcelain is the painting of the *nien hao* (reign mark) in iron red on the glaze rather than in under-glaze blue. One is tempted to think that this was due to the shortage of fine cobalt ore for decoration, for there are pieces on which the body decoration is in under-glaze blue while the *nien hao* is in iron red.

The decorative repertoire in the nineteenth century, apart from the delicate 'Chinese taste' flowers and birds, is very often drawn from both Buddhist and Taoist mythology. Typical of such subjects is the vase illustrated in Figure 7, which shows on one side Shou Lao, the God of Longevity, holding some peaches, an emblem of longevity, and Liu Hai with his three-legged toad spewing *cash*, symbolic of wealth and good fortune.

The moon flask, which derives its name from its shape, showing Hsi Wang-mu, Queen of the Taoist fairyland (Fig. 4), belong to the large group of porcelains which only bear 'hallmarks'. These wares were intended only for palace rooms, pavilions, retreats or similar places. Very often, these 'hallmarks' refer to very fanciful estab-

Sperryn's Ltd

Sotheby Photo

A. C. Cooper

A. C. Cooper

Fig. 5 *Two 'palace bowls',*
Tao-kuang mark and period
(1821–50).
That on the left painted with
famille verte *enamels and a*
dragon amid 'flaming pearls';
that on the right with famille rose
landscape medallions on a blue
graviata *ground, diameter* 5¾ *ins.*
(Sotheby and Co., London.)

Fig. 6 *Lion dancer from a* Noh
play, Arita, probably
mid-nineteenth century. Height
11½ *ins. (Private Collection.)*

Fig. 7 *Vase,* Hsien-eng *mark*
and period (1851–61). Painted in
famille rose *enamels, height* 11¼ *ins.*
(Mrs. E. Hatoum Collection.)

Fig. 8 *Pillow-box,* Arita, *early*
nineteenth century. Blue and
white, width 7 ins.
(Author's Collection.)

bowls', which, unlike their Ming forebears, have lavish decoration (Fig. 5). These bowls are generally painted in fine under-glaze blue on the interior with an elaborate pattern of 'precious' or 'auspicious' emblems, while the exterior is finely enamelled with panels of 'Chinese taste' flowers amid a colourful *graviata* (pattern etched on the enamel) ground enriched with formal foliage; the effect is sumptuous. These pieces were only for palace use and it was not until the lootings in the late nineteenth century that they appeared in Europe.

Among the less familiar wares of this period are those carved and left in the white biscuit state. These pieces are almost exclusively for the scholar's table and include brush-rests and holders, seals and seal-vermilion boxes. Vases occur less frequently. Although these wares are never glazed, they are often enamelled on the biscuit in striking monochrome colours. They are invariably carved with flowers and shrubs in the 'Chinese taste' or landscapes recalling Sung paintings. The most famous exponent of this technique was Wang Ping-jung, who had many imitators, some of whom showed great skill.

In feudal Japan the Tokugawa Shogunate, the hereditary rulers whose powers exceeded that of

the Emperor in whose stead they claimed to rule, enforced total isolation, which was to last from 1603 until their overthrow in 1867. During this period the only intercourse with the outside world was through the port of Imari, where the Dutch kept their warehouses. All other contact was forbidden under pain of death. No foreigner was allowed to travel inland, nor was any Japanese allowed to leave the country, learn a foreign language or introduce foreign customs. For two hundred and fifty years an enforced peace prevailed and the arts flourished. Unlike China, all Japan's kilns were under private patronage and therefore subject to the vagaries of feudalism combined with a limited kind of private enterprise.

At the turn of the nineteenth century the Tokugawa Shogunate had begun to lose its power and influence over the war-lords and therefore over the people. Famine and disease at all levels weakened patronage of the kilns and it was only the very rich *daimyo* (war-lord) who could afford to maintain the luxury of a kiln in such troubled times. The Kutani kiln, under the patronage of the *daimyo* Maeda, collapsed in the closing years of the eighteenth century due to Maeda's fall from favour. In 1816 Yoshidaya Denyemon revived the kiln and for over fifty years continued to produce porcelains inspired by eighteenth-century models. Very few show much originality, and they are generally coarse and vulgar. Typical of these wares are the large plates and dishes with heavy green and egg or mustard yellow enamels combined with black and aubergine. The so-called Yoshidaya revival wares are invariably marked with a two-character Kutani mark which is unrecorded on known eighteenth-century pieces.

The kilns at Arita fared much better during the early nineteenth century and were able to continue making fine porcelain. The fine paste and attractive painting made the unusually shaped pillow-box in Figure 8 a suitable receptacle for a lady's jewels as she slept. As well as these pieces were the typical Imari wares, painted in under-glaze blue and over-glaze iron red and gold. The traditional patterns were continued on the export goods.

The export of porcelain continued to be a valuable source of revenue for the dwindling fortunes of the *daimyo*, and, as demand increased, so quality declined. The Arita kilns continued to make pieces decorated in both the Kakiemon and the Kutani palettes (Fig. 6), some early pieces still being almost indistinguishable from their eighteenth-century counterparts.

As the domestic situation deteriorated in Japan, so the viability of the kilns grew worse. Many craftsmen, unable to make even a living, drifted away from the kilns, and much work that had hitherto been hand painted now became transfer printed. These early transfer-wares show a high degree of skill in the application of the technique, but this soon declined and finally became utterly crude.

The Nabeshima kiln seems to have fared best of all, remaining under strict supervision until the collapse of the Shogunate in 1858–59. The later wares, produced in the first half of the nineteenth century, lost the very fine quality of production but were still well executed, both in potting and in decoration.

Practically overnight, feudal Japan, ruled by the Shogunate, underwent a radical change. Fine manners and taste gave way to unbridled decadence. No longer was the *kimono* the order of the day; now it was a question of aping to an absurd degree the clothes and manners of the Europeans, popularised by the *Nagasaki-e* wood-block prints depicting all manner of European dress and behaviour, by then a commonplace in the city of Nagasaki. The opening of Japan to Europeans, begun by Commander Perry in 1853, spread rapidly, and within two years the introspective Japanese had become so extrovert as to discard without thought its fine traditions, especially in the field of art. The Europeans wanted souvenirs of their travels, especially porcelains. To begin with, they were of fine quality (Fig. 9), even though they were hardly to the taste of the Japanese. Within a few years, however, vases six feet tall found their way to England, heavily encrusted with applied decorations of dragons, flowers and birds. These vases came to be valued almost as highly as the fabled Ming porcelains of China.

The only kiln which seems to have avoided the extreme vulgarity of the Satsuma wares was that of Hirado, where charming toys – small porcelain animals, delicately painted in under-glaze blue and with incised details – were produced. Vases were made, still of the finest porcelain, and decorated with great skill (Fig. 2). Incense-burners, boxes, seals and other scholars' requisites came from this kiln, often finely reticulated with elaborate fret and diaper patterns. How they ever survived the firings still seems something of a miracle.

In the last quarter of the nineteenth century in Japan, European influence was such that under the Meiji Restoration (the Emperor Meiji now ruling in his own right) factory methods were introduced at the kilns in order to produce fine eggshell-porcelain tea-services, bowls and other such wares, not only for export but also for home use. Deliberate copies of Chinese porcelains, especially of the Sung and Ming periods, began to be produced. It is unlikely that these were intended as forgeries, but the degree of skill used often makes it impossible for all but the expert to distinguish them from the originals.

But for the entry of the European into Japan, it is likely that the whole ceramic industry of Japan would have survived the declining years of the Tokugawa Shogunate.

Fig. 9 **Oviform vase,** Satsuma, *second half of the nineteenth century. Gold brocaded shoulders and sides, height 11 ins. The early porcelain 'souvenir' pieces of Japan, such as this decorative vase, were of a fine quality which later descended into extreme vulgarity. (Christie, Manson and Woods.)*

9

A. C. Cooper

FURTHER READING

Japanese Porcelain by Soame Jenyns, London, 1965.
Japanese Ceramics from Ancient to Modern Times edited by Fujio Koyama, Oakland, California, 1961.
Oriental Blue and White by Sir Henry Garner, London, 1954, 3rd edition 1970.
The Ceramic Art of China and Other Countries of the Far East by W. B. Honey, London, 1945.

MUSEUMS AND COLLECTIONS

Chinese and Japanese porcelain of the nineteenth century may be seen at the following:

FRANCE
Paris: Musée Guimet
GREAT BRITAIN
Cambridge: Fitzwilliam Museum
London: British Museum
            Percival David Foundation
            Victoria and Albert Museum
Oxford: Ashmolean Museum
JAPAN
Kyoto: Municipal Museum of Art
Tokyo: National Museum
NETHERLANDS
Amsterdam: Rijksmuseum
The Hague: Haags Gemeentemuseum
U.S.A.
Boston: Boston Museum of Fine Arts
Cambridge: Fogg Art Museum
Cleveland: Museum of Art

SHADOW PLAY PUPPETS

Shelagh Weir

Derived from two great Hindu poems, the shadow-plays of south-east Asia are performed with beautiful hide puppets which are silhouetted against a screen by an oil lamp

There are three distinct shadow-play traditions in Asia: that found throughout the former Ottoman Empire which dramatises the exploits of the comic hero Karagöz (as he is called in Turkey); that of China, which depicts legendary court dramas from Chinese history; and that of India and south-east Asia in which the plays are based on the two great Hindu epic poems, the *Mahabharata* and *Ramayana*. Here we are concerned with the shadow-theatre of south-east Asia.

Some writers have maintained that tales from these epics could have been absorbed into an already existing shadow-theatre in south-east Asia as the influence of Hindu culture spread through that area many centuries ago. However, there is growing evidence that the shadow-play of south-east Asia has its origins in India where, in Andhra Pradesh and other states, plays using large puppets of translucent hide are still performed. The shadow-play has been an important part of south-east Asian culture for so long that it may never be possible to discover the exact pattern of its diffusion through the area.

In south-east Asia there are two types of shadow-puppet: large, non-articulated puppets, which usually contain a small scene with several figures within a frame, found in Thailand and Cambodia; and the better-known single figures, with one or two articulated arms, which are found more generally in southern Thailand, Cambodia, Laos, western Malaysia, Java and Bali. Both types of puppets are made from painted hide, not leather as the skin is not tanned, and both have wooden supports and operating-sticks, except in Java where these are of horn.

In all shadow-play performances these flat, perforated puppets are moved between a light (traditionally an oil lamp) and a white fabric screen so that their shadows are projected on to the screen and can be seen by the audience on the other side. In the plays using the smaller articulated puppets, the puppet-master sits behind the screen and manipulates each puppet, speaks the part of each character, intones the narrative passages and controls the musical accompaniment of the orchestra. The *wayang purwa* of Java and the *wayang siam* of Kelantan in western Malaysia have been the most intensively studied of this type of play, known as the *wayang kulit* (the Malay for 'shadow of hide'). It is not unusual for a *wayang* performance to last all night, or for several hours on consecutive nights, and during the course of the play a host of different characters, each with its distinctive voice and personality, appears on the screen. In the villages of Kelantan where the *wayang* is still a very popular entertainment, the *dalang* (puppet-master) must have a considerable repertoire to be able to draw a good audience every time he plays.

Where the larger puppets forming composite scenes are used – in Thailand the plays are called

1

Fig. 1 *Ravana, from the* nang talung *shadow-play of southern Thailand, mid-twentieth century. Height 22½ ins.*
The demon king of Ceylon in the romantic epic Ramayana, *Ravana, is the main adversary of the noble prince Rama. Note his leaping pose, characteristic of Thai puppets, in sharp contrast to the less dynamic version of the same character known as Mahraja Wana from neighbouring Kelantan in Figure 9.*

A. C. Cooper

2

A. C. Cooper

3

A. C. Cooper

4

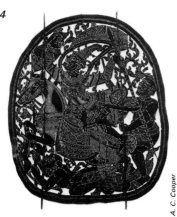

A. C. Cooper

Fig. 2 Left: *Kumbakarna* (probably), Bali, late nineteenth or early twentieth century. Right: *Kumbakarna, Java, early nineteenth century. Height 21 ins. and 33½ ins.*

internecine conflict between the five Pandawa brothers and their cousins the hundred Korawa (Fig. 6). The hero of the play is Arjuna, a noble knight who is advised and helped by the king Kresna (Fig. 10).

It seems likely that plays based on the *Ramayana* were more popular in Java at the beginning of the nineteenth century than they are now, as there are a number of puppets representing characters from that story in the collection made by Sir Stamford Raffles in Java between 1811 and 1816, which is now in the British Museum. There are also in this collection puppets from the *wayang gedog*, a cycle of plays about the adventures of Prince Panji, a legendary Javanese hero. In Bali, it seems that the *Ramayana* is the more popular source for the plays, although in the British Museum collection of Balinese puppets, which dates back to the beginning of this century, there are many representing characters from the Pandawa plays.

A shadow-play is primarily an entertainment, but the performance also contains important religious elements. Religious themes are prominent in the drama where gods frequently intervene in the lives of men; statements are made about the meaning of life which can be of deep significance to the audience; the performance of a play is thought to have a beneficial effect on important events, and plays are performed on occasions such as weddings, circumcisions and birthdays; and rituals to invoke the goodwill of the gods and spirits take place before each performance.

Ornamentation resembling the finest filigree, the colours beautifully and painstakingly applied

Over the centuries, the Hindu epics have been adapted and interpreted by each culture of south-east Asia in its own way. Legends of local origin have been absorbed into the original stories and certain aspects of the Hindu epics have been emphasised and elaborated more than others.

Each culture has also developed its own distinctive style of puppet. The puppets of Java are undoubtedly the most striking of the whole area, representing a remarkably high standard of craftsmanship by the way in which they are chiselled and painted. The excised ornamentation on some puppets resembles the finest filigree, and the colours are beautifully and painstakingly applied even though, as the puppets are opaque, they are not seen by the audience on the other side of the screen.

The general appearance of Javanese puppets is notable for the extended shoulders and elongated arms, and the attenuated facial features of the noble characters. Some writers have attributed this distortion of the human form to the influence of Islam, suggesting that the puppet-theatre was only thus able to survive under a religion which forbids representation of the human form. There is no clear evidence to support this theory, although it would explain the more naturalistic appearance of the puppets in neighbouring Bali, where Islam never took root.

Balinese puppets, although perforated with some precision and attention to detail, do not approach in standard the delicate tracery of those of Java. The paint is crudely applied in large blocks of colour

'nang yai' (Fig. 4), and in Cambodia 'nang sbek' – a number of dancers carry them in sequence across the screen, moving the puppets and their own bodies in a manner appropriate to the figure they are holding. The figure of the dancer as well as the shape of the puppet can be seen as shadows by the audience.

The shadow-plays of south-east Asia are derived from the two great Hindu poems which have inspired the artists of India and most of the Asian continent for more than two thousand years. On the mainland the plays are drawn mainly from the *Ramayana*, a romantic epic in which Sita, the faithful wife of the noble prince Rama, is abducted by the demon king of Ceylon, Ravana (Figs. 1, 8 and 9). The monkey leader Hanoman (Fig. 11) and his monkey army help Rama in the long search for Sita and her eventual rescue. In Java, however, the Pandawa stories from the *Mahabharata* are more popular as a basis for the plays. The dominant theme of these plays is the

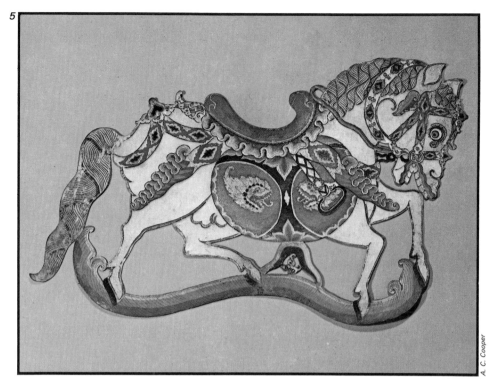

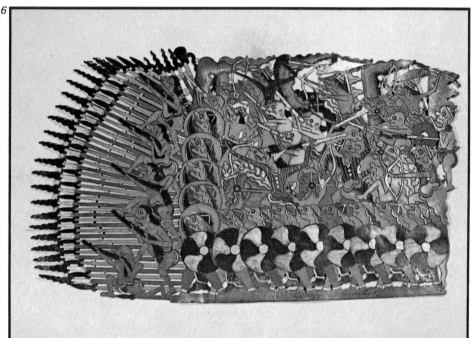

Fig. 3 Left: *Semar, from the* wayang purwa *of Java, early nineteenth century.* Right: *Pak Dogol from the* wayang siam *of Kelantan, western Malaysia, twentieth century. Height 15 ins. and 17½ ins.*
These crude and earthy puppets are the principal clowns of their plays. Despite their antics during the comic interludes in the dramas, they are credited with supernatural powers and are the most sacred of all the figures in a puppet-master's collection.

Fig. 4 *Puppet (detail), depicting a demon on horseback, from the* nang yai *plays in which large puppets forming composite scenes are used, Thailand, late nineteenth or early twentieth century. Height 5 ft.*

Fig. 5 *Horse, with saddle and ornate trappings, Java, early nineteenth century. Height 17 ins.*
Various animals appear in the shadow-plays of south-east Asia, though few compare in beauty with this one.

Fig. 6 *An army in battle, Java, early nineteenth century. Height 16½ ins.*
Battle-scenes are among the most dramatic moments in a shadow-play, and a composite scene such as this might have been used during the great battle between the Pandawa and the Korawa in the wayang purwa.
Interesting features of this piece are the figures holding bows in one hand and aiming spears with the other; and others with coarse facial features holding blow-guns to their mouths – a weapon never native to Java, but used by the tribal peoples of Borneo and the Malay peninsula.

Fig. 7 *Kelana Tunjung Seta, Java, early nineteenth century. Height 20 ins.*
Kelana Tunjung Seta is the enemy of Prince Panji, the hero of the wayang gedog *plays which enact events from Javanese history. Puppets representing characters from these plays are among the finest in the Raffles Collection.*

Fig. 8 *Dasamuka, Java, early nineteenth century. Height 25½ ins.*
Corresponding to Ravana in Thailand (Fig. 1) and to Mahraja Wana in western Malaysia (Fig. 9), Dasamuka is a demon king of the wayang purwa *plays. His status is shown by his ornate crown and clothing, and his evil character by his fanged tooth, red face and aggressive stance.*

with little detailed work, as is also the case throughout the rest of the area. There are, however, as one would expect, many iconographic similarities between the puppets of Java and Bali (Fig. 2).

There are obvious similarities between the different puppets of the mainland in their general appearance and in the ornamental motifs employed, for example, in the head-dresses, types of clothing and bodily decorations. Some of the puppets from Kelantan, near the Malaysian border with Thailand, appear very like those of Thailand and Cambodia, but are less dynamic than the latter, which are usually depicted in a leaping pose reminiscent of their famous national ballets or the sculptures of Angkor Wat. Some Kelantanese puppets, especially the ogre figures, are very similar to their Javanese counterparts.

In the plays of each country there are certain well-defined character types: noble personages, such as knights, princes and kings; demons, giants, ogres, gods and spirits, monkeys, sages, attendants, coarse

A. C. Cooper

Fig. 9 **Puppets** *of the* wayang siam *of Kelantan, western Malaysia, twentieth century. Left:* **Mahraja Wana,** *abductor of Rama's wife Sita Dewi, distinguished by the extra heads concealed in his head-dress. Height 34 ins. Right:* **Seri Rama,** *hero of the plays, distinguished by his green colour and bow. Height 21 ins. Both stand on a* naga *(mythical snake).*

Fig. 10 **Puppets** *of two noble characters from the* Pandawa *cycle of plays, Java, early nineteenth century. Left:* **Arjuna,** *principal hero of the plays. Height 18 ins. Right:* **Kresna,** *the king who watches over the Pandawa brothers. Height 20 ins.*

Fig. 11 Left: **Hanoman,** *leader of the monkeys and ally of Rama, Java, early nineteenth century. Height 22½ ins. Right:* **A monkey character** *from the Rama plays in Bali, early twentieth century. Height 20 ins.*

(All these puppets are from the Ethnography Department of the British Museum, London. Figures 2 right, 3 left, 5, 6, 7, 8, 10 and 11 left are from the Raffles Collection.)

peasants and, not least, clowns (Fig. 3). In any set of puppets, these types can be distinguished by a number of features such as their stance, colouring, size, facial expression, clothing and ornaments. The more important characters from the play usually have particular features which identify them more precisely, for example, a certain weapon or ornament, or a physical peculiarity.

During the performance, when the puppet is speaking or acting in a certain manner, he is immediately recognised by the audience, which is intimately familiar with the story. In museums and illustrations, we see these puppets as static figures, but to their audience they come to life as the legendary heroes and other beings of mythology.

FURTHER READING

Malay Shadow Puppets by Amin Sweeney, British Museum, London, 1972.
Wayang Purwa by U. Ulbricht, Amsterdam, 1971.
Javanese Shadow Puppets by Jeune Scott-Kemball, British Museum, London, 1970.
Shadow Play (The Nang) by H. H. Prince Dhanivat Bridhyakorn, Bangkok, 1968.

MUSEUMS AND COLLECTIONS

South-east Asian puppets are available for study by serious students in the new premises of the Department of Ethnography of the British Museum in Burlington Gardens, London, W.1. Selections will be exhibited from time to time. Other examples may be seen at the following:

GREAT BRITAIN
Cambridge: Museum of Archaeology and Ethnology
London: Horniman Museum
Oxford: Pitt Rivers Museum
NETHERLANDS
Amsterdam: Koninklijk Instituut voor de Tropen
Leyden: Rijksmuseum voor Volkenkunde
Rotterdam: Museum voor Land- en Volkenkunde
WEST GERMANY
Essen: Museum Folkwang
Munich: Münchner Stadtmuseum

A. C. Cooper

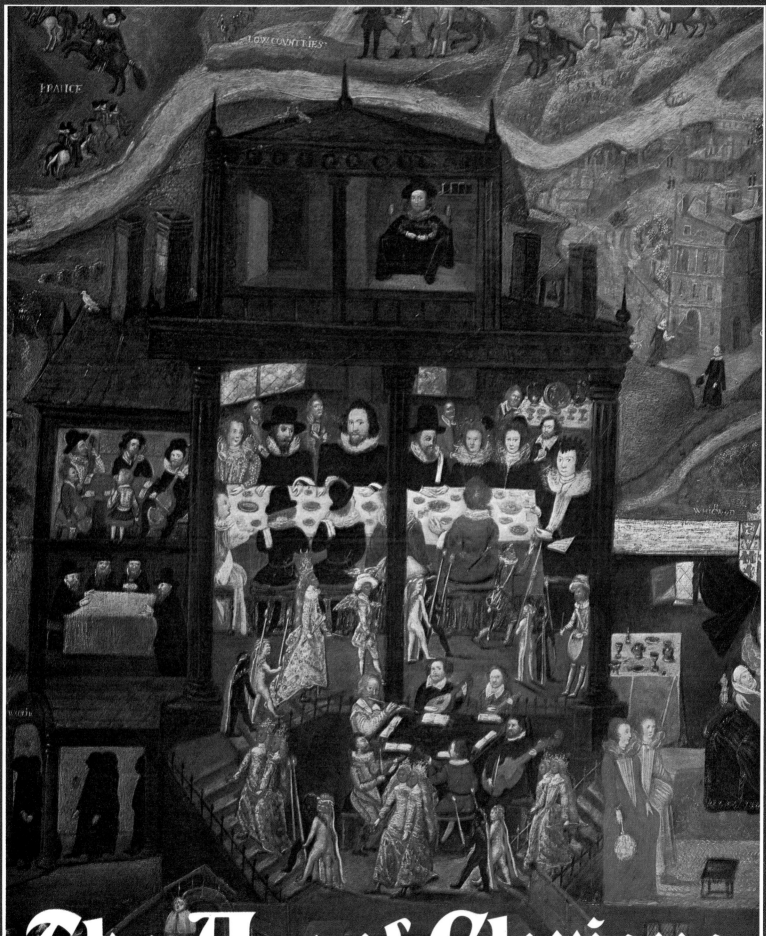

The Age of Gloriana

John Buxton

Queen Elizabeth I
Born 1533
Acceded 1558
Died 1603

Previous Page
Detail from **The Life and Death of Sir Henry Unton,** *English School, c.1596. Oil on panel,* $29\frac{1}{8}$ *x* $64\frac{1}{4}$ *ins.*
(National Portrait Gallery, London.)

The Elizabethans enjoyed the first great period of English domestic building. They built their houses from love and for their families and friends, no longer to keep out enemies. Many of these magnificent houses are still lived in and enjoyed today.

Even after the lapse of four centuries we live still among things which the subjects of the first Queen Elizabeth made and enjoyed. Many of their country houses survive where, in the long galleries, we may see portraits contemporary with the building of the houses. The walls are warm with panelling and tapestries; the heavily decorated fire-places are the true focus of the rooms; the plaster ceilings and friezes once came alive in the varying light of candles. On the beds are the valances and curtains and coverlets which Elizabethan ladies embroidered with the flowers and birds and insects of their gardens. In churches and cathedrals are the gaudy, self-confident monuments with which they commemorated their dead; and in the services of these churches we still repeat in the liturgy and psalms the cadences of Elizabethan prose. In the cathedrals we can hear the music of composers who made Elizabethan England famous throughout Europe as

Monitor

A. F. Kersting

Monitor

Fig. 1 *Montacute House, Somerset, built in the 1590s by W. Arnold for Sir Edward Phelips who later became Speaker in the House.*

Fig. 2 *Wollaton Hall, Nottinghamshire, designed by Robert Smythson during the 1580s.*

Fig. 3 *Gazebo and south wall of the garden at Montacute.*

Fig. 4 *Hardwick Hall, Derbyshire, designed by Robert Smythson under the direction of Bess of Hardwick, 1591–97.*

her poets and dramatists, restricted to the language of one small island, could not.

To the Elizabethans themselves, there can be little doubt that the greatest of their achievements was the Anglican Church – their creation of the means to worship God in their own way, in their own tongue, with their own music. Foreign Protestants were usually astonished to find the Anglican services retaining so much that was Popish, not appreciating the English gift for compromise, even in this. But compromise was also very beneficial in the arts, where it reconciled those two complementary motives of the Renaissance, the wish to follow a European (and therefore classical) tradition and the wish to assert a native (and therefore medieval) tradition. The fine equilibrium here, as in the religious settlement, could scarcely be maintained for more than a generation; but for a time it was the inspiration for many and various achievements.

To the Elizabethans all human problems were, ultimately, problems of man's relation to God, not of man's relation to man. They believed that the world in which they lived was a rationally ordered world, created by divine intelligence and to be comprehended by that gift of reason with which God had distinguished man from his other creatures. 'If we will be men,' wrote Sidney, 'the reasonable part of our soul is to have absolute commandment'. This belief inevitably affected their response to the arts: they did not consider that the artist *imposed* an individual pattern upon experience but that he *revealed* the divine order which underlay it. His personal vision was therefore not very important; but it was important that he should develop his skill, whatever it was, by observation of the good work of his predecessors, especially in ancient Greece or Rome. Hence the constant references to Cicero and Virgil, to Vitruvius and Pheidias and Apelles, or to those who seemed their most successful imitators in modern Italy and France. And since the arts were learned professions, they admired evidence of learning, such as the controlled ingenuity of design in a building, a poem, or a piece of music.

the world is ... 'compared to music, and music to poetry'

Man was the measure of all things, for God had created him in his own image that he might understand the divine order of Creation. 'The world,' said Thomas Campion (who was doctor, poet and musician), 'the world is made by symmetry and proportion, and is in that respect compared to music, and music to poetry'. Sir Henry Wotton (who was diplomat, poet and connoisseur) extends the comparison to architecture by transporting the mathematical proportions that underlie fifth and octave from audible to visible objects, confident, as he says that 'there will indubitably result from either a graceful and harmonious contentment to the eye'. The idea was as old as Pythagoras, whose discovery of the numerical ratios that determine the intervals of the musical scale led him to develop his theory of the numerical basis of universal order. To men of the renaissance, this theory was especially attractive as proof of the rationality of the Universe. It also, of course, made good taste reasonable, and objective. If the proportion 2:3 was pleasing to the ear it must also be pleasing to the eye, and a window or door whose proportions were such must please not merely some of those who saw it, but all. Good taste could then, as it were, be demonstrated with a foot-rule.

The Elizabethans built neither churches nor castles: they had plenty of the one, and did not need the other. They built houses, places where you might invite your friends, not places from which you must keep out your enemies. Sometimes they converted monastic buildings and castles to domestic use as they did Newstead, Longleat and Buckland, Kenilworth, Raglan and Wardour. Generally the former have survived better, for the castles, taking a new lease of life as fortresses in the Civil War, were slighted by the victorious Roundheads, and a charge adequate to render medieval walls indefensible would be more than enough to demolish the flimsier domestic additions. In these houses, whether converted or new built, the first

4

A. F. Kersting

Fig. 5 *The High Great Chamber, Hardwick Hall, showing the arms of Elizabeth I above the fireplace and one of the Brussels tapestries around which Bess of Hardwick is said to have designed the room.*

Fig. 6 *Elizabeth's Procession to Nonsuch, by Hoefnagel. Engraving. Built by Henry VIII, the Palace of Nonsuch was so-called because it was unsurpassed in beauty. Its lavish gold decoration sparkling in the evening sunlight once caused Queen Elizabeth to imagine that it was on fire.*

thing to notice is that the principal rooms have been moved upstairs. Long gallery and great chamber and dining-room have taken priority over the hall of the medieval house, though this remained; they are reserved for the owner and his family and their guests, and are not shared, like the medieval hall, with the household. The long gallery is peculiar to England, and was intended for gentle exercise in bad weather: on its walls were hung the full-length ceremonial portraits, which are also distinctively English. The great chamber was a place to sit in, for conversation or music or for listening to 'long tales of great delight', – *The Countess of Pembroke's Arcadia*, perhaps, or Spenser's *The Faerie Queene*.

Bess of Hardwick and 'the most beautiful room in Europe'

To reach these important rooms there was need of a grand staircase to replace the old vice, a narrow staircase in a turret or in the thickness of the wall. The stairs need not be defended by a man with a sword in his hand; they must allow room for a stately approach in the splendid dresses that the ladies wore. At Burghley House is the first of these grand staircases, in stone, and suggestive of Italy. At Hardwick Hall the staircase is of extreme simplicity, with broad and shallow treads and no hand-rail. It leads from shadow, where no direct light comes in, up into a brilliantly lit space before the High Great Chamber, 'the most beautiful room in Europe' in Sacheverell Sitwell's opinion. Here is a great fireplace of black and white, blue and grey marble, surmounted by the Queen's coat of arms blazoned on the frieze. This frieze continues around the rest of the room and is decorated with Abraham Smith's designs in coloured plaster: hunting in an English landscape – England was then, they said, almost one continuous forest – an allegory of Summer, and scenes with Venus and Diana. The walls below the frieze are hung with tapestries of the Odyssey: they have been there since the room was finished, as has much of the furniture. Thus the poetry of Homer and Greek myth are set side by side with English heraldry and the depiction of English people hunting the deer. The mixture is of the same kind as the mixture of Perpendicular fenestration and classical symmetry in the façade. Hardwick Hall, 'more glass than wall', thus combines native and classical traditions indoors and out.

It is altogether appropriate that this most perfect of Elizabethan houses, and the most complete in its furnishings, should be the work of a woman, Bess of Hardwick, Countess of Shrewsbury. For the civilised life of the age, which had outgrown the military necessities of the Middle Ages, gave scope as never before to the mistress of the house to arrange the interior to suit feminine tastes, just as the writers of poetry and romance more often than not addressed the ladies.

The rooms could be well lit – 'lightsome' was their word – now that there was no need for defence. 'I found no one thing of greater grace,' Burghley told Sir Christopher Hatton after a visit to Holdenby House, 'than your stately ascent from your hall to your Great Chamber; and your chambers answerable with largeness and lightsomeness, that truly a Momus could find no fault.' This effect could be overdone, as Sir Francis Bacon observed: 'You shall have sometimes fair houses so full of glass, that one cannot tell where to become to be out of the sun or cold.' But he delighted nonetheless in the big bay windows where one could retire for private conversation, as he said, or to read a sonnet or to admire a miniature by Hilliard, just received with its secret message from lover to beloved.

Again, one might now enjoy the view from these great windows without scanning the countryside for enemies: at Wollaton, Sir Francis Willoughby built a Prospect Chamber above the central hall which is itself fifty feet high, from which to look out over Nottinghamshire. One might also lay out the garden in the foreground to please the eye from the windows, for the carpet-like patterns of the knots were best seen from above; and in the garden, as at Montacute, the design of medieval fortification could be converted to pure pleasure. 'The gatehouse has become a gateway, the curtain walls open balustrading, the bastions toy temples, the corner towers bower-like pavilions,' and all in the elaborate symmetry which appealed to the Elizabethan eye but had been unthought of by the castle-builders; their concern with the needs of defence and the nature of the site had made functionalism inescapable. Within the garden there would be a fountain with a figure of Hercules, or a relief of Diana and Actaeon, or even one 'standing on pillars under which you may dine and sup', designed by Sir John Harington from a description in *Orlando Furioso*, which he had just translated. Topiary was much admired and the clipped shapes, often geometrical but sometimes representing birds and animals, centaurs and sirens, added to the gay frivolity they sought in their gardens.

'Now the wit of the fox is everywhere on foot'

For they were gay – 'merry England' was a term they used themselves – and for this side of their nature they delighted in making use of the medieval, as in the garden at Montacute. They could not take the Middle Ages seriously: the time seemed to them disorderly and chaotic and irrational, given over to mysticism and superstition and, worse still, to warfare. 'In those days,' the Queen herself said, 'force and arms did prevail; but now the wit of the fox is everywhere on foot.' So when they chose to relax they would imagine themselves living 'like the old Robin Hood of England . . . and fleet the time carelessly', or they would adapt the medieval tournament on state occasions, such as the anniversary of the Queen's accession, which they recalled as the beginning of their new happiness. They converted the medieval to their own purposes in the liturgy, in poems such as *The Faerie Queene*, and in architecture; but always, where they could, they imposed upon it a classical symmetry and rationality. So Bess of Hardwick, having acquired some copes from Lilleshall Abbey for use as hangings, cut out the saints' heads and replaced them with classical heads and then, to prevent confusion, embroidered above them their new names. For men modelled their lives no longer on *Lives of the Saints* but on Plutarch's *Lives of the Noble Grecians and Romans*, by whose examples they were animated to the better service of the Queen, and from whose arts they developed the New Architecture for their, and our, admiration.

A Taste for Riches and Ostentation

Edward T Joy

Fig. 1 **Joined stool**, c.1600.
Oak, height 21 ins.
The stool was still the commonest
form of seat in the Elizabethan
home and this four-legged type
was developed in about 1550.
(Victoria and Albert Museum,
London.)

Fig. 2 **Box-shaped armchair**,
first half of the sixteenth century.
Oak, height 43 ins.
(Victoria and Albert Museum.)

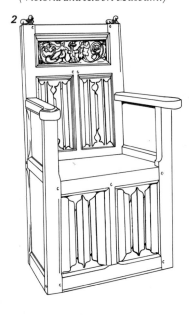

Wealthy Elizabethans wanted comfort and beauty around them, and the quality of their furniture and furnishings reflects their affection for sumptuously decorated beds, tables and chairs.

The England of Elizabeth I was a land of stable government based on a strong monarchy, of material prosperity and of vigorous national self-confidence. Overseas trade and domestic industry were both expanding rapidly and the first adventurous attempts were being made to found colonies. National confidence was strengthened by the successful challenge to the religious leadership of the Pope and the naval might of Philip II of Spain, whose Armada was defeated in 1588 in its attempts to transport troops to conquer England.

The vigour of national life fostered a love of ostentatious decoration

The character of an age tends to be reflected in its furniture; thus we see the rising wealth of Elizabethan England reflected in the increased quantity of furniture and furnishings produced by its craftsmen, while internal security encouraged a greater emphasis than ever before on domestic comfort and the vigour of national life fostered a love of ostentatious decoration.

The Reformation had, to a great extent, kept England from direct contact with Italy and the changes in constructional and decorative techniques in craftsmanship brought about by the classical Renaissance. Cultural contacts were closest with Protestant countries such as Germany and the Low Countries, where the Renaissance was interpreted in a complex and ornate version far removed from the chaste classicism of Italy, but full of appeal to contemporary English taste.

Printed pattern books of architectural and furniture designs from those areas were imported into England. The most celebrated furniture designs of this kind were those published in about 1580 by the Dutch artist Vredeman de Vries (1527–c.1604). It was from such foreign sources that three of the most distinctive kinds of Elizabethan ornament were derived: strap-work (intricate repeated arabesque and geometrical carving in low relief), inlay, or 'markatree' (the insertion of different coloured woods below the surface of the decorated section, to a depth of about one-eighth of an inch, to form floral or geometrical patterns), and bulbs, sometimes of grotesque proportions, on table legs, bed posts and similar supports. Elizabethan furniture remained largely medieval in form, absorbing these new types of decoration as a concession to modern taste. Flemish influence was further increased by numbers of Protestant craftsmen who fled to England to escape persecution in the Netherlands.

The growing affluence and comfort of the time were described by William Harrison in his *Description of England*, written in 1577–87: 'The furniture of our houses also exceedeth and is grown in manner even to passing delicacy; and herein I do not speak of the nobility and gentry only, but likewise of the lowest sort'. The rich, he continues, had 'great provision of tapestry, Turkey-work, pewter, brass, fine linen and thereto costly cupboards of plate, while inferior artificers and many farmers 'had learned' to garnish their cupboards with plate, their joined beds with tapestry and silk hangings and their tables with carpets and fine napery'. The ornate furniture of the rich is clearly shown in the inventories of the household contents of some of the great houses, like those made of Lord John Lumley's possessions in 1590 and 1609.

The principal constructional technique in Tudor furniture-making was that of the panel and frame. The panel, enclosed in a groove within a rigid framework of stiles (i.e. uprights) and rails, was allowed a freedom of movement which prevented the wood from splitting (this occurred when it was fixed by nails or pegs). The frame was made with the mortise and tenon joint, the mortise being the socket or slot into which the projecting tenon fitted exactly. The two pieces were then pegged. The joiner was the craftsman responsible for this technique, but the carver and turner were also important workers engaged on furniture, while the upholsterer saw to such things as the cushions, the fixed coverings of seats and bed curtains and the carpenter made simpler pieces. But highest in prestige was the cofferer, the first furniture craftsman to be permanently employed at Court. This man, as his title shows, at first made travelling trunks and chests for royal use, his particular skill consisting of covering them with leather and other fine materials. Later his activities included chairs, desks and screens. The Court cofferers are the only Elizabethan furniture craftsmen to escape complete oblivion, as references to their work have survived in the royal records preserved in the Public Record Office, London. The best known cofferers of the time were members of the Green family, William, John and Thomas, successively royal cofferers from about 1550 until the end of the century.

Oak was the chief wood for fashionable furniture. Before 1550 joiners had also used other native woods such as walnut, ash and elm. In Elizabeth's reign more use was made of these woods as well as of chestnut, beech, cedar and fir, and at the same time, to make the now fashionable coloured floral and chequer patterns in inlaid decoration, holly, bog oak, poplar, box, sycamore and ebony were employed.

Furniture was a valuable commodity in Tudor England and many Elizabethan houses contained pieces which had been in use from the first half of the century. Among these, special respect was accorded to the panel-back chair (which also had panels beneath the arms and seat), as social convention reserved this type for the master of the house (Fig. 5). The rest of his family sat on stools (Fig. 1) and benches. Another kind of seat was the settle, a bench with arms and back and sometimes a box beneath the seat. A light conversation chair, the caquetoire – from French, *caqueter*, to gossip – (Fig. 3) which had a tall, narrow panelled back and was open beneath its splayed arms and seat, was derived from French prototypes for ladies' use in parlours and bedrooms.

'Cupboard' – an open table for cups and plate

'Cupboard' is a word to treat with caution in its Tudor sense, for it meant originally a cup-board, that is to say, an open table for cups and plate and not, as in modern usage, a structure completely enclosed by doors. Some Tudor cupboards nevertheless were beginning to acquire enclosed sections, and examples of the different kinds – open, closed or partly closed – were being made. Some food cupboards, for instance, had pierced doors for ventilation. On the other hand, it is uncertain whether the livery cupboard, which also held stores of food – in this case the rations doled out daily to servants in large households – had doors or not.

The aumbry, originally a wall recess, then an enclosed space in a piece of furniture, was another term for a receptacle with doors, this time for keeping food for distribution by the almoner to the poor. There were also hall and parlour cupboards in two stages in which the upper stage alone, and sometimes both stages, had doors; while the press cupboard was entirely enclosed by doors. 'Cupboards' as used in Tudor inventories was thus to remain a puzzling term, although by about the end of the Elizabethan period it was beginning to acquire its present meaning.

The most costly piece of Tudor furniture was the great bed, expensive because of its rich hangings, not because of its woodwork. Four corner posts and a panelled headboard to support the tester (the canopy round which the curtains were drawn at night) formed the usual framework after 1550, replacing the canopy formerly hung from the ceiling.

All these pieces were still being made in Elizabeth's reign. The clue to their date lies mainly in their decoration. There were, however, significant changes in some instances in the framework of established types. And finally, there are some distinctly Elizabethan pieces.

The traditional panel-back chair (Fig. 5) is an excellent example of the changes which had occurred by the end of the century. In 1600 the heavy and clumsy early Tudor version had become altogether lighter by the removal of the panels from under the seat and arms. The joiner now had much greater freedom of design. The chair arms curved downwards in the centre for the sitter's elbow and scrolled outwards over the arm supports, while the latter

*Fig. 3 **Caquetoire or conversation chair, late-sixteenth century.** Oak, height 48 ins. This style of light chair, with its single panelled back, was supposedly made for ladies. It derives, as the name suggests, from French models. (Victoria and Albert Museum.)*

*Fig. 4 **Draw table and bench** from Broadway, Somerset, first half of the sixteenth century. Oak, height of table 34½ ins., length of bench 65 ins. (Victoria and Albert Museum.)*

and the front legs (i.e. the former front stiles of the seat panel) were turned in columnar and other forms. The backs of these chairs were often inlaid with floral ornament or perhaps with a coat of arms, and ornamental scrolled sections at the top and sides ('head' and 'ear' pieces) were added both for decoration and to shelter the occupant from draughts.

Towards the end of Elizabeth's reign another type of lighter chair made its appearance, to join the caquetoire. This was the back stool which in contemporary meaning was not a chair at all as it did not have arms, but was literally a stool with a back support raised clear of the seat. It was based on the recently developed joined stool which had four turned legs splayed slightly outwards. The reason for its development is not completely clear. It does, however, coincide with the growing fashion for houses to have a separate small dining parlour. When, in former times, the family dined on the raised dais at one end of the great hall, those who sat on benches or stools could rest their backs against the wall. In the dining parlour, on the other hand, the table was in the centre of the room, and it seems reasonable to suggest that the back stool was a simple expedient for providing the support formerly given by the wall.

'Chairs of clothe of gold, velvet and sylke'

Great houses also had richly upholstered chairs as proved by inventories of the time. In 1590, for instance, Lord Lumley had seventy-six 'chairs of clothe of gold, velvet and sylke' and eighty stools similarly upholstered. Such chairs and stools have all disappeared and it is impossible to say whether they were made abroad or in England. It is likely, however, that many were of the traditional X-frame form, of which one surviving example can be seen in Winchester Cathedral. This is the oak chair, originally covered with blue velvet, which was made in about 1550 and is said to have been used at Queen Mary's wedding to Philip II of Spain.

In sharp contrast to these luxury chairs were the strictly utilitarian turned (or 'thrown') chairs found in the kitchens of large houses and, more generally, in smaller manor houses and in farmhouses. These chairs had their structural members turned in a variety of ways, often in bizarre fashion. The Elizabethans also used a light folding chair which seems to have copied Italian models. This type has been given the name of a Glastonbury chair through the mistaken supposition that it was based on the design of one which belonged to the Abbot of Glastonbury who was executed in Henry VIII's reign.

The dining parlour inspired the introduction of the draw table (Fig. 4), which could be extended to about double its length by pulling out two leaves beneath the top. This saved space when the table was not in use for meals. It is a truly Elizabethan development, for the earliest contemporary reference to one is found in the inventory of the Duke of Somerset's furniture, drawn up in 1552, and it was just the kind of piece to lend itself to the ornate decoration of the time. Minute chequer inlay is sometimes found running round the whole of the frieze, but the outstanding features are the enormous bulbs on the legs. These were often of 'cup and cover' form (so

called because of its similarity to a silver covered cup), and their carved decoration consisted of gadrooning – edging of concave flutes or convex reeds – and acanthus leaves, both taken from Classical sources.

The Great Bed of Ware, wide enough to sleep four couples

Another Elizabethan innovation was the court cupboard. This, a cup-board in the old literal sense, was an open three-tiered side-table. It was the 'prestige-piece' of the period, for the shelves held the family plate when important guests were entertained. The upper and central friezes often contained drawers which were decorated with strap-work. The supports were of bulbous form or in the shape of heraldic beasts, while the base platform had inlaid decoration. The name 'court' remains something of a mystery – perhaps from the French court (short) as these pieces were rarely more than four feet high, or more probably because they may have been first used on formal occasions at Court. Some examples of these cupboards had an enclosed central compartment in the upper stage with canted sides. While, as has been seen, the earlier types of cupboards all continued to be made, food cupboards were now often hung on the wall and had turned spindles in their doors.

Beds sometimes reached enormous proportions. The wooden tester became so heavy that it no longer rested on four posts but on two large foot-posts standing clear of the bed frame, and on an elaborate carved and inlaid headboard. The most famous bed of the time is the Great Bed of Ware (Fig. 6), first mentioned in 1596 and referred to by Shakespeare in Twelfth Night. This bed, and others of the time, often included intarsia work – inlaid perspective views – in their headboard panels. Intarsia was based on Italian techniques, but reached England through imported Flemish pattern books.

Another decorative feature was the split baluster, made of turned pieces split down the middle, then glued to the carcase. One long-established error connected with intarsia (or inlay) work in Elizabeth's reign has arisen over the so-called 'Nonsuch chests', which are decorated with inlaid patterns of formal architectural views supposed to represent Henry VIII's Palace of Nonsuch, Cheam, Surrey, demolished in the seventeenth century. There is no evidence to connect these views with Nonsuch and it now seems clear that the chests were of German or Flemish origin.

Wealthy Elizabethans loved rich and gay upholstery. Cushions, wall hangings, bed curtains and imported tapestries and carpets (the latter being used to cover tables and court cupboards) all added colour and comfort to the interior. One favoured material was Turkey-work which seems to have been produced only in England and was made in the manner of a hand-knotted carpet, copying the designs of the larger carpets imported from the Middle East. In medieval times painted furniture seems to have been common. By Elizabeth's reign this custom was dying out, to be replaced by carved and inlaid decoration or, in the case of plain surfaces, by wax polishing.

5

Fig. 5 Armchair, probably Scottish, c.1550. Oak, height 42¼ ins. This chair illustrates the fusion of gothic and renaissance motifs. (Victoria and Albert Museum.)

6

Museum Photo

Fig. 6 ***The Great Bed of Ware***, *1580. Carved oak with inlaid decoration, length 11 ft. 1 in., width 10 ft. 8½ ins. Wide enough to sleep four couples, it has become one of the most famous beds in English history, and the subject of numerous literary allusions. Sir Toby Belch, in Twelfth Night encouraged Sir Andrew to write 'as many lies as will lie on thy sheet of paper although thy sheet were big enough for the Bed of Ware in England'. It was probably made for Sir Henry Fanshawe of Ware Park but by 1616 it had been moved to an inn. (Victoria and Albert Museum.)*

MUSEUMS AND COLLECTIONS

Elizabethan furniture may be seen at the following:

Derbyshire:	Hardwick Hall
London:	Victoria and Albert Museum
Norfolk:	Strangers' Hall, Norwich
Northamptonshire:	Burghley House
Nottinghamshire:	Wollaton Hall
Somerset:	Montacute House
Warwickshire:	Shakespeare's Birthplace Trust Properties, Stratford-upon-Avon
Wiltshire:	Longleat

FURTHER READING

Furniture 700–1700 by Eric Mercer, Section 4, 'The sixteenth century', London, 1969.

The Connoisseur's Complete Period Guides (ed. by Ralph Edwards and L. G. G. Ramsey), 'Furniture' by John Hunt in **The Tudor Period 1500–1603,** London, 1968.

Furniture in England: The Age of the Joiner by S. W. Wolsey and R. W. P. Luff, London, 1968.

Dictionary of English Furniture (ed. by P. Macquoid and Ralph Edwards), London, 1954. Abridged version, **Shorter Dictionary of English Furniture** (ed. by Ralph Edwards), London, 1964.

The Englishman's Chair by John Gloag, London, 1964.

A Short Dictionary of Furniture by John Gloag, London, 1964.

The Ruff and the Pendant

James Laver

Fig. 1 **The Procession of Elizabeth I,** *attributed to Robert Peake the Elder, c.1600. Oil on canvas, 52 x 75 ins. In order not to appear extravagant to her subjects, Queen Elizabeth who refused to wear any garment more than once, had several identical dresses made in each style she chose. (Collection of Simon Wingfield Digby Esq.)*

Figs. 2 & 3 **Designs for Pendants,** *by Hans Holbein, (1497/8–1543). Pen and ink; left 3⅓ x 2⅙ ins.; right 4½ x 2½ ins. Although many Elizabethan artists designed jewellery, they were rarely involved in the manufacture of the objects. The designs were passed on to a goldsmith who would make up as many copies as he saw fit. (Sloane Collection, British Museum, London.)*

Fig. 4 **The Canning Jewel,** *probably Italian, sixteenth century. The design of this exquisite merman was undoubtedly suggested to the jeweller by the shape of the so-called baroque, or irregular, pearl. The piece was acquired by Lord Canning. (Victoria and Albert Museum, London.)*

Fig. 5 **The Ship Jewel,** *Italian, sixteenth century. After the defeat of the Spanish Armada in 1588, there was a patriotic craze in England for anything to do with ships. This elegant replica, possibly made in Venice, was typical of the time. (Victoria and Albert Museum.)*

Tudor society produced the first generation that can properly be called 'fashion-conscious'. For both sexes this was an age when, as Shakespeare wrote, 'the apparel oft proclaims the man

At the beginning of the sixteenth century clothes both for men and women were still medieval and comparatively plain and sober; but the accession of Henry VIII brought a complete change both in shape and materials. The latter were, for the Court and the upper classes, extremely rich. Contemporary writers speak of cloth of gold, cloth of silver, silver embroidery, figured velvet and 'satin pinselled and overcast with golden threads'. Gowns of taffeta were bordered with the furs of lynxes, weasels, wolves and sables. Much jewellery was worn in the form of rings, bracelets and neck-chains. Stockings were dyed purple or scarlet and were sometimes embroidered and often slashed.

It was as if the stiff and rigid etiquette of the Spanish Court had been imported into England

Slashing indeed was applied to all garments, a curious process which was supposed to be derived from the costume of Swiss mercenaries and German *lanskneckts* and which consisted of cutting slits in the material and drawing the under-material through. Women's clothes were as slashed as those of the men. Until almost the end of Henry VIII's reign this German influence is most marked.

The middle of the century brought a complete change. The German influence faded away and was followed by the almost universal adoption of Spanish fashions. When the English first set eyes on these (at the time of the arrival in England of Philip of Spain in 1554 for his marriage to Mary Tudor), they thought them very strange; for the Spaniards were wearing a doublet, no longer slashed or pierced but fitting closely to the body, and over it a short cloak without sleeves or arm-holes

and with a high turned-up collar. Instead of the flat cap with a brim all the way round, they had a hard hat with a high crown. They also wore long boots of Cordova leather, ending above the knee, and bombasted (or padded) trunk hose. In all this we already see the outline of what we know as Elizabethan costume.

The accession of Elizabeth I put an end to the Spanish alliance, but the strange thing is that Spanish modes continued to dominate English fashion even when the two countries were at war. It was as if the stiff and rigid etiquette of the Spanish Court had been imported into England, with the padded and stiffened garments which were its expression in costume.

The ruff, which is the hallmark of the Spanish style, was derived originally from the string threaded through the upper edge of the shirt. When this was drawn tight an incipient ruff was already in being, but in the second half of the century it increased to such a size that it became a separate article of attire. Ruffs were of various kinds, at first a single layer of gathered linen and later two or even three. These were stiffly starched and kept in place by means of setting-sticks made of ivory, bone or wood.

In Mary's reign women had not worn ruffs; they had instead a white collar open in front and standing up stiffly at the back. The feminine ruff took some time to establish itself and did not last nearly as long as the male ruff, except in the modified form probably introduced by Marguerite of Navarre and adopted by Queen Elizabeth. This innovation consisted of splitting the ruff in front so as to enable it to be worn with a *décolleté* gown; the curious winged effect thus achieved is familiar to us in nearly all portraits of Elizabeth.

The Spanish influence can also be seen in the introduction of the farthingale (Fig. 10). This was a device for expanding women's skirts, sometimes to extraordinary dimensions. In its earliest form it was known as the Spanish farthingale and consisted of an underskirt distended by means of hoops growing wider towards the hem. The new farthingale, or French farthingale, worn by almost every woman after 1580, was shaped like a drum; the skirt was draped horizontally over this and then fell vertically to the ground. The roll farthingale consisted of a padded bolster worn round the hips.

If the trunk hose was cut or pierced in any way, the bran ran out and the wearer was seen visibly to shrink in size

There never was an age in which there was more padding than the Elizabethan Age and it was applied to all kinds of garments. It was, of course, particularly noticeable in the trunk hose worn by men. These were expanded by stuffing them with wool, horsehair and even with bran. The last of these sometimes produced unfortunate results, for if the trunk hose was cut or pierced in any way the bran ran out and the wearer was seen visibly to shrink in size – and importance.

The principal male garment was still the doublet and this too was frequently padded or stuffed. An extreme example was the 'peascod' doublet, a Dutch fashion popular in England from 1575 to the end of the century. The padding produced a bulge which overhung the girdle and sometimes curved down to the fork. It has been preserved up to our own day in the traditional costume of Punch.

In female costume the skirt – known as the kirtle – was now separate from the bodice. Sometimes this was referred to as 'a pair of bodices' since it was made in two parts like a corset and stiffened with wood or whalebone rods known as busks inserted into sheaths in the lining. The bodice was tight-fitting, ending in a point at the waist. The sleeves, up to 1560, were funnel-shaped with a broad turn-back cuff ending at the elbow. For the rest of the century they were usually close-fitting to the wrist, sometimes slashed and puffed and finished with a little ruff. They could be bombasted like the trunk hose of men. From about 1580 the bodice was divided down the middle and the space filled in with a stomacher. This was made of rich material often matching the sleeves but different from the bodice and sometimes elaborately embroidered or studded with jewels. Both the male doublet and the female bodice were indeed settings for a display of jewellery and it is to this that we must now direct our attention.

'Pearls for the Queene's use' at a penny each

Jewellery in the second half of the sixteenth century had a distinctive style of its own. Late medieval jewellery had had a strong ecclesiastical flavour; bishops' rings, pectoral crosses and the like. The Renaissance meant a revival of interest in classical models, but very little actual jewellery of Greece and Rome had survived or been, as yet, discovered. The exception was portrait cameos and these were much imitated in the closing years of the fifteenth century.

Gradually classical motifs began to creep in, influenced by the architecture and interior decoration of the period. Instead of gothic arches and pinnacles, we find niches flanked by columns and crowned by a pediment, and within the niches the gods of antiquity and nymphs and satyrs. There was a close connection between the painting, sculpture and architecture and goldsmiths' work and some of the most famous Italian artists of the time actually began their career in a goldsmith's *bottega*. Even foreign artists like Dürer and Holbein designed jewellery even if they did not make it themselves.

In Henry VIII's time all prosperous citizens wore a collar, rather like that of the modern mayor, and when the wearer was a king the collar was, as might be expected, of great magnificence. Henry had a whole collection of them, and one in particular is represented in several of his portraits. It consisted of a number of flat cut rubies, some square and some oval, in petalled settings, linked by ornaments of richly foliated gold, each studded with two enormous pearls.

In the second half of the sixteenth century there was a gradual transfer of jewellery interest from male to female attire. Men's garments were elaborately embroidered but we do not in general find them sewn and strewn with jewels as they had been in the previous generation. François I had adored jewels and bought large quantities of them. His successor Henri II had more austere taste, in line, as we have noted with the transition all over Europe from the

Fig. 6 *The Judgement of Solomon*, English, sixteenth century. Tapestry. This biblical tale is curiously portrayed in Elizabethan dress. *(Hardwick Hall, Derbyshire.)*

Michael Russell

Museum Photo

Fig. 7 *Sir Walter Raleigh and his Son*, English School, 1602. 78½ x 50½ ins. *The padded look was the height of Elizabethan fashion. (National Portrait Gallery, London.)*

Fig. 8 *Elizabeth I* by Hilliard. *Oil on panel, 31 x 24 ins. The Queen wears a pelican pendant symbolic of her devotion to England. (Walker Art Gallery, Liverpool.)*

Museum Photo

Fig. 11 *The Darnley or Lennox Jewel*, sixteenth century. Formerly in the possession of Horace Walpole, now in the Collection of H.M. the Queen at Windsor.

Fig. 9 *Henry VIII*, School of Holbein, sixteenth century. Oil on panel, 94 x 53 ins. Thought to be a copy of a fresco in the old Whitehall.
(Walker Art Gallery, Liverpool.)

9

Museum Photo

Fig. 10 *The farthingale, or hooped skirt. Fashionable first in Spain, it was common in England by about 1580.*

10

11

By Gracious Permission of H.M. The Queen

exuberance of German modes to the sobriety of Spanish costumes. There was, unfortunately, another reason. The wars of Religion had, to a large extent shattered the economy of France and it is to be feared that many of the treasures of the monarchy were almost perpetually in pawn. The diamonds and pearls of François I were reset by François II in 1559 as a short necklace and only two years later were offered as bribes to Elizabethan courtiers and even to Elizabeth herself in the hope of promoting an alliance with England.

It was quite usual at this period for jewels to be used as investments and means of exchange which was natural enough in an age when bartering, in the modern sense, hardly existed. Ransoms were paid in gems, wars financed in the same manner and all this did much to further international troubles.

Elizabeth had many of the gems worn by her father reset, and her portrait in the National Gallery shows her wearing a splendid carcanet and collar, the latter with a great sapphire in the centre, still in Henry VIII's rose setting. Her belt is of large pearls and her dress is sewn with pearls. Not all of these were real, for a bill of 1569 has survived for 520 'pearls for the Queene's use' at a penny each.

They were presumably made of glass.

Queen Elizabeth is known to have encouraged her courtiers to give her jewels on New Year's Day; we learn for example that in 1584 Sir Christopher Hatton presented her with a head ornament of seven pieces.

Pendants formed an important part of jewellery at this period and some of the elaborate specimens which have survived are miracles of craftsmanship. They were sometimes quite large and consisted of mythological or symbolic figures in a kind of architectural niche. The Virtues were frequently depicted, as can be seen in the Darnley or Lennox jewel (Fig. 11), once in the possession of Horace Walpole and now in the collection of H.M. the Queen. It was made for Lady Margaret Douglas in memory of her husband, the Earl of Lennox, who

was killed in 1571. It is a gold and enamelled heart-shaped pendant which opens to disclose two hearts united by a gold knot. One side is set with a large heart-shaped cabochon sapphire, which in turn opens to reveal two clasped hands with other emblems and a motto.

Victory, crowned by Cupid, stands on deck blowing a horn

The Elizabethan passion for conceits is very much in evidence in the jewellery of the time. As a New Year gift for 1574, the Queen was given a jewel with a figure representing Neptune and on the back some verses making an acrostic of Elizabeth. The rise of England as a maritime power after the defeat of the Armada is reflected in the fashion for pendants in the form of ships. Some of these are of great delicacy with the rigging represented by fine gold wire. There is an exquisite example, thought to be of Venetian workmanship, in the Victoria and Albert Museum (Fig. 5). Another is a jewel said to have been given by Queen Elizabeth to Sir Francis Drake, and now preserved at Berkeley Castle. The hull of the vessel is of ebony, set with a diamond; the masts and rigging are of enamelled gold set with pearls; Victory, crowned by Cupid, stands on deck blowing a horn; a small dinghy hangs below.

Perhaps nothing is more typical of the taste of the time than the pendants made of a baroque (or misshapen) pearl. Such a jewel might suggest the body of a dragon or other monster, the rest of the creature being constructed of goldsmiths' work set with jewels. In the splendid Canning jewel (Fig. 4) the pearl forms the body of a merman. It is probably of Italian workmanship but was found by Lord Canning in India.

Another interesting feature of jewellery at this period is that two or more jewels may exist which have plainly been based upon the same design. The goldsmith worked from a pattern, and this pattern was supplied by what is known as engraved ornament. The original designer engraved a copper-plate from which any number of copies could be printed and these were circulated all over the Continent.

For richness of ornamentation and elaboration of workmanship, the jewellery of the Elizabethan Age has never been surpassed. It was essentially goldsmiths' work, with the setting, if one may so call it, a more important part of the jewel than the precious stone itself. It was not until a century later that the improved techniques for cutting jewels reduced the setting sometimes to a mere claw. It is a happy coincidence that no other age could have provided in its costume so splendid a background for these elaborate jewels.

FURTHER READING

A Concise History of Costume by James Laver, Chapter IV, London, 1969.
A History of Costume in the West by F. Boucher, Chapter VIII. Trans. by John Ross, London, 1967.
Historic Costume (1450–1790) by F. M. Kelly and R. Schwabe, London and New York, 1931.
English Jewellery from the Fifth Century to 1800 by Joan Evans, Chapter IV, London, 1921.

furniture polishes and finishes of the past

From time immemorial almost all furniture has been given some form of surface treatment. Paints, oils, waxes, lacquers, varnishes and polishes of many different types have been used. It is of great importance and value to everyone who owns and loves antique furniture to know a little about the ways in which the original craftsmen gave the final finish to their work. Only then can you know how best to take care of the patina.

During the seventeenth century we know that linseed oil and poppy oil were used on oak furniture, sometimes dyed with alkanet root which gives a reddish colour. The use of oils tended to darken the oak, while polish made from beeswax and turpentine, which was also used at that time, produced a more golden colour.

Walnut furniture made during the late part of the seventeenth century and in the eighteenth century was usually given a thin coat of clear oil varnish before being friction-polished with beeswax. The varnish sealed the fine grain from the wax and so preserved the wood's lighter golden markings.

A more elaborate finish

During the seventeenth century lacquered cabinets and other pieces of furniture were being imported from China. By the end of the century lacquered or 'japanned' work had become so popular that copies in the Chinese style were being made in England. The fashion only remained in vogue for about twenty years, but during this period it was a craze and a number of books were published on how to do your own japanning. The best known was *A Treatise of Japanning and Varnishing* by John Stalker and George Parker, published in 1688. It included a selection of decorative motifs for the amateur to copy, some of which are shown on the left.

Mahogany was not widely used in England until about 1725. At this time it came from the West Indies and was known as Spanish mahogany, a very hard and heavy wood. The Cuban mahogany, which was being imported by the 1750s, was easier to work and also gave a much finer figuring than Spanish mahogany. Linseed

Left: A late seventeenth-century cabinet on a gilt wood stand. It is finished in red japanned lacquer.

Right: A George I secretaire cabinet with a burr walnut veneer finish.

Designs to copy when doing your own japanning, a craze of seventeenth-century England. These motifs appeared in a Treatise of Japanning and Varnishing, 1688.

oil or beeswax were used for polishing both these woods. During the latter half of the eighteenth century England was importing Honduras mahogany in large quantities. It was a much lighter wood with a more open grain and required to have a hard surface built up. Thomas Sheraton in his *Cabinet Dictionary* of 1803 wrote that this was 'the principal kind of mahogany in use among cabinet-makers'. In the same book he says that 'the general mode of polishing plain cabinet work' is to spread linseed oil and brick dust over the surface to make a 'putty under the rubbing cloth' producing 'a fine polish by continued rubbing'.

The 'new look'

French polishing is the only other method of finishing furniture which comes within the category of 'antique'. It is a transparent polish related to oriental lacquer. Nearly all furniture produced in England during the nineteenth century was French polished. This finish was much loved by the Victorians who spoiled many pieces of eighteenth-century furniture by stripping off the original natural patina and giving them the glossy 'new look'.

Looking after the various finishes

The first object in looking after antique furniture is to preserve the patina. First, a few words of warning. It is often said that a

Polishes you can make

For oak furniture, mix one part of beeswax to three parts of genuine turpentine. You can use yellow or brown beeswax for dark oak, but for lighter coloured oak or other light woods use bleached beeswax. If you cannot get genuine turpentine use turps substitute. Dissolve the wax in a tin containing the turpentine. This process can be speeded up by shredding the wax before adding it to the turpentine. Place the tin in a bowl of boiling water and stir until all the wax has dissolved. Do not heat the tin over a naked flame, as is sometimes suggested. When the wax is cold it should be the consistency of soft butter.

To make your own furniture cream for walnut and mahogany furniture, melt the following waxes together: three and a half parts of Japan wax, six parts of fatty grey carnauba wax and one to two parts of paraffin wax. These waxes need melting in a double container over a heat source such as an electric ring, but *great care must be taken*. When the waxes have melted, add about an equal quantity of genuine turpentine and, at the same time, a very small amount of ammonia. Keep the wax in a well sealed tin or pot.

little wax and a lot of elbow grease is the best way of looking after antique furniture, and very true. But when you are rubbing, rub hard with care, especially if is a veneered piece where the duster may snag on a slightly raised edge of cross-banding. Do not try any drastic cleaning treatments without expert advice.

When cleaning old oak furniture which is very dirty, try using warm water to which a little vinegar has been added. Dip a soft rag in the solution and squeeze it out. Then, sprinkle on a few drops of raw linseed oil and rub this over the furniture.

A good wax polish for oak furniture can be made at home. You should use a rag or a brush with medium stiff bristles to apply the wax very thinly, then leave for a while to allow the turps to evaporate. Polish with a coarse cloth.

When polishing walnut furniture, you should use the very minimum of wax polish. Plenty of gentle, firm rubbing with a soft cloth is the secret. A cream-type polish is best for veneered walnut furniture. If you do not make your own, good proprietary ones are available.

Very great care must be taken when dealing with lacquered furniture. If it needs cleaning, make up a paste of plain white flour and olive oil, apply with a very soft cloth, wipe off and polish very gently with a piece of fine, soft silk.

For cleaning mahogany furniture, if it is in a very dirty state, make up a mixture of equal parts of raw linseed oil, genuine turpentine and turpentine with a quarter part of methylated spirit. Patience and gentle rubbing with a soft cloth dipped in this solution will remove most of the dirt. For polishing use a suitable proprietary wax such as Antiquax or your own. Use only a very little wax.

Too much wax on French polished furniture can give it a sticky, dull, patchy appearance. To remove this, use a soft cloth wrung out in warm soapy water, then dry the piece thoroughly. To revive the French polish use the following recipe. Dissolve two ounces of good quality soap in half a pint of boiling distilled water. Add this to half a pint of genuine turpentine in which one ounce of bleached beeswax and one ounce of paraffin wax have been dissolved by heating in a tin placed in boiling water. Leave this mixture for a day before using. With a soft cloth pad rub this into the furniture and finish off with a dry soft cloth. After this treatment use a furniture cream very sparingly for all future polishing.

DENNIS YOUNG

Market Trends

18th CENTURY EUROPEAN PORCELAIN

Porcelain is perhaps one of the main fields of collecting which divides neatly into the purely pretty pieces bought solely for decoration and those which are really only appreciated by enthusiasts. Eighteenth-century European porcelain is now, of course, comparatively rare, and collectors who start buying with the idea of putting together a small group of good quality examples as either a decorative scheme or as an investment often find themselves drawn into a study of their collection. This leads inevitably to a rapid specialisation, and rarely does one come across a collector of any more than one or two factories today.

Capodimonte

Often pieces of soft-paste Capodimonte seem dull to the amateur, but to many collectors examples of the pieces made at this short-lived factory are ultimately desirable. The soft but very vigorous modelling of the clean white clay, and the subjects, perhaps especially those of the Italian Comedy, so typically period in their flavour, and their rare and costly appearance on the market, contribute to this. In May, 1956 a tiny scent bottle modelled as a Callot dwarf sitting on a turtle made £180 while a larger and amusing group of a mother scolding her child made £620. In July, 1960 a fine figure of Pierrot eating Macaroni made £760 while a more brightly coloured, but less attractive, Mezzetin holding a letter only realised £580.

Gricc Models

The models of Giuseppe Gricc have always been especially sought after, and in April 1962 the rare Bird Catcher (from a set of

poveri which he modelled between 1743-45) realised £1,750. In the same sale a group of peasant dancers, also modelled by Gricc, made only £550; a tiny Bull Terrier by him made £340 in May 1963, while his Porcelain Seller, from the set of poveri, made a high £4,310 in April, 1964. All these pieces were in good condition, but we see the graph rise steeply from this time onwards for even damaged examples. A group of The Proposal in which both the shy girl's arms were missing, still made £945 in March, 1965, while a brilliant group of The Rabbit Hunters only 6½ ins. high made £9,450 in March, 1968. This trend was confirmed in March, 1969 when three important groups, all modelled by Gricc, appeared at Christie's in the same sale, and £4,200 was paid for a not badly damaged group of Peasants Drinking, £9,450 for a brilliant Italian Comedy group, and the same high figure for a pair of Masked Strolling Lovers. Today, as with all other rare and fine quality examples of early European porcelain, these Capodimonte pieces would be worth more!

ANTHONY DERHAM

THE ARTS OF CENTRAL EUROPE

Even a casual glance through a reference book such as Feuchtmuller and Mrazek's monumental Kunst in Oster-reich 1860-1918 (Vienna, 1964) reveals the astonishing variety and originality of design and craftsmanship during the last years of the Dual Monarchy. It makes one regret all the more that so few artefacts with this provenance appear in London salerooms, and that interest in them should be confined to a comparatively small number of specialists, whether dealers or collectors.

Silver

The artists of the Secession were not renowned for the scale of their output, and their products scarcely ever appear at auction in London. In March 1971 Sotheby's handled an extremely fine tea- and coffee-service by the silversmith Eduard Friedmann. Friedmann commissioned a number of designs from avant garde artists such as Otto Prutscher and Hans Bolek, and both services and individual pieces from their house are eagerly sought after. There was a hope that the exhibition devoted to the Secession shown at the Royal Academy in 1970 might send a tremor of activity through the salerooms. There is no evidence that this has been the case, and it seems that the trend of the last few years will continue; a small number of keen collectors competing vigorously for the few pieces that appear at auction.

A silver-mounted Loetz vase, the dimpled body tapering into a slender cylindrical neck, in combed blue lustre glass applied with a stylised silver plant and tendril decoration, the base engraved 'Loetz Austria'. This vase was sold for £100 at Sotheby's Belgravia in November 1971.

Sotheby's Belgravia

Furniture

Thonet furniture is also virtually unknown in London salerooms. Sotheby's Belgravia occasionally handle bentwood furniture, and there is a chance that some pieces will come up for sale later in 1972.

Glass

Loetz glass is the one exception to this trend. It appears very often, both in London and in America, and its popularity with collectors is on the increase. A Loetz silver-mounted rosewater sprinkler, the dimpled gold glass body decorated in an iridescent pale blue-green, sold for £85 at Sotheby's in July 1971. A few months later, in November 1971 a silver-mounted vase of combed blue lustre glass fetched £100 at Sotheby's Belgravia saleroom. There is, of course, a very great difference between the prices paid for items which are definitely by Loetz, and those that are merely attributed. Of two vases sold at Sotheby's Belgravia recently, one attributed to Loetz sold for £40, and the other carrying the words 'Loetz Austria', fetched £95. This type of glass is still plentiful, and prices are still going up; it is probably the most collectable product of late nineteenth-century Austria, if not the most exciting.

DAMASCUS HOBNAIL

ORIENTAL PORCELAIN AND SWORDS

The Ming Dynasty lasted nearly three hundred years, from 1368 to 1644, and during that time the contemporary value of porcelain was on the level of diplomatic gifts exchanged between Emperor and Sultan. An example of this—probably made for the Persian market—is an Arabic-inscribed blue and white dish painted in underglaze blue, which was included in the second part of the Eumorfopoulos collection dispersed in May, 1940. It was made during the reign of Ch'eng Te and realised less than one hundred pounds. In 1968 the same dish fetched £20,000. Although the first European excavations in China started in 1923, a general interest in this subject only emerged after the great exhibition at Burlington House in 1935. It is over the past twenty years that prices have soared. Ming porcelain today is obviously fashionable; it is the art of the recognisably expensive. In addition, it is a field that has attracted the investment collector. The extraordinary increase in value is due to a combination of the Japanese interest vying against the American tax loss donations, as well as the rich private collector. And so those without this kind of wealth have turned to the porcelain of the provincial kilns, the Southern Chinese kilns of Swatow province, and the export porcelain of the Malay Archipelago. Some of these provincial wares are of good quality and the demand for them is considerable. If they show little aesthetic merit and are coarsely potted, there is always a late Ming blue and white bowl, which may not fetch more than £50.

Swords

In the Western world there remains a startling ignorance about Japanese swords. Because it is technically one of the most difficult subjects in which to gauge quality and therefore price, this may well persist. It is therefore a worthwhile field for those who are prepared to acquire assiduously the necessary knowledge. Up until 1968 a fine Japanese sword would fetch less than £300; since that date an exceptional example may realise several thousand pounds. A price barrier has been broken, which is not surprising in view of the fact that the Japanese themselves will on occasion pay £5,000 for a good blade. In 1970 two magnificent early fourteenth-century swords attributed to Kaneuji were sold for £5,670 and £4,725. A year earlier an attractive Wakizashi blade with hilt and scabbard of green and gold lacquer had made £168. The difference in quality between these examples would not be discernible to the amateur and yet it is to be hoped that the difference in price will encourage a more academic understanding of the Japanese sword.   TOM MILNES GASKELL

One of a pair of Kraak porcelain blue and white dishes, Wanli period, sold at Christie's for £120 in January, 1970.

CHINOISERIE

While the taste for 'Chinoiserie' has often been fashionable in the West since the late Middle Ages, it was only in the late seventeenth and early eighteenth centuries that the rapidly expanding East India Companies fed this market. In the eighteenth century, England especially enjoyed a wild vogue for nearly anything which originated in the Far East (no distinctions were made between China, Japan or the odd pieces which any East Indiaman could pick up along his voyages through Indo-China) or could be remodelled or repainted here in the Oriental manner. 'Japanning' furniture was a pastime many ladies of quality enjoyed and excelled at; services of porcelain were ordered from Canton with the coats of arms of English families, sometimes to commemorate a marriage, and often in shapes and sizes directly taken from the fashionable English silver of the day. Perhaps the elaborate frames for the mirrors and imported paintings on glass typify this period of fashionable taste better than most, and show how, along with most top quality objects appearing at various moments on the London market, they have become increasingly valuable as the machine age turns our appreciation of many objects from one of contemplating admiration for workmanship and detail to one of instantly recognisable visual impact.

Mirror Paintings

In early 1960, a mirror painting with a typical scene of Chinese figures resting in a harbour landscape, among exotic and unlikely long-tailed birds and flowering trees, in a 'Chippendale' gilt-wood frame composed of flame mouldings outlined with leaves and C-scrolls, made 400 guineas; later that year, an elaborate mirror, made up of two brilliantly painted panels of Chinese and golden pheasant, again amongst tree peonies and rocks, came up at Christie's. In May 1962, a set of four panels of paintings on glass made £1,750, a high price justified by the fact that each was in the original gessoed hardwood frame, and, although definitively Chinese in technique, the composition owed a lot to Western painting, a point which must have charmed the first buyer into parting with a lot of money. In November 1963, an overmantel, of a mirror picture set over a panel of plain mirror and framed in an exotic way, made 1,200 guineas, while in 1965, the great mirror from Harewood House made 10,000 guineas, an extremely high figure based on the quality of the paintings, the fact that the frame was by Thomas Chippendale from a design by Robert Adam, and of course, the provenance.

Wallpaper

Naturally as a background to any room, the brightly coloured wallpapers imported with every shipment were very popular and, while fine reproductions are expensively available today, the price of these early pieces of decorative painting has soared, obviously partly because taking them off walls poses large problems and risks. In 1957 a set of ten large panels totalling 360 square feet of paper dated to the early nineteenth-century Emperor Chia-ch'ing made only £200; in 1960 a fine set of seven panels of pheasants on bright blue grounds made a high £2,100. In 1968 a series of ten pieces of various widths made 1,000 guineas; the panel illustrated shows the quality and clarity of these wallpapers. An extraordinary series of twenty-four pieces, many unused, made a high 2,600 guineas in 1969, and these would certainly realise much more today.   ANTHONY DERHAM

JAPANESE ART FORMS

Of all the Japanese art forms, only prints have been appreciated in the West for any great length of time. Prints themselves have increased enormously in price in the last few years mainly due to the increased activity of Japanese collectors in European and American salerooms. The highest price so far recorded at auction outside Japan for any single plate is the £3,333 paid in New York in April this year for *The Courtesan with Attendant* by Okumura Masanobu, the great early eighteenth-century master whose works are now rarely seen on the market. Outstanding prints by Utamaro and Hiroshige, probably the two most famous Japanese names in the West, can fetch upward of £1,000, especially the large heads by the former and the landscape views, such as the fifty-three stations on the Tokaido Road and the eight views of Lake Biwa, by the latter. Many prints, especially attractive examples by Hiroshige, can be bought for under £150, however, although the collector should always ensure that they are in fine condition.

Netsuke

Netsuke, the small toggles carved usually in wood, bone or ivory have been far more popular as works of art in Europe for the last two or three years than they have ever been in Japan. The finest pieces, by such craftsmen as the eighteenth-century artists Masanao of Kyoto, and Tomotada and the great nineteenth-century master Kwaigyokusai, can fetch between £1,000 and £3,000 at auction today, while the best pieces by fine makers from less important schools such as Ikkwan of Nagoya, Mitsuhiro of Osaka and Okatomo of Kyoto, can make between £200 and £1,000. Beautiful examples by unknown artists, especially middling quality pieces of the Tokyo school, can be bought for between £50 and £200. In general, wood is less popular as a medium than ivory, whilst the best-liked subjects are animals.

Inro

Inro, whilst being more popular in Japan than netsuke, have never enjoyed the same level of popularity in Europe. The main problem is that the finest inro are made of lacquer, a notoriously difficult substance to display as it almost invariably warps in central heating, while the colours fade if subjected to light for prolonged periods. The two greatest makers are Shibata Zeshin, some of whose pieces have made more than £1,500 at auction in Europe, and Ritsuo. It is unlikely that a good piece by either of these two could be purchased for less than £500. These are the exceptions, however, and most pieces of inro make less than £250 at auction. Although a difficult subject which requires a good deal of expertise and experience, there is still great opportunity in this field for the collector on a modest budget.

Porcelain

Until very recently, Japanese porcelain of good quality was rarely seen at auction in Europe and when it did appear, prices were, by comparison with those paid for Chinese pieces, very low. Recently, however, there have been some particularly good examples of eighteenth-century Nabeshima ware at Sotheby's and prices for three pieces, £1,450, £1,600 and £1,700, were ten times as high as any similar piece has previously fetched at auction in London. Again, it is probably the large numbers of new Japanese collectors who are responsible. The Kakiemon and Kutani wares of the seventeenth century are also rising very rapidly in value, while good examples of Arita and Imari wares of the eighteenth and nineteenth centuries can still be purchased for between £20 and £150 depending on their condition and the quality of the decoration.

KEITH POWNETT

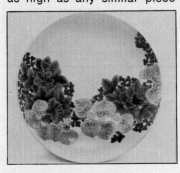

18th century Nabeshima dish, sold at Sotheby's in 1970 for £1,450.

CERAMICS AND PRINTS OF THE ORIENT

It is a curious but apparently accepted fact that more Chinese and Japanese ceramics change hands in Britain every year than ceramics from any other country and than perhaps any other type of antique. A large proportion of the pieces sold are nineteenth-century pieces, although there are regrettably a good many dealers who make it their business to persuade the unwary or inexperienced customer that they were made a hundred years before.

Japanese Ceramics

This is such a crowded and popular field for collectors that there is little doubt that prices will continue to rise as they have done in the past few years. Japanese ceramics are marginally cheaper to buy than Chinese. A fine moulded Japanese vase, the oviform body in unglazed biscuit with multicoloured mottled glazes running over the shoulders, made in the late nineteenth century, sold for only £12 at Sotheby's Belgravia in 1971. A fine pair of Imari vases sold for £26 and a *cloisonné* enamel dish decorated with cranes wading in a lake made c.1880 fetched £12 at the same sale. If a piece carries the mark of a well-known maker, it will obviously fetch more. A large yellow-ground vase enamelled in green with dragons and a phoenix sold for £72 at Sotheby's in 1971, bearing as it did the mark of Ryosensei with the rebus of Fujiyama.

A fine Japanese cloisonné enamel vase made c.1880 depicting dragons in combat on a prussian blue ground, which sold at Sotheby's Belgravia for £120 in November 1971.

Sotheby's Belgravia

Chinese Ceramics

Chinese ceramics of the same standard and date tend to fetch a rather higher price. A pair of blue and white jars and covers of baluster shape, decorated with flowers and stylised *shou* characters made at the end of the last century, sold for £54 at Sotheby's in 1971. Another blue and white vase of elongated ovoid form painted with stylised floral scrolls made £18 at the same sale. *Famille-rose* vases seem to command higher prices and arouse greater interest than the commoner blue and white pattern. A pair of Canton *famille-rose* vases of hexagonal section and baluster form, each applied on the shoulders with four green and gilt salamanders, sold for £440 at Sotheby's Belgravia in 1971. Another pair of *famille-rose* vases, the bodies painted with panels of warriors made near the end of the last century, sold for £88 at another Sotheby sale in 1971. Although this is such a crowded field, there is no reason why a collector with a reasonable knowledge of ceramics shouldn't be able to find some very attractive pieces at a fairly low cost. Buy now, while there is still some reluctance to acknowledge the merits of nineteenth-century products.

Prints

As with ceramics, Chinese and Japanese prints have been among the most sought after items in London salerooms in recent years. Although the discerning collector may be lucky enough to find Japanese prints for about £50 in some of London's many print-shops, almost everything of even average quality ends up in the salerooms. There such items command very high prices. At Sotheby's in November 1971 a print of the head and shoulders of a young girl drinking from a European wineglass, signed Utamaro Hitsu and with the publisher's mark Ezaki-ya, sold for £680 despite some crease-marks near the margin. A fine Hokusai print of two cranes on a snow-laden pine tree sold for £780 at the same sale. There will be no slackening in the interest shown in these prints.

DAMASCUS HOBNAIL

ELIZABETHAN ANTIQUES

Elizabethan furniture over the past couple of years has become much more expensive and there is every indication that this boom will continue, for this solid oak furniture has been long neglected. But there is another reason besides scarcity that has attracted collectors to this type of furniture; the best quality walnut and mahogany of the eighteenth century has outpaced all but the richest collector, whereas country-made Elizabethan chairs and tables are within the price range of many. An imposing court cupboard nearly four feet high, decorated with carved reeding and strap-work and mounted on typical baluster supports, fetched £460 at Sotheby's in December 1969 and an oak games table of a rare type realised 600 guineas at Christie's two months earlier. An attractive and small oak chest of 1600 with four drawers and geometrically panelled front made only 75 guineas last July at Christie's. But naturally any upward trend in a branch of the art market attracts the unscrupulous who are deft in tampering with an old piece to make it appear more valuable or who, by using well-seasoned oak, create a brand new 'antique.' So before spending a great deal on, say, a magnificent four-poster bed—a fine example was sold by Christie's in February this year for 2,600 guineas—have it vetted first by an independent expert.

Silver

On the other hand, silver of this period has long been regarded as desirable and although fine bell salts will usually cost several thousand pounds, an East Anglian example made only £950 in 1967. But one avenue for the smaller collector remains open—spoons. These were extensively produced in wood, pewter and base metal, as well as silver, with variations in finials such as *maidenhead, apostle, lion sejant* or the rare *moor's head.* Occasionally they are engraved with a coat of arms and more commonly with the initials of the original owner. Provincial made spoons are sometimes unmarked and, for those who want a genuine piece of Elizabethan silver at a low price, then these are something to go for. A good seal-top spoon with the London hallmarks for 1570 made £145 in July 1966; a year later a *maidenhead* spoon by Richard Orange of Sherborne of about 1600 fetched £75. More recently, in December 1969, two fine *lion sejant* spoons of 1589 sold for £390 at Christie's.

Miniatures

Portrait miniature prices reached their zenith with the dispersal during 1967/68 of the De la Hey collection at Sotheby's in three parts. Since that time few outstanding miniatures have appeared on the market. A miniature of *An Unknown Young Girl* attributed to Holbein the Younger was sold at Sotheby's last season for £21,000, a colossal price in view of the serious doubts attached to the authenticity of this piece. The sitter was depicted wearing French costume of the period and an attribution to Clouet or another artist of the French School of miniaturists seems much more likely. Should a Holbein miniature in good condition come on the market, I would expect it to fetch anything up to £50,000.

Costume

Occasionally Elizabethan costume is to be found in the auction rooms. The hat illustrated, of plum-coloured knotted silk embroidery on a woollen felt ground and with a green plume, may be mid-sixteenth century, but there is always difficulty in arriving at an accurate dating of such a rare piece. It was sold by Christie's in March 1969 for 720 guineas. TOM MILNES GASKELL

George, fourteenth Earl of Sutherland, a fine portrait miniature by Nicholas Dixon, which realised £1,050 at auction in December 1967.

Photos: Christie's

720 guineas was paid in March 1969 for this felt hat decorated with silk embroidery and a plume, which is probably sixteenth century.